School Crisis Response: Ref
written, informative, and eas
make more concrete how the PR̶E̶P̶a̶R̶E̶ model can be applied to a
variety of crisis situations.

Stephen E. Brock, Ph.D., NCSP, LEP
California State University, Sacramento
President, National Association of School Psychologists (2014-15)
Co-Author,
School Crisis Prevention and Intervention: The PREP<u>a</u>RE Model

In *School Crisis Response: Reflections of a Team Leader,*
Dr. Roth offers valuable information regarding school crisis team
planning, formation, development, and maintenance. I recom-
mend this book for all professionals preparing for school crisis
response activities.

Shane R. Jimerson, Ph.D., NCSP
University of California, Santa Barbara
Co-Author,
Best Practices in School Crisis Prevention and Intervention
President, International School Psychology Association

School Crisis Response: Reflections of a Team Leader is a
great resource to assist school-based mental health professionals
learn the ins and outs of responding to emergencies. Dr. Roth
interweaves the mental health theory with practical examples of
what happens during each response. The book **demonstrates the
benefit of training** school staff in PREP<u>a</u>RE Crisis Prevention
and Intervention, and other techniques. School staff can use this
book to learn how to create a crisis team; how to respond; and
how to determine who needs assistance after a crisis. It does not
neglect care for the crisis responder. This is a great resource for
any school crisis responder!

Christina Conolly, Psy.D., NCSP
Coordinator, Division of Psychological Services
Montgomery County Public Schools, MD
PREP<u>a</u>RE Workgroup

Unique aspects come together beautifully in Dr. Roth's book to paint a realistic picture of what school crisis prevention, response, and recovery look, feel, and sound like. Each chapter begins with an abstract that segues into a case vignette, providing the reader with the story of each crisis from start to finish. This structure captures and holds interest.

The book's most distinguishing characteristic is in the way the author gives examples of statements that can be made when one does not know what to say in the midst of and after a crisis. Each experience concludes with reflective questions. Ethnic and cultural differences can make situations temporarily more difficult. The author's personal mistakes are teachable moments that can help mental health professionals dig deeper into personal bias and cultural awareness.

Bibliotherapy—an extensive list of resources organized by topic (e.g., loss of a pet, natural disasters)—is so detailed that all school mental health professionals can benefit from having this at their immediate disposal. I recommend this book for multiple audiences.

Victoria A. Comerchero, Ph.D., NCSP
Assistant Professor and Director, School Psychology
Touro College, New York, NY
Co-Chair, Grief and Bereavement Interest Group, NASP

Dr. Roth's reflections are revealing and insightful. He provides resources that are both plentiful and of high quality.

Richard A. Lieberman, M.A., NCSP
Los Angeles Unified School District
National Emergency Assistance Team
Co-Author,
School Crisis Prevention and Intervention: The PREPaRE Model

For years, Dr. Jeffrey Roth has supported students and school-based staff in responding to crises. While providing an honest and valuable reflection of his experiences, he is simultaneously humble in reflecting upon what he would do differently. This is an effective learning tool. The book is comprehensive, providing guidance and resources on how to respond to a variety of crises—from the death of a teacher to the drowning of a student. Tips for school psychologists and other professionals are integrated throughout the book, along with valuable letters and memo-templates to distribute following a crisis. Reflection questions and a comprehensive list of books for a variety of ages, death, and other losses are included. *School Crisis Response: Reflections of a Team Leader* will be an invaluable resource for school psychologists and graduate students.

Jacqueline A. Brown, Ph.D., NCSP
Assistant Professor, Department of Psychology
University of Montana
Co-Chair, Grief and Bereavement Interest Group, NASP

This book is a bridge between theory and practice and a fleshing out of best practices during a situation. It addresses real world issues—challenges, doubts, frustrations, and decisions, touching anyone who has responded to a crisis. It was reassuring to reflect on earlier challenges to see that I felt similar doubts and frustrations, but in the end we all did the best job we could. This book is a must for school crisis responders. In it, I found a number of approaches we can integrate into what we are doing to bolster our program.

Ben Fernandez, NCSP
Lead School Psychologist, Office of Diagnostic and Prevention Services
Loudoun County Public Schools, Virginia
PREPaRE Workgroup

Dr. Roth's book is a powerful resource for trainers who are preparing graduate students and professionals new to crisis intervention. His insights illustrate the growth and pain that seasoned responders experience but sometimes do not share when training novice responders. New responders will see the need to plan and to engage in best practices. The sample questions after each case study can stimulate discussion during training. I value the tips and sample letters. I plan to incorporate Dr. Roth's book into my crisis intervention curriculum.

Sara Castro-Olivo, Ph.D., NCSP
Associate Professor and MACP Director
Department of Psychology and Communication
Texas A&M International University, Laredo, Texas

The National Association of School Psychologists developed our own training model, called PREP_aRE, for crisis intervention. Knowing the model well, Dr. Roth provides extensive insights and practical examples. He outlines the levels of crisis intervention, offering examples of collaborative efforts among school personnel to assist when a crisis occurs. This deeply researched and practical book should be on the desk of school administrators and support personnel to serve as their guide for when the inevitable crisis happens.

Dr. Scott Poland, NCSP, LP
Nova Southeastern University
Co-Director of the Suicide and Violence Prevention Office
Co-Author: *Suicide in Schools*

Few school psychologists have experienced the number and range of school crises as has Dr. Roth, and I know of no other who has written about them. In *School Crisis Response: Reflections of a Team Leader* Dr. Roth reflects on how he and other members of the school crisis teams he served with for more than twenty years handled crises caused by tragic deaths from shootings, suicides, automobile accidents, home fires, and more natural causes. Dr. Roth's review of how schools responded to these crises, and especially his reflections about what worked and the lessons learned, provide an insightful read for mental health workers, educators, and others.

School Crisis Response: Reflections of a Team Leader is of particular value to those learning and implementing the NASP PREPaRE model for crisis intervention. In the cases presented, Dr. Roth connects his reflections and insights with the PREPaRE model, providing valuable guidance on the model's application to unfolding crises.

George Bear, Ph.D., NCSP
Professor, School Psychology
University of Delaware
Author,
School Discipline and Self-Discipline: A Practical Guide

School Crisis Response

Reflections of a Team Leader

Jeffrey C. Roth

Hickory Run Press

Library of Congress Control Number: 2015908599

School Crisis Response: Reflections of a Team Leader by Jeffrey
C. Roth

ISBN 13: 978-0-9908927-9-3

ISBN 10: 0990892794

First Edition, August 2015

Printed in the United States of America

Published by Hickory Run Press
Wilmington, DE

For orders, contact: HickoryRunPress@gmail.com

http://www.schoolcrisisteams.com/

Editing and design by Bonnie Britt

Cover image by © Michaeljung | Dreamstime

Back cover author image by Danny Schweers

Manufactured in the United States

Dedication

Dedicated to crisis responders everywhere.

Table of Contents

Section 4: Team Maintenance—Sharing Leadership, Expanding Knowledge, Ongoing Challenges

Appendices

Foreword

" It will never happen here" is a phrase we often hear as no one wants to think their school is vulnerable to a tragic event. Unfortunately, the reality is that tragedy and violence have no boundaries. This book is a collection of lessons learned over a two-decade career doing one of the hardest jobs possible, helping students, parents, and educators through a crisis event. The personal and often raw self-reflections by Dr. Roth provide unique insight into the feelings underlying school crisis response and the skills needed to do this work with integrity and competence. His honesty about mistakes made and lessons learned provide a powerful and moving tribute to both the victims and survivors of school-related crises. It is through lessons learned that we honor those affected, ensuring we don't make the same mistakes twice and providing the best supports possible in the aftermath of a school crisis.

The practical advice and insights are unparalleled in any other book I have read on this topic. From early struggles in trying to form a school crisis response team to subsequent struggles in providing crisis intervention without training in a school-based model, this book shows that determination, persistence, and passion can triumph over adversity and roadblocks to ensure that mental health needs are met. Dr. Roth demonstrates the valuable connection between theory and practice by applying salient concepts of the PREPaRE model at various phases of crisis response. This book also speaks to the uniqueness of school settings that require a specialized skill set. Mental health professionals involved in school crisis intervention need to be structured, yet flexible; kind, yet firm; recognize the details, yet see the larger picture; be able to work with youth, yet also work with adults; and have good communication skills to work one to one, yet be proficient at facilitating small and large group interventions. They must be masters in collaboration.

Dr. Roth speaks of unique variables that can complicate school crisis response, such as deciding on the appropriateness of memorials, working with children with special needs and families of diverse cultural backgrounds and languages. He speaks of the daunting challenge of doing this work when school professionals and responders are often as emotionally or physically affected by the event as the students. They are expected to "hold it together" while simultaneously helping others. No easy task.

Dr. Roth's personal journey is filled with excellent guidance and resources as to how we can best prepare for and respond to a crisis event. Learning from his experiences is a journey worth taking as his years of "working in the trenches" cannot be replaced by theory alone. Dr. Roth's work honors those victims and survivors whose legacies will continue to live on in the work we all do to help students, families, and school professionals see that even in some of the darkest moments, the light can shine.

Melissa A. Louvar Reeves, Ph.D., NCSP, LPC
Nationally Certified School Psychologist, Licensed Professional Counselor, Licensed Special Education Teacher
Co-Author, NASP PREPaRE School Crisis Prevention & Intervention Curriculum
Lecturer, Winthrop University, Rock Hill, S.C.
President-elect, National Association of School Psychologists. Tenure begins July 2016.

Preface

What a pleasant surprise when I learned that our daughter Leah, a talented second year high school English teacher was on her way from work to our house for dinner. Traffic was unusually "backed up", but she would soon join Carol and me. Her husband Raleigh was attending graduate classes in school counseling that evening.

We invariably discussed her students—a source of both challenge and satisfaction for her. It was obvious she cared about them and took a personal interest. As Leah prepared to leave our house, the cell phone call came. Traffic had been "backed up" because of an accident. A horrible accident. Two eleventh graders, a young man and a young woman were killed. The former was a current student of Leah's; the latter had been her student the previous year. Through her tears she said, "We told him not to speed. We told him to slow down."

I was thankful the call had not come moments later when Leah would have been on the road. The irony, the pain of seeing my daughter experience the kind of suffering I had often seen as a crisis responder will stay with me. Leah and I talked. I gave her some literature. She got back on the phone with another colleague and they talked for a long time. I think that helped the most.

The Appreciation and the Bond

Leading the crisis response team was clearly the most difficult — and most meaningful work— of my career as a school psychologist and district coordinator. There were times when the help we offered to school communities was so critical and necessary, it was palpable. We saw children struggle to make sense of sad and terrible events, and to begin the process of healing. Sometimes, they drew comfort simply from seeing that caring adults were present for them during a devastating time. Often, our response was just hard work — sometimes wishing we could be somewhere else, but knowing we needed to be there. Constantly trying to figure things out, finding meaning and order in events that made no sense and that triggered emotional pain and suffering for many people.

I developed a profound appreciation for the work of our crisis response team — comprised of people always ready when called upon to help. There was the counselor who neglected to eat (until we persuaded her otherwise) because she would not stop seeing children when so many needed to be seen. There was the school psychologist who gave a constructive voice to the anger of a violated community. There was the social worker who knew just the right book to read to kindergarten students whose classmate suddenly was not there anymore and would never be there again. And, there was the counselor who could not cope with death, disappeared, but persevered and came back as present and able as any of us. These were among the counselors, school psychologists, social workers, nurses, educators, and other responders we relied on.

We bonded like sisters and brothers. We trusted each other, depended on each other, found strength in each other. Our work could be exhausting. After one, two, three days in a traumatized school, I sometimes felt physically and emotionally drained. We were tired but needed to maintain our energy and to renew our spirit and strength. We needed to be able to think and communicate with each other, with teachers, and of course, with children. As I reflect on our work, which mercifully was occasional and a relatively small portion of our everyday jobs, my respect and admiration extends ten fold to the police, troopers, firefighters, EMTs, trauma counselors, volunteers and others constantly responding to stressful circumstances.

This book is dedicated to the thousands of crisis responders, who hope they will not need to be called, but stand ready to help people begin to recover after traumatic incidents occur.

Mistakes as Opportunities for Learning

Early in my public education, I learned the valuable lesson that we learn from our mistakes. During the years of crisis response, I made mistakes and so did the team. I believe we learned from most of them — at least those we recognized. An example of one mistake that influenced the team's learning and well being was that we did not often require debriefings at the conclusion of responses, especially in the early years.

In most of our work, district and school administrators could not have been more cooperative. Early chapters provide criticism of some administrative actions before we had established credibility and a formal team. The purpose of these case studies is to tell what happened and provide opportunities for learning. While striving to follow best practices, we accept that mistakes are inevitable. We are human and therefore fallible. We are thankful when mistakes cause no harm, or we can remedy any harm.

Confidentiality

Consistent with American Psychological Association guidelines, I have exercised care in maintaining confidentiality and the privacy of individuals and groups described in the case studies and reflections in this book. I have tried also to balance the need for reasonable confidentiality of events and interventions with the need to include honest, substantive educational material for those learning about or providing school crisis response.

Transcripts have been edited to remove the names of students, staff members, and schools involved in each response. Selected dialogue, drawn from multiple interviews and representative of typical intervention themes has been included for educational purposes, but edited to protect the privacy of individuals and groups. The names of response team colleagues and school staff have been either included by permission, replaced by pseudonyms, or identified only by job title.

While the nature of this book, documenting events in one school district, may lead some individuals to recognize themselves, editing has attempted to prevent others from recognizing them. I hope that those who recognize themselves will understand that my purpose is to inform and educate those engaging in, or learning about school crisis response, so they can better care for others and themselves.

Introduction

Natural and accidental disasters, gun violence, and other catastrophic events are tragic reminders of the need for training in school crisis response. While the most dramatic events lead to national headlines, lower profile, yet devastating crises occur in schools every day. This book focuses on the development of a crisis team and response to a variety of traumatic incidents in a large urban-suburban school district.

- We are called to an elementary school after the rape and murder of a third grader, accosted as she walked to her bus stop.
- When a popular middle school student suddenly collapses in the classroom, his classmates witness the school nurse trying to revive him.
- The murder of a high school senior is the most recent in a cycle of community violence that devastates students and staff.
- When a teacher revered for his work in Latino neighborhoods suffers an accidental death, the response team becomes a mobile crisis unit, demonstrating developmental and cultural sensitivity.
- A teacher shocks the conscience by raping a student. Her betrayal of trust and manipulation of students and staff victimizes the entire school community.

Purpose

Professionals working in schools inevitably confront crises, and must be trained to respond effectively. Traumatic incidents share common themes, although unique problems require creative solutions. A purpose of this book is to provide case studies to enhance the training, professional development, and service delivery of school psychologists, counselors, social workers, nurses, teachers, and administrators. Reflection on essential elements of crisis response is encouraged, to develop and strengthen university students, practitioners, and teams serving under the most difficult circumstances.

Textbooks and manuals describe how to respond to crises. Few describe the thoughts and emotions that guide the responder's application of concepts and skills in the field. Vivid illustrations provide a powerful training resource that transports the reader into the trenches, to confront the facts, feelings, difficult decisions, and unanticipated challenges of real crises. This book documents the process of multidimensional response to stabilize reactions, mitigate the effects of trauma, and support resilience and recovery.

Chapters also document the formation of a district crisis team, including the initial advocacy that brought it into being, and the ongoing work necessary for it to thrive. Insights are shared about the author's professional growth and self-acceptance as a team leader over a period of twenty years. Anecdotes document the personal journey of a school psychologist leading a crisis team. The author hopes this book will contribute to the effectivness and welfare of school crisis teams and caregivers.

Organization

Phases of Team Development

To orient the reader, *case study* and *reflection topic* chapters are presented within four sections corresponding to phases of team development described in chapter 4, *Establishing a Crisis Response Team*. The case studies are presented in the chronological order in which the traumatic incidents occurred.

Section 1: Team Planning and Advocacy—Establishing a Crisis Response Team describes the painful struggle of responding to crises without a team and without a plan. It reflects the challenges associated with advocating and planning for a crisis team.

Section 2: Team Formation—Implementing the Team and Establishing Credibility describes some of the new team's early responses, when lessons were learned without the benefit of previous experience, and credibility was sought with each intervention.

Reflections tackle issues related to knowledge and skill building in essential elements of crisis response.

Section 3: Team Development—Building Skills, Caring for Clients and Ourselves reveals how severely traumatic incidents mold character and blend experience with growing knowledge and skills. Reflections explore practical considerations such as addressing the media, planning memorials, being present, and caring for the caregiver.

Section 4: Team Maintenance—Sharing Leadership, Expanding Knowledge, Ongoing Challenges addresses the task of keeping a long-established team vital, coordinated, and interested in continuing to learn and develop skills. Reflections elaborate on evolving factors such as how best to disengage, leadership and teamwork, and awareness of how systems of people and processes interact during a crisis.

Case Studies and Reflections

The *case studies* with lessons learned describe responses to school crises from the perspective of a team leader. Interspersed with the case studies are *reflection* topics that discuss essential elements of response and apply evidence-based literature. These chapters elaborate on what was learned, and they describe the team's effort to educate and take care of itself.

The case study format begins with an *Abstract* to orient the reader to key issues in the response. The *Introduction* describes the traumatic incident, and in some cases, the school history and culture. To present a consistent framework for each unfolding event, case studies are organized by the four phases of crisis planning (Office of Safe and Drug Free Schools, U.S. Department of Education, 2007). The phases are **1)** *prevention/ mitigation,* **2)** *preparedness,* **3)** *response,* and **4)** *recovery.* Each case study concludes with *Lessons Learned: Reflection and Discussion.*

Note: The first three case studies, describing responses *before* a trained, coordinated team was formed, are not organized by headings of the four phases of crisis planning.

Prevention/Mitigation

Prevention involves creating a safe, supportive school climate with school-wide programs to enact violence prevention, anti-bullying, positive behavior supports, and social skills. *Mitigation* consists of ongoing actions that reduce or eliminate risks to people and property, thereby decreasing the likelihood of tragic events. Mitigation takes inventory of potential hazards, identifies ways to reduce injury or damage, assesses climate and perceived safety, and increases capacity to meet physical and emotional needs during a response (Reeves et al., 2010).

Preparedness

Preparedness addresses school and district readiness to coordinate effective crisis response. Preparedness involves proactively forming trained crisis teams, command systems and locations, community partnerships, materials, drills and practice (Reeves et al., 2010).

Response

Response involves mobilizing, evaluating, and implementing appropriate resources and interventions to minimize traumatic effects and restore adaptive coping. Assessing the situation and intervening consistent with need is critical, and can include such factors as coordinating school and district teams, implementing appropriate leadership, and conducting physical and psychological triage. As the response unfolds, flexible application of resources, leadership, and needed interventions is vital to achieve positive outcomes (Reeves et al., 2010).

Recovery

Recovery involves restoring, as quickly as possible, the physical and psychological safety and perceived security of students, staff, and community. During the response, a school provides multi-tiered interventions needed to stabilize students and staff, support coping, and re-establish pre-crisis capacity for learning. To the extent needed, a good recovery plan may include *psycho-*

education for school staff and family caregivers, ongoing psychological triage to support emotional needs, appropriate memorial activities, flexible and sustained recovery efforts, and examination of response effectiveness (Reeves et al., 2010).

PREPaRE Model

Within the organizational structure of each case study, the conceptual and skill development approach most often applied is the National Association of School Psychologists' (NASP) comprehensive, PREPaRE Model (Brock, 2011; Brock et al., 2009; Reeves et al., 2011). While most of the case studies occurred before, or during the early years of PREPaRE curriculum development, many of its concepts and lessons are applied for educational purposes. The PREPaRE Model presents a full range of coordinated, evidence-based crisis planning, prevention, intervention, and recovery concepts, designs, and strategies.

The PREPaRE Model (Brock et al., 2009) emphasizes that, as members of a school safety and crisis team, school mental health professionals must be involved in the following specific hierarchical and sequential set of activities:

P—**Prevent** and PREPaRE for psychological trauma

R—**Reaffirm** physical health and perceptions of security and safety

E—**Evaluate** psychological trauma risk

P—**Provide** interventions

a—**and**

R—**Respond** to psychological needs

E—**Examine** the effectiveness of crisis prevention and intervention.

Section 1

Team Planning and Advocacy: Establishing a Crisis Response Team

1   Accidental Death of a Student

2   Responding Alone to Death of a Colleague

3   Homicide of an Elementary School Student

4   Establishing a Crisis Response Team

5   Roles of Team Members

I

Accidental Death
of a Student

Abstract

This is the first of three case studies describing the frustrations encountered responding to a crisis before establishing a district team. It describes what happened at a high school after a popular student died. His high-risk behavior resulted in his electrocution. Crisis responders were unprepared to deal with the grieving students. Alienated from the larger school population, many of them had special needs. Responders helped the students work through grief, but rather than being debriefed as the response concluded, they were chastised by a supervisor for mistakes. *Aspects of this study include 1) counseling students with special needs and/or who are alienated; 2) understanding perspectives given minimal administrative support; 3) handling criticism in lieu of debriefing.*

I walked into a hot room crowded with about thirty high school students, some sitting in chairs, most huddled on the floor. They had been herded into this chamber adjoining the counseling suite because some had witnessed and others had heard about the death of a friend and fellow student the night before. After climbing a high voltage electrical tower, he was electrocuted.

Was this simply another of his risky pranks, or was it a gesture of defiant disdain for life? No one knew for certain, but most believed it was a cruel accident rather than a suicide. When he touched the transformer, an arc of 69,000 volts coursed through his body. Some said he was still alive after falling to the ground. Some even claimed he said something before dying.

We did not arrive as a team. Individual crisis responders were summoned to the high school by a phone call from a district office secretary. There was no district crisis team, no training or planning, no discussion with the principal, and little knowledge of, or opportunity for triage. I recall no briefing or faculty meeting. I do not recall whether there was a school-wide announcement, or an offer of counseling for students.

I believe the high school administration wanted to care for the grieving students but they were unprepared for crisis response. This negatively affected the administration's interface with the district psychologists, counselors, and social workers who entered the school as strangers without the cohesion or credibility of being part of a team. To me, it felt like we were tolerated rather than accepted.

Crisis Counseling with Alienated Students

The gathered students were some of the school's most disaffected—the "leather jacket crowd," alienated and segregated from most of the school population. To some, these students were more an annoyance than adolescents needing care. Many were from the Intensive Learning Center (ILC), which was designed for students with learning difficulties and behavior problems. They grieved their friend, a fellow ILC student not well known to most of the student body but popular among his peers.

I entered the crowded room and saw several of my colleagues among the bereaved students. I sat on the floor with students where quiet was interrupted by occasional sighs and sobbing. The young people had lost someone they admired.

Some of these students had earned a reputation for disruptive behavior and based perhaps on previous experience, the administration seemed to distrust them, treating them as though they needed to be controlled rather than counseled. In retrospect, this hardened lot grieved much like other traumatized adolescents.

4

The difference was that the present horror was the most recent in a succession of painful life experiences.

Some sat in quiet grief, without words to express their sorrow. Others appeared angry and agitated. It was as if all of the Kubler-Ross stages of grief (1997) were simultaneously in progress. Several girls sobbed in each other's arms while others leaned on comforting shoulders. A boy cursed in anger that something so senseless and tragic could have happened. Some sat bewildered and in denial, incredulous that it had happened at all. Some bargained with God for a different outcome. The room was a crucible of contradictory emotions.

The students found a focus as they talked about the accident details but were unable to separate rumor from fact. As responders, we could offer little information because we did not know the facts. When called to the school, I was told that a student had been accidentally electrocuted—nothing more. The school psychologist was skilled and caring but appeared immobilized. The school's counselors cared but they were more familiar with helping students file college applications than comforting alienated students. They had not formed relationships with our sad troop and showed little inclination to try.

We could do little other than be with them and listen as they spoke of the student who had died. "He was such a good person." "Why did he do it?" Angrily, "What a dumb thing to do." A theme of conflicted feelings emerged in their words. Sadness that they had lost a friend. Anger, not only at his death, but at his reckless actions that led to it. There was guilt. How could they feel so angry toward someone they valued and grieved? How could he do something so stupid?

I reflected, "It's okay to feel angry about what he did and still be sad that someone you care about died." There was silence, then more words. A colleague suggested the students share memories of their fallen friend. I thought, "No, too soon." But many shared anecdotes, some of them funny. There was ice-breaking laughter and it was okay.

No Comfortable Place

An assistant administrator moved the group to another location. We weren't sure where we were going, but ended up in the auditorium, which seemed like a terrible place to counsel students. Sitting face forward in seats, they were more isolated than before. It was nearly impossible for them to physically lean on each other for support though they continued clinging to each other emotionally and sharing memories. Just before lunch, someone suggested moving into the hallway, forming a circle and joining hands. Some spoke while others remained silent. The students seemed comforted, calmer than before. Then they were escorted to the chaos of the cafeteria for lunch.

After lunch, the students returned to the crowded room next to the counseling suite. We asked the administration for a larger, more appropriate space but none was available. The suite connected to a corridor leading outside to a grass lawn split by a concrete walk. Off campus, the street, cars, houses, and life were visible. We escorted the students outside where they could walk, talk, and get fresh air.

We stood on the lawn with the young people allowed a respite from the confined grief room inside. Two responders, reinforced by school counselors, patrolled the area. However, it seemed like no one was in control and that leadership was lacking. Rather than a crisis team, we were a loose band of skilled onlookers.

The vacuum in response leadership must have been apparent to the students, many of whom, after years of trouble, were sensitive to the adult climate around them. Several students standing at the far end of the lawn broke open a pack of cigarettes and began smoking. We looked the other way, pretending not to see. They puffed. We let it happen. With a clearer sense of leadership, with a longer standing relationship, would we have squelched the smoking? Probably. Under the circumstances of that first day, it was easy to look the other way though it would have been appropriate to caution the students against turning to alcohol or illegal substances to ease their pain. Right or wrong, we allowed the smokers the comfort of their cigarettes before leading them back inside. Several responders came up with a solution. We raided the school store and bought all the chewing gum in sight, and distributed it as an alternative to tobacco. Later we were criticized because students were chewing gum in class.

Constructive Direction

Eventually, we directed some of the student energy toward constructive acts, such as writing letters to create a memory book for the family. Other students plotted less constructive ways to empower themselves. By the time we realized the victim's possessions needed safeguarding, his jacket had disappeared. We were concerned that his locker might become a monument not to his memory, but to his final, high-risk act. There were rumors that students would smuggle his classroom chair off campus. We did not want it to become a throne celebrating his impulsive, possibly suicidal gesture. The room was monitored, and when not in use, locked.

A source of anger for some students was that the school, ostensibly because it had not received official notification, did not formally recognize the death. A couple of rebels were furious that the school did not adequately acknowledge their fallen comrade. They tried to remedy that condition. On the second day of our tentative, unassertive response, someone noticed that the United States flag flew in front of the school at half-staff. It was not long before one of the faculty, a former Girl Scout leader, complained to the school administration, citing clear directives about appropriate circumstances for flying a flag at half-staff. She was right. The flag was correctly restored to its normal height. Some students took this as a slap in the face—a sign of disrespect toward them.

Impact on Students with Special Needs

Awareness of the impact of school crises on special needs populations is apparent in literature and practice (Bates & Spears, 2010; Lavin, 1998; Susan, 2010). Special needs include physical and learning disabilities, cognitive and developmental disabilities, autism spectrum disorders, and behavioral and emotional disturbances. Students with special needs often feel the impact of trauma more personally, more intensely than others, and may need special support and treatment to understand and recover from crises. Special needs populations may have relatively poor problem-solving and coping skills. Most of the high school students with whom we worked had been diagnosed with learning or emotional problems. Their previous experiences made them more vulnerable to intense reactions after the death of an admired peer. Their status in the ILC signaled that they were a troubled, but tight-knit group. Surprisingly, some assumed remarkable leadership roles supporting others in their group.

What We Accomplished

During the two days of our response, our interventions yielded mixed results. We did our best to provide support, emotional first aid, and crisis counseling for the affected students. Fearing they would be unable to concentrate, we advocated, unsuccessfully, for several girls seeking to be excused from an exam. By telephone, we contacted parents of those identified as most severely affected. We listened to the students, sat and walked with them, guided them through a difficult time toward coping, constructive action, and normalcy. We encouraged them to return to class.

We established a degree of rapport with some of the more stable and the most troubled students. Some began privately sharing information about their lives, including struggles they faced. I don't believe we did much more than actively listen to their stories, being present for them, reflecting their feelings, showing that we cared. As we neared the conclusion of the response, something unusual happened. Several of the students walked up to responders and individually thanked them for being there. In many years of crisis response that followed, we never expected direct expressions of appreciation from students and rarely got them. I felt this response was difficult and disjointed. We could have been more helpful, yet they thanked us.

An Attempt to Support a Colleague

Early on the morning after the school had returned to routine, I returned to the school alone. I sensed my fellow school psychologist, assigned to the high school, needed more support, perhaps a chance to talk. As I sat waiting in the "grief room" adjoining the counseling suite, the principal suddenly appeared and asked, "What are you doing here?"

I felt like the enemy, an unwelcome alien. "I'm here to see Laura," I replied. "She's not here today," he said. I left.

Minimal Administrative Support

It is helpful to try to understand various perspectives during a crisis. I was unable to grasp the perspective of the principal then although the passage of time has fostered understanding. For years, the principal had been an effective old school, no-nonsense administrator. Many of the affected students had been troublesome, and some were capable of violent behavior and suspected of using illegal substances on campus. The principal either chose not to, or was unable to change his attitude relative to these students. He remained the disciplinarian, with control the priority over trust. In a sense, perhaps he was right. Some students needed the secure structure of an authority figure while we did our grief counseling.

Still, it felt bad for us, perceiving that both students and responders were sometimes treated like the enemy. Lack of acceptance precluded our joining the school administration and staff in a consultative relationship to plan a coherent response. Without a district or school team, there was no clarity regarding the expected roles of the administration, staff, or crisis responders.

Debriefed or Chastised?

About a week after the response, our district supervisor met with the responders in a high school conference room. No one was told the reason for the meeting. Would our supervisor preside over a debriefing to examine lessons learned? Not exactly. She criticized responders for a litany of indiscretions including the cigarettes, the flag, the chewing gum, the lack of discipline. We listened incredulously. Apparently, she had been briefed about what we did wrong but not what we did right. We were not invited to share our feelings. This humiliation was our "care for the caregiver."

The way crisis responders were perceived and treated was not the fault of the school or the administration or even the supervisor. It was the fault of a system unprepared for a traumatic incident. This was the national norm before mandates requiring crisis response preparation were issued after the Columbine tragedy.

Lessons Learned: Reflection and Discussion

1. After traumatic events, there is a need for trained, skilled school and district crisis team collaboration to meet student and staff needs. *What are some disadvantages of entering a school in crisis without teams or plans?*

2. It is imperative to pre-plan a comfortable location for triage and crisis counseling with areas for group and individual interventions. *What messages do students get from not having an appropriate place to be together, grieve, and receive support?*

3. Students challenged with special needs are vulnerable during traumatic events, and benefit from clear boundaries, but are also capable of empathy and support for others. They also need respect to support constructive grieving and progress toward recovery. *Describe ways that students with special needs are at risk in crises, and how their physical and emotional needs can be met.*

4. School administration support for the crisis team and the team's support for administration is a two-way street. After a traumatic incident, the principal faces tremendous pressure and multiple tasks. The crisis team can offer emotional support, foster communication, and share responsibilities with the principal. *Describe ways the crisis team can approach a principal and offer support.*

5. Debriefing caregivers after a traumatic incident is important. Recognizing effective aspects of the response helps the team examine difficulties and ways to improve. *How can administrators learn about the needs of those affected as well as caregiver needs during and after response?*

2

Responding Alone
to Death of a Colleague

Abstract

This, the second of three case studies on responding to a crisis
before establishing a district team, describes the aftermath of
the sudden death of a mentor and friend. The author, a young
psychologist, copes with his own grief while responding to the
needs of students and staff, gaining insights and helping students
alleviate feelings of guilt caused by magical thinking. He learns
first hand the importance of cultural sensitivity. *Themes are:
1) responding without a district crisis team, 2) counseling students
while grieving, 3) magical thinking and guilt, 4) cultural sensitivity:
unprepared for a funeral..*

Janet Newsome was an educational diagnostician. I was
new to the district and to the profession and she became
my mentor and friend. We worked together closely in two
schools where I was the assigned school psychologist. Her greatest
strength was forming relationships with students, including
those struggling with academics and challenging behavior. She
liked them and they responded. Each morning, before the start
of classes, a steady stream of Asian, Black, Latino, and White
students flowed in and out of her office. Their color or ethnicity
did not matter. Some had progress reports to be signed. Others
just needed her help or encouragement.

"The kids always come first," she often said.

Janet helped me realize that morning hall duty was a real opportunity to get to know some of more than a thousand pupils as they entered school each day.

"Think how many students you can see arriving. Start their day with a smile," she coaxed.

I began to look forward to standing in the hallway, greeting students as they poured in, some chatting with friends, most trudging in mechanically, like little robots. If a student came within five feet of me, I would smile and say, "Good morning" or "Hello" or "Welcome." I rarely got a response or even eye contact. I persisted and, after awhile, some replied with "Hi" or a smile. Occasionally a student entered crying or with a frown or a scowl. I could give them attention and point them toward a counselor.

One day Janet suggested we go out to lunch. After we ordered food she said, "You know you are being watched."

"Being watched? What do you mean?"

"The black teachers, especially [an older, veteran male teacher] are watching to see how you are with black students. Do you treat them differently? Do you see mostly white students and ignore black students?"

"Wow, I had no idea," I replied, feeling uncomfortable.

I tested more than 100 students a year doing psychoeducational assessments. Too many were African American. Too many were being tested, regardless of race. But Janet was not referring to those being tested. She was referring to the students with whom I was forming relationships, encouraging, consulting with teachers and caring about. Janet's strength was forming helping relationships because "the kids always come first."

"How am I doing?"

"You are doing fine, but remember, you are being watched."

As winter break approached, we were tired, but excited about some well-deserved time off. On the last day before break, the school had nearly emptied. I looked for Janet to wish her a happy holiday but couldn't find her. I locked my office door and walked to the parking lot. With a veil of light snow covering the cars, there was my friend brushing snow from her car. I sauntered over and helped finish the job. We hugged and wished each other a happy holiday. Janet reminded me to come to the Christmas party at her house. We said, "Goodbye." That was the last time I saw her alive.

A school secretary called the next day with news that Janet, who was 48, had collapsed at home while shoveling snow and died.

The rest of that holiday was a blur. The first day back, the faculty was called into the library. The principal shared what everyone knew. I was feeling distracted and grieving when the principal appropriately asked me, the school psychologist, to say a few words to the faculty. Taken by surprise, I recall making eye contact with the veteran African American teacher and feeling his silent strength and support. He was no longer watching me in judgment. He was with me in sorrow. It is difficult to remember exactly what I said or whether I was able to hold back tears.

"Janet was my friend—this is a hard time for all of us. We need to lean on each other for support. Janet often said, 'The kids always come first.' Let's be vigilant for those who need help. Send them to me or to the counselors."

Magical Thinking and Guilt

Soon, two tearful fifth-grade girls came to my office, one black, one white. The friends were inconsolable, explaining that they argued a lot and Ms. Newsome had advised them not to fight. She wanted them to learn how to get along better, but they argued again just before winter break. They thought it was their fault that she died. I remained calm, but did not hold back tears. In clinical studies, I had learned about magical thinking that young children sometimes exhibit, especially during crises. It is a false belief that there is a causal relationship between a discrete action by a person and a specific event. These girls believed their argument caused Janet's death. Their magical thinking was a source of pain much too heavy to bear any longer. Through my sorrow, I was elated that they came to me.

Waiting until they were calm enough to hear me, I spoke clearly and directly to them, even invoking some expertise.

"Listen, I am a school psychologist. I know about these things. I am taught to understand feelings. It is not your fault that Ms. Newsome died. You are not to blame."

"Do you hear what I am saying?"

"Yes," they both nodded, relaxing just a bit.

"Your fighting had nothing to do with Ms. Newsome dying. It is not your fault. She had a serious illness. Ms. Newsome cared about both of you, whether you argued or not. Friends sometimes argue. It is normal. Maybe you can get help figuring out how to argue less. Working out your disagreements and getting along better is one way to honor Ms. Newsome's memory."

Their burden seemed lighter as they left the office. They seemed to believe me and I felt okay that we had grieved together. They saw my tears, but they also saw I was in control of those emotions to the extent that the kids came first.

I phoned the district supervisor of school psychologists and reached voicemail. I left a message asking for help. I was seeing students and staff, but needed help for them and for me. I don't know if anyone listened to the voicemail. I never heard back. I never got the help. It was my job to do the best I could. It was my school. Besides, I was too busy to think about it after that call. Much later, I became conscious of the resentment I felt that my request brought no help. It may be that my voicemail never reached the ears of my supervisor. I will never know for sure. What I do know is that I was essentially on my own, grieving with a school in grief.

Cultural Sensitivity: the Funeral

I had a hard time at Janet's funeral. Full of 'fire and brimstone,' the minister seemed angry, and he seemed to exclude people having other beliefs. He shouted and chanted a message that seemed threatening. Janet wasn't like this. Janet's caring was inclusive. It didn't matter about race or religion or ethnicity. Her message was kindness for all—kindness to children. I wanted to stand up and describe the Janet I knew—what she valued. I was sitting next to the principal. She saw that I was agitated.

"I need to get up and say something about Janet."

"No, stay here. This is the way the service was planned. This is comforting for the family. Leave it alone."

She was right. I was unprepared for this kind of funeral. I was not sensitive to the religious and cultural differences of the African-American Baptist service. It took awhile for the lesson to sink in, but I learned something about the need to help others prepare for religious and cultural differences in the expression of grief, mourning, and the associated rituals. I still think Janet might have wanted another message at her funeral service, but what I thought wasn't important. I'll always remember Janet and her message, "The kids always come first."

Lessons Learned: Reflection and Discussion

1. Staff responders in a school where a traumatic incident occurs are likely to need emotional and logistical support to help them work effectively with students and colleagues. *What are ways to provide support for crisis responders and staff so they are stabilized and able to care for students?*

2. School and district responders should be prepared with information and handouts to help teachers recognize and address the needs of students affected by a traumatic incident. *What would you say to a grieving school staff gathered for a briefing after the sudden death of an admired student or teacher?*

3. Recognizing and addressing rumors, misinformation, and false beliefs such as magical thinking can aid the crisis counseling process and foster recovery. *How is it beneficial to debunk rumors and correct students' false beliefs?*

4. Proactive planning for culturally sensitive understanding of funeral rituals can reduce stress and promote healing. *What are some ways that students and staff can be prepared for cultural differences at a funeral or other events they attend?*

3

Homicide
of an
Elementary School Student

Abstract

This is the last of three cases where we responded to a crisis before establishing a district team. It describes what happened after a third grader was abducted while walking to the school bus. Even untrained responders were a welcome sight for the beleaguered school psychologist who was caring for many distraught children. *Themes include 1) responding without a district crisis team, 2) reaffirming children's safety and security, 3) explaining death to children. The section concludes with a useful handout.*

A colleague and I joined the school psychologist at a small elementary school where a third grader had been raped and murdered in the woods near her home. She was last seen walking in the early morning to the school bus.

We found the school psychologist in his office with three third graders, all crying inconsolably. His pained expression was the only communication possible as the girls wailed. He was relieved to see us. We began seeing small groups and individual students. We triaged to discover the most needy—those who had seen the police and EMT first responders and those who had seen the victim's body. Some even said they knew the perpetrator. Law enforcement personnel would interview them. In the meantime, we applied psychological first aid, invited discussion about death and grieving, provided drawing materials complements of the art teacher, helped the principal compose a letter to the school community, and we flew mostly by the seat of our pants.

Reaffirming Safety and Security

We reassured the children that sad and horrific events sometimes happen, but they are rare. We reminded them that caring adults (their parents and guardians) at home and at school are determined to protect them and keep them safe. We shared and discussed with them what they could do to stay safe.

While young children need to grieve, it is most important that initial psychological intervention recognize and address their fears with honest reassurance.

Lessons Learned: Reflection and Discussion

1. Reaffirming children's perceptions of safety and security and reuniting them with support networks in the family, school, and community are basic and powerful interventions in many responses to tragic events. *What are honest ways to reassure children that they are safe and protected while also encouraging them to feel capable of taking initiative in addressing their fears?*

2. In many crises, it is imperative to educate families regarding children's typical reactions, useful adult listening skills, stress management, coping strategies, and the possible need for referral. *Consider ways (resources and opportunities) that needed psychoeducation can be provided for families in an impacted community.*

∽

A tragedy of this magnitude occurred while I served at a parochial school in Philadelphia. The following letter, edited for confidentiality, was distributed to the school and at a community meeting.

Words of Support

We are brought together tonight by the tragic death of
_____. As teachers, counselors, parents, and friends of the
_____ school community, we feel many emotions in the
face of the violent loss of this ____ year old student. We
are angry, sad, shocked, and frustrated over this senseless
death. We share a sense of anguish and outrage.

As parents, you are concerned about your children and
may be asking, "How can we help them through this difficult time? How can we assure them of their safety, allay
their fears, and answer their questions."

As parents, indeed as adults, our natural inclination is
often to shield and protect children from a trauma like this.
And yet, *a tragic reality* has become part of their world and
school community.

As adults we often worry about finding the *right words*
or saying the *right thing* to children who seem so vulnerable. We know from our experience working with children
after a crisis how helpful an honest "I don't know why"—
simply and caringly stated, can be. An explanation that
sometimes mom, dad, teacher, and counselor do **not** have
all the answers, especially to the most profound questions.
There are many things parents can do within the family,
such as reassuring the children of your love and your ability
to care for and protect them. Repeat this many times. Children need to hear that what happened is most unusual—a
rare event to counter their fantasies about how such a thing
could have happened. Their fantasies will be expressed in
various ways, depending on the child's age and development.

**Listen to the children and respond to their feelings,
validating them and letting them know they are not alone
with their scary thoughts and sad and angry feelings.**

The [counseling] staff has met with the faculty to assist
teachers in helping students cope with this crisis.

Additionally, the counseling staff has met with each

19

5th grade class and one 4th grade class. In these meetings, the students had an opportunity to share their feelings, questions, concerns and memories of _____. The children responded well to this opportunity.

I would like to be more specific about what we have learned in dealing with similar crises.

Consider the following points, which we can discuss in the question and answer period.

- Children need to be reassured that they are safe and that caring adults at home and in school are determined to maintain their security. When children ask or indicate a need to understand, it is important to give them correct, age-appropriate information to the degree that we know it, but without disturbing or unnecessary details. As hard as it is to talk about the death of a classmate, if an attempt is made to conceal the incident, it will create confusion for children who may already have heard many different details.

- Children express their grief differently than adults. Their sadness is often short-lived, giving the impression that they are indifferent, or unaffected. Children may have difficulty putting their feelings into words. When behavioral changes are observed by adults, they can ask but not force children to express their underlying feelings.

- Grieving children can experience behavioral changes as a result of their upset and anxiety. Contrary to the behavior seen in adults, they are frequently mischievous, angry, boisterous and noisy. These changes should be viewed as transient. Teachers and parents can respond with understanding and patience. For example, you might say, "I know you are upset and it's hard for you to concentrate but you have to try to do your homework (or your seatwork, etc.)"

- Elementary school children may see death as a form of punishment. They need to be reassured that death doesn't happen if you do something bad. Children often think about death in terms of their own responsibility. They have a kind of magical thinking and need to be told that nobody can cause the death of someone else by having bad thoughts or feelings. Children may not ask about this because they're afraid of the answer.

- We don't believe that death happens as a form of punishment. This did not happen to the victim as a consequence of something she did. The victim is not responsible.
- Parents may respond consistent with their religious or spiritual beliefs. Sometimes children fear that God has chosen certain people to die. The problem this can create for children is anger toward God and difficulty perceiving God as a loving figure. This is a tragic event for which there is no rational explanation. It is okay to say, "I don't know."
- Children may tend to imitate their parents' coping behaviors. When parents are able to cope calmly and directly, children are in a better position to cope. Parents and families have their own style of dealing with crises. Know your style and address the issues within that framework.
- Feel free to call and speak with the counselors.

4

Establishing a Crisis Response Team

Reflections

Psychological First Aid

Brock (2002a, 2012) describes some of the characteristics of crisis events, including that 1) they are perceived as extremely negative (Carlson, 1997) and cause extreme physical or psychological pain; 2) they are uncontrollable, thus generating "feelings of helplessness, powerlessness, and entrapment" (APA, 2000); and 3) they often occur suddenly and without warning (APA, 2000). The suddenness and unpredictability of a crisis tends to increase the traumatic effect since there is little time to prepare or adapt to problems generated by the crisis (Carlson, 1997; Saylor et al., 1997).

The functional goals of crisis intervention—called psychological first aid—include 1) stabilizing symptoms to avert the worsening of distress and impairment reactions; 2) reducing symptoms by supporting constructive grieving and recovery; and 3) reestablishing functional capacity, or referring for more intensive treatment (Everly, 1999; Everly & Mitchell, 2003). Brock et al. (2009) emphasize that in the school setting, "the primary goal of... intervention is to help restore the crisis-exposed student's basic problem-solving abilities and in doing so to return them to their precrisis levels of functioning" (Brock, 2012; Sandoval & Brock, 2009).

Need for School Crisis Response Teams

Establishing and preparing crisis response teams is a vital need in schools, given the vulnerability of young people, the prevalence of traumatic incidents, the nature of relationships, and the unique constellation of consequences after school crises. Crisis teams not only respond during and after a crisis, they are involved in proactive preparation and prevention of incidents (PREPaRE Model: School Crisis Teams/ Preventing and Preparing for Psychological Trauma). Rossen and Cowan (2013) emphasize that schools can provide trained, caring adults; a learning environment that develops resilience and coping skills; and partnerships with families and community resources that offer comprehensive systems of support (Blaustein, 2013; Nickerson & Heath, 2008; Reeves et al., 2012; Reeves et al., 2010).

Tragic events that affect schoolchildren underscore the need for district-level response capability. When there is a sudden traumatic event that affects groups of students and staff, the ability to evaluate situations and make decisions can be compromised. Severe trauma can quickly exhaust a school's resources. The availability of trained district or regional teams is critical. An experienced team with proactive plans is likely to perform efficiently and effectively when a school needs supplemental services. The first three days are critical, when responders evaluate psychological trauma, mitigate stress reactions, and contribute to long-term recovery (Kennedy-Paine et al., 2014).

Prior to establishing a district team, our school psychologists responded individually to crises. We grew frustrated without collaboration or an action plan. We were unprepared when a teenager died and yet again when a young girl was killed. In both situations, a trained team would have offered a more skilled response. Our district psychologists resolved to form a planning committee, write a proposal, and establish a team.

Initial Request Denied

Our first request to form a district-level team was turned down perhaps due to long-standing district norms dictating that the principal is the autocratic leader whose territory shall not be infringed. Institutional denial is another obstacle that occurs when an organization denies the potential for the occurrence of a traumatic event, adopting the myth that not talking about possible future crises will prevent them from happening. "If we just ignore the painful reality that something bad might happen, everything will be all right." This false belief leads to being unprepared when the inevitable crisis occurs.

Futility of Re-Inventing the Wheel

Our team shares a heritage common to many budding crisis teams. The impetus for team formation came not from wisdom of a desire to prevent and plan for school crises, but rather from the frustration of repeated responses without a plan or coordination. It came from our realization of the futility of "re-inventing the wheel" in difficult circumstances.

Brock et al. (1996) advise not to become frustrated if there is resistance to crisis team proposals. They suggest continuing self-education and development efforts until crises change attitudes. We were fortunate to have a small group of committed individuals with a desire to make the case for a team and to educate others. Dwyer and Jimerson (2002) emphasize the importance of ensuring a system of support either in the form of a directive or at least permission from top-level administrators to begin the process. We lobbied for months, finally receiving permission to proceed. Our team began a long journey toward competence and acceptance.

Reflections on Early History

Several years after our team was established, I reflected on our team's history in an address to crisis responders. Here's what I said.

> Sometimes when you deal with crises, you forget to eat. We've learned that responders need to take care of each other. So it is appropriate that we have this dinner meeting as part of our training. The atmosphere here is relaxed and crisis free. Let's enjoy that peace and remember we must also

nurture ourselves when there is a crisis.

Some years ago, if there was a traumatic event and a school required outside help, one or two school psychologists or counselors would get a phone call from a district secretary saying, "There is an emergency at _____ School. Can you get over there? Imagine arriving at the school and being informed that a girl had been murdered on the way to the bus stop. Imagine walking into a room where her friends cry inconsolably, surrounding a school psychologist who manages only a forlorn expression. We begin reflexively to react—triage with no plan... smaller groups... individual counseling... let them talk... let them draw... call home... get through the day.

Responding to crises in those days often meant:
- Feeling uninvited
- Feeling chaos
- Feeling helpless
- Working with colleagues without a plan
- Reinventing the wheel every time
- Doing some extraordinary work without coordinated preparation
- Being exhausted without a network of support
- Having some knowledge, but not enough
- Having individual skills, but not enough collaboration
- Feeling that something needed to happen.

At the Delaware Association of School Psychologists (DASP) Conference in May, 1992, I gave a presentation on crisis teams. Afterward, a group of school psychologists sat around a café table. We resolved to educate ourselves and form a competent, district-level team. Joan English wrote a proposal for team formation.

Guess what happened? We were told, "No, you may not proceed."

There were reasonable concerns about usurping authority from school administrators. We persisted because of our experience and belief in the need. We lobbied and reassured administrators. A skeptical administrator became our advisor, then our advocate.

We addressed the concerns.

- District team will be invited only at the discretion of the principal;
- Principal maintains leadership of the process with option to designate authority;
- District team will consult with the building team that knows their students;
- Building and district teams will blend, sharing observed needs through briefings.

We received the go-ahead to organize a district team and sought training opportunities. They were also thrust upon us with each response.

We continue to learn from every incident and to educate students and staff using many teachable moments presented by adversity.

Phases of Crisis Team Development

Reflecting on the establishment of our team, four phases of development are evident. The points under each phase are relevant to the development of most school crisis teams. The following phases constitute the four sections of this book:

Phase I: Team Planning and Advocacy

A small core group, disenchanted with unpreparedness, advocate for developing a crisis team.

We wrote a proposal and talked with district administrators to gain support. We included a budget.

Administrative approval is critical for team formation to proceed.

Phase II: Team Formation

We recruited team members, compiled phone lists, and assigned member roles. We developed response checklists, planned meetings, and wrote a manual.

Our goal was to include representatives of elementary and secondary grades, administrators, school psychologists, counselors, social workers, and nurses.

Coordinators share leadership roles. Generally coordinators are a school psychologist, a counselor, and/or a social worker. We planned responders' roles and functions in a way that was flexible enough to adapt to the specific needs of each unique crisis.

While a nucleus of responders is on call, the school principal can request additional trained staff when needed. In larger districts, capacity can expand to several teams.

We planned logistics and procedures for team notification and mobilization and we planned school and district-team collaboration-protocols for consulting with and joining schools in crisis.

We refined the crisis manual and distributed it to schools to publicize the district team and to support forming teams in the schools. We offered to consult on establishing school teams. We gave the manuals to police and firefighters.

We established a regular schedule of team meetings and training.

Phase III: Team Development

We provided school administrators with a description of the district team's mission, membership list, and contact numbers. We also provided them with the procedure to initiate consultation and mobilization of the district team.

Team coordinators facilitate regularly scheduled meetings with member input. The team identifies training needs and sets annual developmental goals.

The team defines itself as a Crisis Response Team. Identification as a team develops during formation, but is forged through the first responses and many that follow. Team members begin trusting each other, assuming necessary functions, communicating constructively, supporting, and caring for one another.

The processes of briefing and debriefing during and after responses become a vehicle for ongoing team learning and development.

School principals and administrators begin to request and accept district team involvement. Credibility as a team spreads through helpful responses and by word of mouth between school administrators and staff.

The district team sponsors workshops for administrators, support staff, and teachers. District team continues to coordinate and consult as every school develops its own crisis team.

Phase IV: Team Maintenance

A dynamic work group that clings to the status quo risks stagnation. Even the most effective teams require maintenance to remain viable. Maintenance requires continuous learning, improvement, and development.

We scheduled periodic meetings to assess and address current needs and to provide relevant discussion and training. Our members held demanding jobs and there was pressure to cancel meetings. Determined team leaders continued to schedule meetings on a regular basis.

After assessing needs, we followed with relevant training, both for team members and district personnel. Drills and practice are difficult to organize, but vital. Collaboration with other agencies can be useful in providing drills.

We used crisis briefings and debriefings for ongoing learning; to facilitate responders' recovery; and to examine ways to improve effectiveness.

We rotated team leadership and membership, as needed, to guard against burnout and to monitor members for symptoms of stress reactions. Some members maintain resilience for many years, while others need periodic rotation off the team for a respite of a year or more. A large responder pool allows rotation, and the option to mobilize two or more teams.

We tried to offer care for the caregiver during and after responses to traumatic events. Debriefings should become a regular part of response closure. We noticed that members with a pattern of avoiding closure debriefings were sometimes raising red flags that needed attention.

We engaged in ongoing communication with school and district administrators. We began each school year distributing updated information about the team's mission, membership, contact numbers, and consultation and mobilization procedures.

We made opportunities for training and workshops available within and outside the school district. The PREPaRE curriculum training is highly recommended.

We recommend team-building activities that are fun and energizing although finding time for such events is difficult.

Appreciation and acknowledgement mean a lot. Team members often praise and reinforce each other's efforts during and after a response. We appreciated the recognition and thanks received from school administrators, teachers, district administrators, and occasionally from parents.

An Ongoing Challenge

Crisis response readiness is now generally accepted. Educators have access to the National Association of School Psychologists' comprehensive PREPaRE training (Brock et al., 2009). However, team maintenance remains a challenge. In many states, mandates to form crisis teams can become fading echoes in the hallways of schools preoccupied with high-stakes test scores. While school districts no longer obstruct the formation of crisis teams, they sometimes forget the need to support them, or, with competing pressures, they sometimes set an unrealistically low priority for crisis prevention, preparedness, and response.

5

Roles of Team Members

Reflections

Qualities, Functions, and Development

Significant benefits are derived from team training, planning, practice, and discussion of role responsibilities and leadership functions. Roles and functions must be clear, but also flexible and subject to change as a crisis unfolds. Team members often repeat the same role for multiple crises, but roles may change, given the unique demands of each crisis. Increased comfort with crisis response generally flows from a combination of training, knowledge, skill development, and productive experience. Having or developing certain personal qualities and skills can be a vital resource during response.

Develop Qualities, Skills in Team Members
- Feel comfortable talking with children about trauma and death in disturbing surroundings.
- Have appropriate knowledge, training, and practice in crisis evaluation and response, grief reactions, and post-traumatic stress.
- Have the ability to be with survivors of emotional trauma without trying to make them feel better immediately.
- Understand developmental grief and stress reactions and needs.
- Have the ability to establish rapport quickly, but respond patiently, according to each child's pace and needs.

- Are sensitive to cultural differences and feel comfortable working with consultants and language interpreters, when needed.
- Have knowledge, training, and practice using interventions such as psychological first aid and triage.
- Have the ability to work well with others, be flexible, take initiative, share leadership functions, and solve problems collaboratively in difficult, rapidly changing circumstances.
- Have the ability to monitor system-wide needs, including managing personal stress and that of fellow responders.
- Are resilient, appreciate even small gains, and enjoy empowering others.

School Level Crisis Team Membership

Within schools, team membership is comprised of staff members who have an interest in and want to develop skills in response preparedness. For administrators, counselors, psychologists, social workers and nurses, school team membership is a natural extension of their usual work roles.

Suggested members of a building crisis team:
- Principal
- Assistant Principal or designee
- School Counselor(s)
- Faculty Member
- Security Officer
- School Psychologist
- School Nurse

Source: Petersen & Staub, 1992.

Major Responsibilities of Key Personnel

School Principal

- Direct intervention.
- Be visible, available, supportive and empowering.
- Direct teachers on how much to set aside curriculum and postpone tests.

32

- Communicate with central administration and other affected schools.
- In the event of death, contact family of the deceased.
- Inform staff and students about funeral arrangements.
- Ensure that memorials are appropriate.

Counselor/School Psychologist/Social Worker

- Be available and prepared to cancel other activities.
- Locate additional counseling assistance, including local resources (district, community).
- Provide crisis counseling for individuals and groups.
- Contact parents of affected students with suggestions for support or referral.
- Contact other affected schools.
- In the event of death, follow the schedule of the deceased and visit classrooms.
- Support the faculty, providing counseling as needed.
- Keep records of affected students, providing follow-up and referral services.

Teacher

- Provide accurate information to students (without unnecessary or violent details).
- Lead classroom discussions that help students cope with loss.
- Dispel rumors.
- Recognize the varying religious beliefs held by students.
- Model an appropriate response.
- Give permission for a range of emotions.
- Identify students who need counseling and refer to building crisis team.
- Provide activities such as art work, music, and writing to reduce trauma.
- Set aside the academic curriculum as needed.
- Discuss funeral procedures and expectations.
- Use "teachable moments" for prevention and safety planning.

Source: Poland, 1997.

PREP<u>a</u>RE's Incident Command System

Team Structure and Member Roles

The PREP<u>a</u>RE Model is an outstanding resource for planning crisis team organization, roles and functions (Brock et al., 2009). The following summarizes the Incident Command System adapted from the National Incident Management System (2004)).

Incident Commander (IC)

Administrator-in-charge (e.g. superintendent, principal, site administrator or designee, or crisis team coordinator) has overall responsibility for the response.

Planning/Intelligence Section ("Thinkers")

Crisis Team Chair/Coordinator (e.g. assistant principal, school psychologist, counselor, or designee)

Operations Section ("Doers")

School Security and Safety Coordinator/Officer (e.g. school resource officer, school security, or designee)
Student Care/Mental Health Officer (e.g. school psychologist, social worker, counselor, community mental health, or designee)
Emergency Medical Care Coordinator (e.g. nurse)
Translation and Cultural Mediator Coordinator/Liaisons (e.g. community liaison)

Logistics Section ("Getters")

Facilities (e.g. building engineer)
Supplies and Equipment (e.g. office personnel)
Staff and Community Volunteer Assignment/Coordinator
Communications (e.g. public information officer or designee)

Finance Section ("Payers")

For a more detailed description of role responsibilities, review the functions outlined in PREP<u>a</u>RE. Even better, secure PREP<u>a</u>RE training!

The PREP<u>a</u>RE team organization of roles and functions provides a useful guide, but may prove difficult to fully implement in some districts. In practice, the leadership command structure may be a more flexible, collaborative blend of building and district thinkers, doers, and getters. In small or fiscally struggling districts, individuals may perform multiple roles. For all districts, the PREPaRE Model provides a useful checklist to make certain that significant team member roles and responsibilities are considered. Application of any model should proceed with the understanding that one size does not fit all. Schools, districts, and crises require that models be adapted for available resources and unique challenges.

Leadership Functions and Reciprocal Support

Effective communication with a supportive, inviting school administration is crucial for the crisis team. Support must also flow from the team to the administrators. The principal, more than anyone, feels responsible for what happens in the school building and may need special support after a traumatic incident. Leadership within the blended school and district teams can be distributed among one or more coordinators consulting with the principal or a designee. The team can have many functional leaders in various areas of a multidimensional response. There are opportunities for team members to exert leadership as unanticipated needs or tasks arise during debriefing sessions. Coordination of the response should always respect the principal's authority and demanding role during a crisis (Poland & Poland, 2004).

Multiple Roles of School Counselors

Fein et al. (2008) addressed the specific role of school counselors during the response to school shootings. Counselors were concerned that they were inadequately prepared for multiple roles during crises *beyond* direct care of students. A survey of school counselors identified the need for preparation in four areas:

1. To assume leadership roles;
2. To resolve role conflicts, i.e. exerting authority that "outranks" a principal or superintendent during a crisis and then returns to pre-crisis position;

35

3. To employ subtle counseling to support peer responders and administrators;

4. To debrief; to recognize the danger of secondary trauma; and to care for one's self.

A Model for Forming a District Team

Members of the district team are drawn from individuals throughout the district whose job skills contribute to response and who are available to be on call. In my experience, district team membership was voluntary with little need for recruitment. Personnel new to the district often have a professional and personal interest in serving.

Large or combined school districts with a sufficient member pool can provide the option of rotating membership. Team members can choose to remain on the crisis team while others prefer to rotate off, with the option of returning after a break.

Our district formed three distinct teams, all led by the same coordinators. The breadth and intensity of a crisis determines whether one, two, or all three teams mobilize to the same location. This plan provides flexibility, as separate teams can be deployed to multiple schools, if necessary. It also provides an opportunity to rotate mobilization among the teams in order to allow more time for members to recover between incidents. Multiple teams can focus on either elementary or secondary populations.

Questions for Discussion and Planning

This section raises questions for discussion on planning for a crisis response team and the roles and responsibilities of its members.

I. Team Levels and Functions

What are the team levels and the function of each level? Teams may be national, regional, district or school level and they may interact with other teams such as law enforcement, firefighters, and emergency medical. While we recommend proactive planning with outside teams, the focus here is the interface between district and school-level teams.

2. District- and School-Level Team Member Responsibilities

What are the differences in district and school level team membership and role responsibilities? District and school teams should plan for coordinated, collaborative services during a crisis. A traumatic incident may negatively affect the capacity of a school team to respond, requiring the resources and support of a district-level team.

3. Group and Individual Member Qualities

What qualities are worth developing in the group and among individual team members? Are there differences and similarities in desirable qualities of district and school level teams?

4. Training and Skills for District and School Team Members

What training and skills are needed to develop the members of district and school level teams?

5. Role Responsibilities Assumed by Key School Personnel

What are the role responsibilities assumed by key school personnel when a crisis requires that their usual duties expand to crisis team member? How do the building principal, counselor, psychologist, and teachers fit into the overall response structure?

6. Availability of Team Members

What is the availability of team members in the event of a crisis? Is there flexibility for mobilizing a small or large number of responders, depending upon incident needs? How quickly can responders be mobilized? Are there plans for both short- and long-term response, and reinforcements, if needed?

7. Team Structure, Roles, and Functions

What is the structure, roles and functions of district level and other externally based teams providing crisis response in school settings? How will the need for intervention by district and regional teams be determined?

8. Structure and Sharing of Leadership

What is the structure of team leadership and how is it shared? Who has been identified to lead during a catastrophic emergency and other critical incidents? How is leadership coordinated among Incident Command Structure, school, district and regional response?

9. Team Member Commitment and Transition

What constitutes team member commitment and how does membership, energy, revitalization, and transition or rotation of membership and leadership work?

10. Team Membership in Small Districts and Schools

How do small districts and schools develop and maintain sufficient membership when there is a limited pool for drawing members? Some small districts have only a few counselors and perhaps one or two school psychologists. There are clear benefits for small district teams to have reciprocal agreements to partner with neighboring or larger school districts (PREPaRE Model: School Crisis Teams: Collaboration with Crisis Response Partners).

Each district and school can use best practices, crisis response literature and checklists to take inventory of its resources, needs, and problems while forming teams that have quality membership, training, and numbers to establish and sustain response capacity.

Section 2

Team Formation: Implementing the Team and Establishing Credibility

6

Training and Team Building

Reflections

While attending graduate school, I taught at a community alternative school in Philadelphia called Project Learn. I worked with a talented and caring teacher, who taught the five and six year old student group. When a high school was started, I began working with its lead teacher, Judy Diamondstone, who was as precious as her name. She loved to teach and believed in the students.

One day, as we walked toward the small high school building with a large group of students, we noticed a woman, grief-stricken and loudly calling for help. Her car was stopped in the middle of the street, an elderly woman lying in front of it. After confirming that emergency medical service had been called, Judy asked me to get blankets from her car to warm the seriously injured woman. Nearby, students stood in shock, holding onto each other. As I delivered the blankets, Judy asked me to escort the students back to their classroom building. The woman lay there, crumpled and bloody, moaning softly in pain. I remember Judy calmly saying, "She's like a broken little bird," as she covered and comforted the injured woman.

The high school students were reluctant to move. I yelled at them to follow me to school, fearing they would not follow. Inside the building, I yelled at them again, "Stay here in school. Nobody leave. Nobody go back to the street."

I could have said it calmly. I could have even recognized their feelings, invited them to talk. I did not. I later heard that one of those sensitive students said, "Jeff must have been scared." She was right. I was scared. I was angry. Why did something like this have to happen? Why did the kids need to see the specter of death on my watch? The day had been sunny, almost serene. I enjoyed my time with the high schoolers in this idyllic alternative school. This incident was not fair to them or to me. I wanted to shield them—to protect them. I wanted to care for them. Instead, I yelled at them.

∽

Training to Respond to Trauma

Once a crisis response team is established, the need for trained team members to maintain a calm, coordinated, caring response is vital (Adamson & Peacock, 2007; Brock & Jimerson, 2004; Brock et al., 2009). The reactions of caregivers, including their demeanor, body language, verbal and nonverbal messages influence children's perceptions of the severity of an event (Brock et al., 2009; Brymer et al., 2012a; Dyregrov & Yule, 2006; Eksi et al., 2007). If a multitude of responders bring chaos rather than calm to a school campus, the level of student stress will likely escalate (Klingman & Cohen, 2004).

Since the *level of response* can also influence perceived severity, it should match the level of need generated by the incident. Over-response as well as under-response can be damaging. Included in the PREPaRE Model is a detailed assessment of crisis severity for schools, and psychological triage variables for individuals. In order to match the level of response with the degree of crisis severity, response can be *minimal* (staff members in their normal roles), *building level* (school staff assuming their crisis team roles), *district level* (blended district and building crisis teams), or *regional* (resources from beyond the district, joining with the district and building teams) (Brock et al., 2009) (PREPaRE Model: Levels of School Crisis Response).

Risk Assessment and Intervention Training

During triage, factors considered in assessing risk for psychological trauma include *predictability, intensity,* and *consequences* of the traumatic incident, and *duration* of exposure. Interacting with the nature and circumstances of the incident are personal vulnerability factors such as *physical proximity* to the event, *emotional proximity* to the victim, *internal personal vulnerability, external personal vulnerability,* and *perception of threat.* Evaluating the varying impact of a crisis on students, and ongoing vigilance for *warning signs* of traumatic stress is a key aspect of designing interventions that meet individual needs. See Chapter 10 for more on assessing risk. Training is essential to understanding and implementing assessment concepts and processes (Brock, 2012; Brock et al., 2009; DiRaddo & Brock, 2012; Reeves et al., 2010; Reeves et al., 2012) (PREPaRE Model: Evaluating Psychological Trauma).

Educate the Team, Educate Others

The goal of our new district team was to train ourselves and then to provide training. We had to educate *ourselves* first. We met three times a year, although monthly or bi-monthly meetings would have been better. We tried to use our time wisely, with team coordinator planning and member input to set agendas. Our initial project was to write and distribute a crisis response manual to address our district's needs. Eventually, we designed a simplified emergency flip chart.

While PREPaRE Model training is highly recommended, it was not available when we formed our team (Brock, 2011; Brock et al., 2009; Reeves et al., 2011). At meetings, we distributed and discussed books, articles, and topics of interest. A school nurse provided training sessions for certification in CPR, defibrillation, and first aid techniques. We invited presenters such as a fire marshall, state trooper, police, and counselors discussing intervention techniques, stress management, the grief process, and care for the caregiver. We served as consultants supporting the formation of school level teams.

We sent a contingent from our district team to National Emergency Assistance Team (NEAT) and National Organization for Victim Assistance (NOVA) training. Our trained groups then prepared a major dinner presentation for a target audience of over one hundred district and school administrators, and members of school crisis teams. A purpose of our agenda was not merely to provide information and food—it was to jump-start the formation of school teams, and to publicize and establish credibility for our district team. By empowering others, we empowered ourselves as a team.

A District Training Event

The Lower Merion Elementary School Tragedy

Our team developed another district training idea that targeted building administrators. The daughter of school psychologist (and team member) Phyllis Tallos attended Lower Merion Elementary School on Thursday, April 5, 1991 when a helicopter and an airplane collided in the sky above the playground during noon recess. When the flaming wreckage hit the ground, seven were dead, including two first grade girls, the popular United States Senator, John Heinz, two pilots, and two other passengers. Three more children and two school employees were seriously injured when they were burned by the wreckage. One boy was critically burned. Phyllis suggested inviting the retired principal, Dr. Marvin Gold, to address our district. He accepted the invitation.

While school administrators were the target audience of Dr. Gold's presentation, we welcomed all staff interested in attending. Phyllis introduced Dr. Gold. She told us what it felt like being the parent of a child attending the elementary school on that day. The shock, fear, panic. Was my child among the injured? Who were the children? No parent should have to experience the horror, the uncertainty. They were compelled to get to the school.

Dr. Gold sat in a chair facing the large audience. He calmly told the story of the tragedy, recounting what I imagine was the worst day in his life. As he spoke, he wove in lessons learned, which he thought would be helpful for us. I remember anxiously hoping that the audience would be receptive. They were so quiet, you could close your eyes and imagine there was no one present except Dr. Gold. They were present, listening intently. Then they asked questions and Dr. Gold responded.

Many years have passed since that presentation. The message was so powerful, it stayed with me. Early in his talk, Dr. Gold made a couple of practical points—perhaps because they are so obvious, they could easily be overlooked in crisis planning. The first challenge is to keep major routes to the scene of an incident open for firefighters, police, ambulance, and medical personnel. It did not take long after the crash for hundreds of parents, relatives, media and curious onlookers to converge on the scene. All roads, small and large, leading to the elementary school were soon blocked. Eventually, emergency responders made it through, but time was precious, and much had been lost.

"Is it possible to prepare for a disaster of this magnitude?"

If an access route can be identified, and police, firefighters, and district personnel are prepared, the identified route can be dedicated to emergency responders and be kept open. Similarly, if media trucks, so intrusive in this situation, can be directed to an area near or across from the school, but not in front, space needed for response can be reserved.

The second immediate challenge recounted by Dr. Gold was the need to accommodate very large numbers of distraught parents. How to counsel them, to reunite them with their children in an orderly, efficient manner, and to document the process. Having a parking area to direct vehicles of parents/guardians and a large, comfortable area for parents to congregate is helpful. In that area, they could be asked to provide proof of identity and be given information and counseling until their children are dismissed into their care. Imagine a school where parents, and possibly strangers, are running through hallways, into classrooms, and grabbing children with no organized procedure. Out of the chaos, there must arise some order, some structure of support. Proactive school crisis planning can make a difference.

Whatever the district's preparation, the response described by Dr. Gold was broad-based and comprehensive. The community rallied to the aid of the stricken school. "Pupil Services got us through it," he said. Trusted school psychologists, counselors and social workers gathered to lead the crisis intervention. Classes were cancelled and counseling sessions were made available the rest of the day and into the night. Classes were cancelled the next day as trauma experts counseled teachers and staff. Counseling remained available throughout the weekend for children and adults. Drop-in centers were established at other schools in the district and counselors also made home visits.

Beginning the following Monday, and every morning of that week, students were divided into small groups and encouraged to "talk and talk and talk." They were familiar with the magic circle format – a time that fosters a sense of belonging when children can express feelings and set goals related to meaningful topics – often used prior to the tragedy. School psychologists, counselors, and social workers continued to be available to work with the most affected children. Ongoing counseling was also provided for staff, including teachers, custodians, and cafeteria workers exposed directly to the aftermath of the midair collision. Discussion groups formed for those who needed to be involved. One month after the incident, counseling teams still went into the community.

Re-entry for an Injured Student

The young student who had suffered severe burns was treated in Delaware at the duPont Hospital for Children. As his condition improved, counselors prepared students for his return to school. The hospital presented a program for the children about burn injury and recovery. Before the injured student returned, the school nurse spent four or five mornings in his classroom, educating and supporting his classmates. When the recovering student returned wearing a hat to cover his scars, his entire class wore hats in solidarity with him. A welcome back party the morning of his return dismissed fear and apprehension.

Memorials and Ongoing Support

There remained the sad task of memorializing those who had died. The empty desks of the first grade girls remained through the Monday following the event. They were removed as work on memorials began. Each grade decided how to memorialize the event in its own way. Children throughout the school planned and created a memorial garden—a living tribute to those who died. Brief memorial ceremonies were held annually on the anniversary date for four more years, until the affected class graduated.

Classrooms, grade levels, school, and community formed concentric circles of support. "How much is too much? How little is too little?" Dr. Gold asked.

Counseling was available for months throughout the school district and community, upon referral or request. Memorials were held annually for years. Many years after the tragedy, Dr. Marvin Gold brought us vivid images of trauma, death, survival, and healing. A large measure of his healing involved recognizing the help provided to so many.

A Training Model For Schools

School Crisis Prevention and Intervention: The PREPaRE Model is designed especially for schools to help teams build a framework of efficient, effective response (Brock et al., 2009). This practical, evidence-based training model and curriculum is valued for providing the supportive structure necessary to glean order from the chaos of a disaster. It includes two workshops, *Prevention and Preparedness – The Comprehensive School Crisis Team* (Reeves et al., 2011) and *Crisis Intervention and Recovery – The Roles of School-Based Mental Health Professionals* (Brock, 2011). PREPaRE guides schools through the establishment of crisis teams, member roles, crisis prevention, preparedness, evaluation, intervention, recovery, and examination of the response. Reeves and Cowan (2008) offer suggestions to "make your case to administrators" to secure PREPaRE training.

Workshops our team attended before and after the availability of PREPaRE training validated our work. Training also provided new ideas we could translate into improved practice.

Occasionally, reflecting on our response, we learned that some things needed to be done differently. We expanded our knowledge and developed our skills. We began feeling a sense of identity and validity as a team (Nickerson & Heath, 2008).

Team Identity: Badges

What symbolic gesture makes team membership more official than conferring a badge? Eventually, every team member got one. For the security and comfort of those receiving aid, we wanted to easily identify the crisis responders. Our badges were designed simply for clip-on or neck lanyards. At the top of the laminated badge was the responder's name. Beneath the name, in larger letters were the words, RESPONSE TEAM. Below was a photo of the responder, school district name and logo. We purposely omitted the words CRISIS or EMERGENCY in front of RESPONSE TEAM, figuring that people would know they were dealing with a crisis without advertising on our badges.

Drills and Practice

Challenging to Organize, but Worth the Effort

Looking back, our team did not meet the important task of organizing drills and practice to prepare for responses. The literature includes extensive descriptions of a wide array of exercises and drills, and how to develop them (Brickman et al., 2004; Brock et al., 2001; Brock et al., 2009; Dorn et al., 2004; Freeman & Spears, 2009; Reeves et al., 2010; Reeves et al., 2011; Taylor, 2006; Zhe & Nickerson, 2007). Tabletop drills and discussion would have been preferable to learning from mistakes during real events. In reality, instituting drills requires determined leadership and coordination, team buy in, and support from district and school administrators. We discussed drills and tabletop exercises, but did not follow through (PREPaRE Model: Exercising School Crisis Plans).

We recognized the need for practice and maintainance of skills, collaboration, and team building. We had precious little time for perceived luxuries, given our full-time, often multifaceted jobs. At one point, to our delight, an administrator planned a full-scale, district-wide crisis drill. We put it on our calendars. First, it was postponed. Then, it was cancelled. Then it was forgotten. Nevertheless, it is emphasized that periodic, carefully planned drills are crucial, and can save lives.

Team Building Activities

We had some success with team-building activities. We planned a spring canoe trip on the Brandywine River. Only four of us showed up—Nancy Carney, Elliot Davis, Marty Tracy and I. Two canoes with two paddlers each floating into the most tranquil part of the school year. We had a much better turnout when team member/school counselor Paul Iaboni led us through the high ropes course at his middle school. In addition to seeing how well we all looked in hard hats, it was an exciting, self-confidence and trust-building experience. Thank goodness, with Paul's expertise, we all survived.

Before each school year began, I hoped we would not be called for crisis response but usually, inevitably, we were called more than once each year. It is ironic that an aspect of our job requiring a relatively small percentage of time, constituted some of our most meaningful work. Over the years, the most powerful team-building came from the experience of working together during crises. Katzenbach and Smith (1993), point out "as teams evolve, their stories often progress through a series of galvanizing events—often unplanned and sometimes 'failures' – that propel team performance." Cooperative effort in pursuit of shared goals can be extremely unifying. In crisis response, the team is constantly dealing with unique experiences and new information requiring creativity, collaborative problem solving, and the development of new skills. Trained team members helping people deal with tragic circumstances often develop appreciation for one another, and express that appreciation in direct and subtle ways that help keep the team going (Nickerson & Heath, 2008).

7

House Fire

Abstract

Early in the experience of the district crisis team, four siblings died in a house fire. Three were students at the elementary school. Some fellow students witnessed the fire. The principal wrote a detailed chronology afterward. Extraordinary leadership by the principal and school counselor serve as models for administrators and staff. Sample letters and an agenda for a community meeting are included. *Themes are: 1) reaffirming children's safety and security; 2) coping with death, grief, and guilt; 3) explaining death to children; 4) community meetings and support; 5) care for school staff and caregivers.*

INTRODUCTION

We often hear about fires, often with loss of life, in poor urban areas where faulty wiring in old houses and cheap, unsafe heating alternatives are recipes for disaster. In the present case study, a community was traumatized after four children lost their lives in a house fire. Three of the four attended one elementary school. Neighborhood children witnessed the fire, rescue efforts, and loss of life.

PREVENTION/MITIGATION

The affected elementary school had a positive school climate and strong, effective leadership by the principal. The school was perceived as a safe, caring place with minimal physical hazards. Students and staff practiced requisite fire drills but the school was unprepared for a neighborhood catastrophe. Three factors compounded the risk for psychological trauma. They are: 1) the nature of sudden trauma; 2) that some children witnessed the removal of bodies, and; 3) the early emotional and cognitive development of the student population (Jimerson et al., 2012a, 2012b).

PREPAREDNESS

School and district crisis teams were in the process of being formed when the fire occurred. The district team had little formal training and little response experience. The team had several coordinators, but leadership roles were unclear, in that they predated PREPaRE's useful Incident Command Structure and division of roles described by Brock et al. (2009). The inexperienced team worked closely with the principal and counselor to coordinate an effective response.

RESPONSE

The school principal could not have been better organized or more inviting to the district crisis team. She actively supported collaborative efforts to meet the needs of students, staff, and community. She moved beyond her own feelings to care for others and exert leadership. The school counselor stepped forward, as well, to provide extraordinary service to the community, assume a leadership role, and blend easily into a collaborative relationship with the district team.

A well-coordinated combination of school administrator and crisis team with a district, or regional team can be a powerful and effective response to disaster (Brock et al., 2009; Reeves et al., 2010; Reeves et al., 2011). Conversely, a poorly coordinated combination of school and outside resources can add to trauma after a disaster. Before the formation of school and district crisis teams, responders had experienced confusion rather than coordination more than once. Having no prepared teams meant indecision, lack of acceptance and respect, and ineffective communication of needs. That is not what transpired in this instance, thanks to the confluence of circumstances.

During the response, I grew in experience. As one of several colleagues who coordinated the district team, I did not perceive myself as a team leader until a respected administrator approached me, made eye contact, and said, "You are in charge." He smiled gently. I realized he was serious as he left the school and returned to district office. While reflecting upon my role and continuing to share leadership, I more readily accepted the responsibility of being a primary team leader.

At the conclusion of our response to the loss of children in the house fire, the principal wrote a detailed chronology, which served as a vehicle to inform her district and school administrators about the response. The chronology was helpful in debriefing the crisis team and served to support the credibility of our new district team. Used with permission, here is an edited summary of that chronology.

First day of crisis response

Early Monday morning in late January, after the children's identities are confirmed, the principal requests crisis team response from the district office.

Team members arrive and there is an emergency staff meeting to clarify information and give instructions for the morning.

Children from the neighborhood of the fire arrive by bus and are met in the cafeteria by the school counselor, principal, and selected staff. They move to the library to get information and discuss their feelings about the fire and the deaths. Children who need immediate attention are identified.

The library is selected as the counseling center and location for crisis team briefings throughout the day. District crisis coordinators Marty Tracy and Jeff Roth organize arriving responders.

At the staff meeting, we give teachers suggestions on how to discuss the death of the children. We ask them to call the office

53

to have any distraught children brought to the counseling center. Teachers who are uncomfortable discussing death with their classes are identified for assistance. Counselor and principal visit the three affected classrooms to discuss the news 9– 9:30 am.

We give the secretary a script for phone inquiries and ask that media questions be referred to the principal.

9:30 am. School and district crisis teams meet in the library to divide responsibilities. Two school psychologists and two counselors are assigned to work with individual students, small groups, classes, and individual staff members.

Marty Tracy remains on site for two days as district liaison.

Jeff Roth remains to assist the school counselor in coordinating counseling services.

Kittie Rehrig, district social worker and crisis team member, reports to the Parent Community Center to assist families affected by the fire and to prepare for a counseling session at 4:30 pm. A meeting for parents is at 7 pm the next evening.

We plan to contact other schools with neighborhood students who are possibly affected by the fire and its aftermath.

The team sets 8 am and 1:30 pm as daily debriefing times. After school, debriefing is scheduled as needed. Superintendent and district directors return to district.

10 am. Principal notifies counselor at neighboring elementary school where Odyssey gifted and talented students study. Principal contacts the director of transportation to bring Odyssey students in at 2:15 pm for counseling. She asks transportation director to cover neighborhood bus stops after school to prevent media from approaching students.

The principal, Jeff Roth, and Marty Tracy prepare staff information packets and letters to parents to send home with students.

Principal gives phone interview to the *News Journal*.

11:30 am. Principal contacts district graphics department for assistance in printing letters and packets, which Marty Tracy takes to the district office. District secretary types the letter to parents.

1:30 pm. At the debriefing, the team reviews status of children and the classes team met with. Counselors plan to contact parents of especially affected students. Plans are finalized for two parent meetings.

2:15 pm. Principal meets with returning Odyssey students. Letters and packets are distributed to students to take home.

3:15 pm. Staff meeting: Principal updates information about the circumstances of the fire. Staff packets are distributed and strategies reviewed. The school counselor leaves to visit the mother of the deceased students. Crisis counselors remain for staff counseling.

4:30 pm. At the parent center counseling session, our team is composed of the principal, school nurse, counselor, psychologist, Jeff Roth, Marty Tracy, Kittie Rehrig, a district school psychologist, a district principal, a community liaison, and a kindergarten teacher from the feeder school.

Second day of crisis response

8 am. The principal, Jeff Roth, Marty Tracy, and the counseling team meet with teachers of the three children to plan closure activities and release of student belongings. One teacher becomes distraught. The principal calls in a floating substitute for the day to relieve staff members for counseling, as needed.

9 am–3 pm. The counseling team meets with individual children and small groups throughout the day. The principal talks with students, monitors staff, and organizes school response for assistance with funeral arrangements.

1:30 pm. Debriefing. Counselors triage three basic levels of need among students 1) who witnessed the fire, 2) who fear for their safety, and/or 3) who feel guilt for having had disagreements with classmates who later died.

Counseling includes lots of listening, reassurance, psychological first aid, and crayon drawings. The children frequently draw pictures of fire, which are used to elicit their stories, thoughts, and feelings. Students who choose to draw images need a range of colors. We talk about fire safety and ways to feel better. We reassure children who are feeling guilt that disagreements are normal and have nothing to do with the fire or the deaths. We say often to the children that adults at home and in school are determined to make sure they remain safe (PREPaRE Model: Reaffirm Physical Health and Safety/ Ensure Perceptions of Safety and Security).

7 pm. At evening counseling meeting with parents, we discuss children's stress reactions and coping strategies. We talk about how to be supportive and when to refer for counseling. We answer parents' questions. Radio station interviews the principal and school psychologist.

Third day of crisis response

8:15 am. Staff meets for update on funeral arrangements, and to identify staff who will attend funeral. Principal prepares staff for anticipated highly emotional funeral.

9 am–3 pm. Principal writes to parents and guardians about funeral arrangements and donations to cover funeral expenses. Parents are told that district personnel (and substitutes) will cover classes while staff is at funeral. Two teachers and the school nurse volunteer to coordinate fundraising with parents. The Parent Teacher Association coordinates food donations for reception at neighborhood community center. The principal issues a form letter for donation requests. Local supermarket and businesses are called for donations. With district supervisor, the principal coordinates substitutes and administrative coverage for the funeral. The school district pays the substitutes. Teachers' absences are coded as professional days and are not charged against the school's allotment. Jeff Roth arranges for additional counselors on the day of the funeral and the day after. One counselor is requested specifically for staff on the day after the funeral. A representative of a private counseling center offers free counseling services, and we refer one parent there. That center is also scheduled to consult at a faculty meeting. The number of children seeking help or showing anxiety is decreasing. The district crisis team remains on call, but is no longer onsite.

Fourth and fifth days

These are relatively normal days, with normal schedules. Children in the three affected classrooms participate in closure activities—cards, drawings, books for the family. Staff identifies students who will attend funeral and counselors prepare them for what to expect. The principal keeps staff informed.

Sixth day (the funeral)

9–11 am. Staff meets with substitutes, and then leaves in small groups for the funeral.

School nurse, counselor, and principal identify students who are absent, and probably at funeral. Counselor sees students with concerns in school. We give names of those students to crisis team members. The principal visits each classroom to establish a normal tone for the day. Later, at the church, the principal is interviewed by a television crew.

2:45 pm. The principal and counselor return to the building for crisis team debriefing.

Seventh day

Crisis team is on site the day after the funeral. Students are coping well, with a few referrals. Some staff members who had attended the funeral are feeling worse. A counselor from the crisis team is assigned to work with the adults.

Eighth day

7:45–8:15 am. School hosts a breakfast to thank district personnel, crisis response team members, support personnel, and parents who helped the school through the tragedy. The purpose is to bring closure to staff and allow them to return to teaching.

Elaboration on several points in the chronology follows.

When fire struck a neighborhood home, the impact on the elementary school and the community was devastating. In addition to counseling provided to students who exhibited one or more of the "three basic levels of need" (those who witnessed the fire; those who feared for their safety; those feeling guilt for disagreements) many other students were seen. The latter were from classes having no contact with the deceased children, but intensely affected by the fire, or by earlier trauma and loss in their own lives (PREPaRE Model: Evaluating Psychological Trauma).

RECOVERY

Recovery efforts involved ongoing vigilance for the emotional needs of the students, staff, and community (PREPaRE Model: Tertiary Triage: Evaluating Psychological Trauma). The purpose of two parent/guardian meetings – one in the school and one in the urban community, was to educate adults about trauma and grief reactions and when to seek more intensive help (PREPaRE Model: Caregiver Training). The response concluded with an appreciation breakfast that recognized school and district caregivers.

Agenda
for School Community Meeting

1. Welcome and Introductions by Principal
   - Thanks to parents, PTA, staff, school district family.
   - Update: plan for support, funeral, donations.
2. Children at home: school counselor and school psychologist.
   - What to look for, normal reactions, red flags.
   - How to respond, support recovery, and when to refer.
3. Panel discussion with school counselor, school psychologist, crisis team coordinator, and social worker. Team uses small focus groups when necessary.
4. Closure: Principal
   - Resources, contact numbers

Care for the Caregiver

Any description of this saga must include recognition of the dedicated work of the school counselor. Throughout the response, she kept seeing student after student, group after group, classroom after classroom. As a crisis team, we recognized that something remarkable was happening. We also realized that it was probably not a good thing that the school counselor did not appear to be resting, sleeping, or eating. We finally made her sit quietly talking, and we made sure she ate. We talked about how we could give her support and relief. She accepted some help, but continued her incredible work with the students. For years after, she became our continuing reminder of the decisive need to "care for the caregiver" (PREP_aRE Model: Caring for the Caregiver).

Lessons Learned: Reflection and Discussion

1. Effective collaboration and coordination with school administration is a critical component of effective crisis response. *How did the principal's initiative make this response more effective?*

2. Care for caregivers, including administrators, counselors, teachers, and others is essential for maintaining the ability to care for students. *What pitfalls could obstruct caring for caregivers, and what are steps to assure the provision of care during and after a response?*

3. Briefing and debriefing sessions as part of triage can be a significant resource to identify the level of system and student need. While need for intervention in the present case was initially determined by association with the incident or children who died, some students having no direct connection were intensely affected. *After a traumatic incident, what are some ways of identifying emotionally vulnerable students throughout a school community?*

4. System-wide planning in the present case study resulted in students, teachers, parents/guardians, and responders being provided with information and emotional support. *What are specific ways to provide information and care for multiple subgroups during crisis response?*

Sample Letters and Memos Sent after Tragedy
School / District Letterhead

Dear Parents,

I want to share with you the sad news that three of our students, along with their younger brother, died in a house fire on [day]. The student's names are _____, first grade,

_____, second grade, _____, third grade. Our deepest sympathy is extended to the children's mother, Mrs. _____ and her family.

The [School] staff wishes to be supportive of all students and their families in helping them cope with this tragedy. Counselors, our nurse, psychologists, social workers from [School] and the district, and district administration are onsite meeting with children both in classroom groups and individually when needed. Both the district and building staff will continue to work closely to identify children who may need attention that is more individual. Counseling staff are contacting the parents of children who appear to need more follow-up.

I am enclosing some material that may be useful in understanding how your child may be feeling. If you or your child has concerns or anxiety, please call [School] at [phone number].

For additional support, we are planning two meetings for parents to share information and discuss strategies to assist children. The meetings are:

Monday, 4:30 pm, _____School District Parent Center [address], [phone number]

Tuesday, 7 pm, _____ Elementary School [address], [phone number]

Thank you for your understanding as members of the [School] family work through this difficult time.

Sincerely,

Principal

∿

Helping Children Cope after Schoolmate Dies
Children's Perceptions of Death

Ages 1–5 Preschool age children are unable to appreciate death as final. They often think dead people will wake up and return to life. It is important to distinguish the difference between being dead and being asleep to avoid confusion and fear.

Ages 6-9 Children between the ages of 6 and 9 are better able to understand the true nature of death. They imagine death to be something outside themselves and may think about death as a monster, ghost, or skeleton that can come to get them.

After age 9, children can believe that death is final and will happen to everyone eventually, but usually when people are sick and elderly.

Suggestions for helping children cope with death

1. Children need to be reassured they are safe and that caring adults at home and in school are determined to maintain their security. This reassurance may need to be repeated. When children ask or indicate a need to understand, it is important to give them age-appropriate, correct information to the degree that we know it, but without disturbing or unnecessary details. We know at this point that these children died in a house fire. As hard as it is to talk about the incident with children, if an attempt is made to conceal it, confusion may be created for children who have already heard many different things.

2. Children express their grief differently than adults. Their sadness is often short-lived, giving the impression that they are indifferent, or unaffected. Children may have difficulty putting their feelings into words. Adults can be helpful when they see behavioral changes. Parents can try and encourage, but not force children to express their underlying feelings.

3. Grieving children can experience behavioral changes because of their upset and anxiety. Contrary to the behavior seen in adults, they are frequently mischievous, angry, boisterous, and noisy. These changes should be viewed as transient and need to be responded to with understanding by teachers and parents. For example, you might say, "I know you are upset and it's hard for you to concentrate but you have to try to do your homework (or your seatwork, etc.)"

4. Children of elementary school age may see death as a form of punishment. They need to be reassured that death doesn't happen if you do something bad. Children often think about death in terms of their own responsibility. They have a kind of magical

thinking and need to be told that nobody can cause the death of someone else by having bad thoughts or feelings. Children may not ask about this because they're afraid of the answer.

5. Parents may respond consistent with their religious beliefs. Sometimes children fear that God has chosen certain people to die. The problem this can create for children is anger and difficulty perceiving God as a loving figure. This is a tragic event for which there is no rational explanation. It's okay to say, "I don't know."

6. Parents and families have their own style of dealing with crises. It helps to know your style and deal with these issues within that framework. Children may tend to imitate the coping behaviors of their parents. If parents are able to deal with the situation calmly and directly, children are in a better position to deal with it.

If you are having particular difficulties or have specific concerns, please feel free to call [School] Elementary, [phone number].

∿

District / School Letterhead

Dear Parents of Mrs. _____'s class,

In working through this sad event, we are being particularly attentive to the classmates of the children who died. We ask that you be especially vigilant with your child in looking for signs of anxiety and concern. We emphasize that we will remain available as resources for you and your child. We encourage you to attend one of our parent meetings if you feel this would be helpful for you.

Sincerely,
Principal

HOUSE FIRE

~

District / School Letterhead

Dear Parents,

On behalf of the staff and children of [School], I would like to thank you for your support this week as we have helped each other work through our loss of [Child's Name/Names]. Your many expressions of concern and offers of assistance have been heart-warming.

I want to share information with you about the funeral arrangements and about the agencies coordinating donations for the family. Services for [Child's Name/Names] will be held on at the [location] [address].

Viewing (open caskets): [time]

Funeral Service: [time]

Burial in _____

Reception at _____

Several members of the [School] staff will be attending the services on [Day]. District Office administrative staff will be providing coverage for our classroom teachers. Counselors will continue to be available to support our children as needed.

Contributions may be sent to the [Family Name] Fund [bank name and address] to help defray funeral expenses. Donations of furniture or clothing can be made by contacting _____.

Our PTA is donating a food tray for the _____reception, contributing to the [Family] Fund, and is sending flowers. Our staff and PTA are working together to plan a commemoration of the children here at [School].

We hope this information has been helpful. Again, our staff is grateful to the [School] community for your caring response to the needs of our children and of Mrs. _____ and her family.

Sincerely,

Principal

~

An Invitation

In appreciation for your assistance and caring support, the staff of [School] Elementary invites you to join us for breakfast on Wednesday, [Date], 7:45-8:15 a.m. in our school library. We are deeply grateful for the gifts of time, guidance, and moral support that we received from our District family.

8

Essential Elements of Crisis Response

Reflections

A new school crisis team must be prepared and flexible to address many essential elements of response. The goal here is to review essential elements from a team leader's perspective.

The Usefulness of a Framework

Each response to a crisis presents similar themes and needs, but also unique circumstances and unexpected challenges. The responder must be ready for anything. Flexibility, creativity, and thinking on the spot are helpful qualities. A trained crisis team using a conceptual framework adjusts more smoothly when coping with the unexpected—especially under duress. A flexible structure helps the team find order in chaos, analyze the situation, and more effectively adapt as an incident unfolds. Understanding the essential elements helps the team navigate a situation that initially seems random and senseless. The literature outlines many useful frameworks, protocols, and checklists describing the essential elements of school crisis response. None is more comprehensive than the PREPaRE Model (Brock, 2011; Brock et al., 2009; Reeves et al., 2011).

Proactive Safety Measures

While this book focuses mainly on what a trained crisis team does in a school after a traumatic incident, prevention and pre-planning are crucial (PREPaRE Model: Preventing and Preparing for Psychological Trauma).

School Climate

Discussion of primary prevention and preparation for crises begins with establishing a school climate that fosters norms of open communication, enthusiasm for learning, shared influence, and caring support among students and staff. When a crisis strikes a school with a positive climate, students tend to be more resilient and to recover more quickly. (Bear, 2010; Bradshaw et al., 2010; Charney, 1992; Doll et al., 2014; Durlak et al., 2011; Gilman et al., 2009; Reeves et al., 2010; Ristuccia, 2013; Roth & Curtis, 1993; Sugai & Horner, 2006)

Emergency Student Lists and Go Kits

Preparation includes having multiple student lists with emergency contact phone numbers and addresses. Lists should be located in the nurse's office, where they can be put on a carrier with wheels, and in the school office. They should be mobile and accessible, if there is quick evacuation or the need to take inventory of students and their whereabouts.

Classroom teachers' student rolls should also be handy and included in a mobile "go kit" with helpful emergency items (Reeves et al., 2010). Kits may include first aid materials, hat to identify teacher, confidential list of students having special needs (allergies, medications, etc.), charged cell phone, batteries, whistle, duct tape, masking tape, markers, flashlights, paper and crayons, etc. (Masking tape and markers are useful for quick labeling of persons or materials.) Go kits in the school office and nurse's office should contain district and agency contact numbers, the school floor plan with classroom numbers, and a list of students' special needs such as medications. A bullhorn and battery-powered radio are also recommended.

Evacuation/Lockdown Procedures

It is important that staff and students be familiar with how to complete an evacuation or lockdown efficiently, and that they practice periodic drills (PREPaRE Model: Exercising School Crisis Plans).

Evacuation

If there is a sudden crisis with the possibility of injury or violence such as a fire or bomb threat, the school should activate its plan for evacuation or re-location of students. It is recommended that a staff response plan be placed in every classroom—a user-friendly flip chart hung next to the door. It is critical that the plan include accommodations required for students with special needs. A plan must take into account that elevators may be unsafe or unavailable during evacuation such as for fire, necessitating an alternative method for students with physical disabilities or wheelchairs.

In the event of a bomb threat or a similar terroristic threat, more than one evacuation route is recommended—a primary site and at least one alternate location. There should be indoor and outdoor options in case of inclement weather or other crisis considerations. School buses can be used as evacuation holding sites, with the advantage of mobile capability. It is also advisable to have a "buddy school" with capacity to house students in the event of prolonged evacuation.

If evacuation is to a designated outdoor location, students and staff must be a safe distance and facing away from the building. Proceed with caution in case a potential shooter or other violent perpetrator triggers evacuation as a ploy to injure students and staff while outdoors or in transit. An efficient "reverse evacuation" plan for students and staff is wise to have for rapidly reentering the school to seek shelter.

For a bomb, or similar threat, document as much detail as possible (PREPaRE provides a form), including the person's words and voice description on a phone call. Attempt caller identification and note the sending phone number.

Evacuation Procedures

When a fire alarm sounds, or a school administrator gives a verbal signal, each teacher must:

- Take class list, visitor list, and "go kit."
- Turn off lights.
- Follow last person out of room.
- Close door.
- Report to designated area, depending on the emergency (fire, tornado, bomb threat).
- Take attendance.

      1. List those who are not physically present and their possible location.

      2. List those who are present, but assigned to another class or group.

- Unassigned teachers/staff meet at identified area outside (or shelter in the event of tornado).
- Remain in designated area until advised by proper authority.
- Return to classroom when directed by proper authority.

Source: Brandywine School District Crisis Response Manual

Lockdown

A lockdown is necessary when there is an incident or intruders enter the school or school grounds posing a threat to students and staff. The possibility of sudden violence (such as by a potential shooter) should activate a prepared plan for lockdown. A straightforward announcement to go into classroom lockdown mode is recommended, with a description and location of the intruder/threatening persons if possible. This type of announcement is generally considered preferable to code words or phrases like "Code Red" or "The janitor lost his keys" that may be missed by the teaching staff or substitute teachers. The preferred announcement may sound like "Lockdown, Lockdown. Please go into immediate lockdown procedure," and may continue, "An intruder, an unauthorized male possibly wearing a blue sweatshirt and red baseball cap has been spotted in the main second floor corridor. Please remain in lockdown mode until further notice.

Police have been notified." Such an announcement could result in the intruder immediately leaving the school premises without doing harm. The purpose of lockdown—protecting students and staff—is accomplished, with apprehension of the suspect still possible off campus.

When lockdown is called, hallways should be swept, if possible, to make sure students are not in vulnerable areas. Schools should consider planning lockdown options for large groups of students in spaces such as the cafeteria or library. An office or command center must be locked and secure, with intact communication capacity to the school, the district, and law enforcement. Include communication options such as dedicated cell phones, intercom, walkie-talkies, and bullhorns. A secure back-up command center is a good idea.

Lockdown Procedures

When making announcements, do not use codes—Might say, "Lockdown. Lockdown. There is an emergency in the building... (Give location/facts)."

- From doorway—check immediate area (hallway) for students
- Lock doors, pull shades, turn off lights, place barricade if necessary
- Get students on floor away from door, behind desks if necessary
- Follow instructions given by administrator or command center
- Release no one except by direction of proper authority
- No restroom breaks (a toilet, or bucket and plastic bags is suggested).
- Ignore class change bells.
- Ignore fire alarm unless smell of smoke and emergency announcement.
- Maintain strict silence.
- Silence all cell phones.

- No use of radio or television.
- Take attendance.
- List those not physically present and their possible location.
- List persons present, but assigned to another classroom group.
- Move if directed by proper authority – lockdown may transition to evacuate.
- Take class and absence list, and safety "go kit."
- Call only vital information to office (i.e. injuries).
- Be prepared to stay in lockdown for an extended time.
- In lockdown, maintain calm control with students. Use short messages, such as:

"Get down now."… "Don't move."… "Be quiet."

"I won't leave you." (Teacher reassures students.)

"I'll stay with you." (Teacher reassures students.)

- Non-assigned staff stay in secure area until notified by proper authority.

Source: Brandywine School District Crisis Response Manual

Communication Capacity

Communication lines should be kept open between school and district as effectively as possible—especially between command centers, and between school, families, police, and fire departments. It is advisable to have dedicated phone lines and extra cell phones to remain operative when many calls must be made. Some phones may be used only for outgoing calls and others only for incoming calls. When cell phone calls jam due to high call volume during a crisis, text messages may work. When many students carry cell phones, they will be calling and texting, so parents may hear about an incident from their children, rather than the school.

Reunification with Primary Caregivers

Traffic and Crowd Control Plans

Events such as news of an impending natural disaster, the

aftermath of a school shooting or catastrophic accident, the threat of a bomb, or mass violence can lead to large numbers of parents quickly descending upon a school. This will challenge resources already extended by a difficult situation. Traffic and crowd control is imperative, including planning to keep roads open and procedures to dismiss students safely to family members. An orderly reunification plan can pay dividends when frantic crowds arrive for their children (Brock et al., 2009; Reeves et al., 2010). Since parking and waiting areas can be difficult to manage, attention to details can facilitate the process. An example is placing a sign on the school's main entry door directing parents to a location and stating "IDENTIFICATION REQUIRED" in multiple languages as needed (Brock et al., 2009). Consider having a parent reunification page on the school's website.

Planning for reunification to take place inside or outside of the school building, or an off site location can make a difference during the chaos of a crisis. Visible signs above tables, indicating alphabetical letters of the last names of people being served, can be helpful. After checking identification, release forms can be given to parents/guardians for presentation to teachers. Alternately, "runners" can safely escort students from classrooms or a secure, off-school site to waiting parents/guardians.

Crisis preparation should include who is responsible for directing traffic, including media vehicles, and maintaining locations where parents/guardians can wait. Having proactive discussions with local police and fire departments to plan to keep routes open, and control traffic, crowds and media can be extremely beneficial.

Mobilization: Initial Phase of Response

The crisis event triggers planned mobilization procedures. It is important to determine the appropriate level of response, depending upon the severity of the traumatic incident. Levels of response are minimal, building level, district level, and regional level (Brock et al., 2009; Reeves et al., 2011). The decision regarding the level of response is generally made by the school principal in consultation with district administration, school counselors, and coordinators of the district crisis team, using multiple sources of data (police, family, students). Under-response can be harmful since there are insufficient resources to help, while over-response is harmful in that it may serve as an unintended cue for the perception of increased severity (DiRaddo & Brock, 2012).

Initial Briefing for Response Planning

Gathering/Sharing Information

During briefings and debriefings, the team gathers information, senses needs to plan interventions, and plans timely movement toward "normalcy" and recovery. The initial briefing ideally happens before initiating interventions. It could take place after school, early in the morning before students arrive, or over the weekend.

Ongoing Contact with the Family

Gathering and sharing information involves maintaining contact with the family or families of injured or deceased persons. Generally, the principal or a designee maintains this contact and offers the school's support. The family, if able, is a significant source of information about the status of someone who is ill or injured, or if there is a death, information about funeral arrangements and wishes.

Important Items for the Initial Crisis Team Briefing

- Get the facts—collect information, confirm death, clarify details.
- Get the circulating rumors in order to dispel them.
- Discuss what to say and not to say to students and staff, including need to protect confidentiality.
- Plan for culturally competent response—nearly every aspect can be strengthened or weakened by the degree of cultural sensitivity.
- Plan to meet with, inform, and prepare staff with resources to care for students.
- What are the main points to emphasize when intervening with students?

- Who specifically will perform the various tasks and functions of the response?
- What is the plan to inform students, school-wide? Will each teacher be provided with a copy of the same written statement?
- What is the plan to reach students and perform triage (hall sweeps, teacher/student referral)?
- Initiate primary triage to identify those expected to be most affected. Use brainstorming, risk variables, vulnerability checklists, and/or mapping to aid this process (Brock et al., 2009).
- Determine locations for triage and crisis intervention counseling.
- Plan for intervention, including individual, small group, and classroom visits as needed.
- Plan for contact with family or families of the injured, ill, or deceased to exchange information and offer support.
- Plan to notify parents and other guardians of the most affected students; inform and educate the school community by phone and letter.
- Sense and then plan to respond to needs that are unique to the situation.
- Establish a tentative timeline for interventions to support recovery.
- Establish tentative time and location for next debriefing.

Prepare Teachers and Support Staff

In the initial stages of a crisis, begin by informing and stabilizing the school staff, enabling them to care for the students (PREPaRE Model: Ensure Perceptions of Safety and Security). Notify school staff by phone tree, call alert system, or e-mail. The team can meet with staff to prepare a response in the morning before students arrive, or after school. Provide pertinent information, including handouts for school staff. Rather than being out of the loop, teachers appreciate being informed and supported, so they can support their students and each other.

Planning Items for Staff Meetings

Working with Students

- Inform staff about the incident, including rumors to be dispelled. Teachers should be honest with students, but share developmentally appropriate information, avoiding disturbing details.
- Discuss what to say and not say to students. This information is often driven by the nature of the event and the need to protect confidentiality. Teachers may be given a uniform statement to read in classrooms at a set time, with responder support, if needed. Public address announcements are less personal and a last resort.
- Discuss grief reactions and student referrals to crisis counselors (Johnson, 2004). Encourage patient and careful response. Advance teacher training is beneficial.
- Plan appropriate cultural responses.
- Provide handouts with information for teachers about reactions to trauma, how to discuss events, how to listen and show support, suggested activities and options for dealing with students' feelings (Johnson, 2004).
- Suggest reestablishing normal routines to the extent possible, while understanding that facilitated discussion may be helpful and concentration on academic tasks and tests may be compromised.
- Encourage students to connect with social support systems including family, friends, religious community, and in school, with peer groups (team, band, club) including teachers, counselors, psychologists, and other meaningful staff.

Support for Teachers and Other Staff

- Determine whether teachers are emotionally able to talk with students, or need classroom support. Students take cues from adults, who can model calmness, reassure about safety, and recognize students' emotional needs.

- Offer support to teachers and staff, including floating substitutes if needed, private areas for quiet or counseling, and resources for counseling referral, when needed. Emotions are okay to feel, express, and manage.
- Provide support for secretarial staff, including scripted statements for telephone and visitor inquiries.

Logistics for Teachers and Other Staff

- Discuss logistics of schedule changes, student referral for intervention, escorting students to triage or crisis counseling, intervention locations, support in designated classrooms, and information distribution to parents/guardians.
- Caution teachers not to dismiss a student to the restroom to grieve. Students must be escorted to the counseling/triage area for intervention.
- Provide appropriate ongoing communication for staff, students, parents and guardians with medical updates, funeral arrangements, and memorial plans (phone contacts, text messages, letters, e-mails, meetings).
- Share plan for managing media, crowds, and traffic.
- Plan staff meeting at day's end, or later.

Triage

The PREPaRE Model (Brock et al., 2009) suggests multiple phases of psychological triage—primary, secondary, and tertiary. Triage is an ongoing process of evaluation to provide appropriate interventions for affected students beginning with initial crisis briefings (primary evaluation), continuing during interventions (secondary evaluation), and during response conclusion (tertiary evaluation). Throughout triage, names of those needing more intensive help can be generated by teachers, students, responders, and others. Triage is ongoing, because for some, symptoms of the need for intervention only become clear over time (Brymer et al., 2012a). It is also important to recognize normal reactions and the capacity for resilience, natural coping resources, and recovery, without imposing interventions on those who are minimally affected (Bonnano, 2004; Brymer et al., 2012b; Flynn & Norwood, 2004; Johnson, 2006; Levine & Kline, 2007; Sandoval & Brock, 2009). PREPaRE provides useful forms for screening and referral during the triage process, with degree of risk for psychological trauma helping to indicate the type of interventions needed (PREPaRE Model: Triage: Psychological Trauma Screening Tools). Chapter 10 contains a more detailed discussion of triage.

Locations for Psychological Triage and Crisis Intervention

The crisis team arranges comfortable spaces for students needing intervention. Spaces for triage and interventions should include a large area to accommodate multiple groups as well as nearby smaller rooms for crisis counseling with individuals or small groups. A critical aspect of triage is to have sufficient space to form homogeneous large and small groups—that is, grouping students with others having similar reactions for conducting interventions. Students may also be seen in classroom groups, according to need.

Documenting Student Contacts

Crisis counselors should document names of students seen, family contact information, estimated need for follow-up (referral and screening forms are useful), and themes discussed during intervention. Responders should be aware of the need to protect the confidentiality of student contacts and documentation.

Contacting Parents/Guardians

As soon as reasonably possible, team members share the task of contacting parents/guardians of students the team determines are emotionally "at risk." They are given information about monitoring, supporting, and referring their child for assessment, counseling, or immediate treatment if necessary.

Contacting Schools

The search for students who are most deeply affected often extends to schools throughout the district. As soon as reasonably possible, team members share the task of contacting other schools to discuss students who may need screening or intervention.

Crisis Interventions and Counseling

General Considerations

Generally, reactions to traumatic incidents are developmentally and culturally mediated, but the need to reaffirm perceptions of safety and security is universal, across age and ethnic groups (Brock et al., 2009; Reeves et al., 2010). The mantra of reassurance is relevant, to the extent that reassurance can honestly be given. Children can be reminded that adults at home and in school are determined to take care of them, and keep them safe. It may be helpful to invite expression of feelings, sharing of stories, questioning, and creative arts (Brymer et al., 2012a). Interventions afford an opportunity to engage in secondary triage. (Brock et al., 2009)

For middle and high school students, the peer group, carefully guided, can offer a powerful source of support. Groups of older students can benefit from time to express grief together, vent emotions, talk about the traumatic event, and plan ways to manage stress and other actions that support recovery. Crisis counselors may need to focus the expression of grief and discussion of the experience in constructive directions. Based upon psychological triage variables, groups should be designed for relative homogeneity of stress reactions to prevent vicarious trauma and possible contagion of mildly affected students by exposure to those more severely traumatized.

Empowerment often flows from involvement in constructive, creative actions such as writing or drawing for a memory book for the grieving family, planning a memorial, or joining a group to address a problem such as depression or substance or alcohol abuse. This kind of empowerment supports recovery and return to the normal routine (PREPaRE Model: Providing Opportunities to Take Action).

Structured Approaches

Throughout primary, secondary, and tertiary triage, there is an attempt to assess and match individuals' degree of risk for stress reactions with appropriate interventions (Brock et al.,

2009; Nickerson et al., 2009; Reeves et al., 2010). Brock et al. (2009) adapt a three tiered model (Gordon, 1983) matching Tier 1 universal interventions, Tier 2 selected interventions, or Tier 3 indicated interventions with students' varying degrees of risk for stress reactions (PREPaRE Model: Levels of School Crisis Interventions). Chapter 12 contains more information about the three tiered intervention model.

Other useful strategies and interventions include bibliotherapy, play therapy, art activities, story telling, memorial activities (memory books and letters), and other structured counseling interventions (Brock, 2011; Brock et al., 2009; Dugger & Carlson, 2007; Johnson, 1998: La Greca et al., 2002; Osofsky, 2004, 2011; Ruzek et al., 2007; Vernberg et al., 2008; Webber & Mascari, 2010; Worden, 2009).

Death by Suicide

In the event of a death by suicide, crisis counselors should engage in practices designed to prevent contagion—the intent of others, influenced by an earlier suicide, to complete their own suicide (Brent et al., 2013; Erbacher et al., 2015; Hart, 2012; Jellinek & Okoli, 2012; Lieberman & Davis, 2002; Ruof & Harris, 1988; Vaillancourt & Gibson, 2014; Zenere, 2009a). Chapter 12 contains information on preventive measures to minimize contagion. A section of Chapter 16 addresses information about planning memorials after a death by suicide.

Letters for Parents/Guardians

The principal, often with consultation from school counselors and the crisis team leader, develops a letter to be sent home to parents/guardians. Letters provide information about the incident and about what reactions to expect, how to listen and be supportive, and how to seek help if needed. Sample letters are often helpful in developing letters. A letter is sent to the entire school community and sometimes, a separate letter is sent to families of students whose classroom was most affected. Letters can indicate that more information such as funeral or memorial arrangements will be shared when available. Often, a crisis team member working with the district graphics department can reduce the school's burden by getting copies and helping prepare them for mailing or distribution to students.

Content of letters to parents/guardians

- A brief description of what happened, with condolences to family members and others
- Steps the school is taking to address the incident, emphasizing support for students and staff, efforts to restore safe, secure routine, and any necessary problem-solving to address needs
- What is happening next—possibly a community meeting or in the event of a death, funeral arrangements consistent with the family's wishes.
- Brief description of developmentally appropriate, typical student reactions to crises.
- Suggestions about how to listen to and support children, and "red flags" indicating possible need for referral.
- Contacts at school, if parents have concerns they wish to discuss.

Continue Informing Staff, Parents, Community

Throughout the course of the response, collaboration with significant stakeholders is crucial. While care for students is primary, experienced caregivers balance the need to inform and care for the school staff, parents/guardians, the community, and themselves. Effective communication with the school community is a key to reducing tension and encouraging a climate of understanding and support. Tragic events can create a crucible of strong, irrational feelings. When information is appropriate for sharing but not disseminated, feelings of exclusion and resentments arise that can hinder recovery.

Media Control and Cooperation

A proactive plan for communicating with and setting limits for the media (PREPaRE Model: Collaborating with the Media) begins with establishing boundaries for the street location of media vans and declaring the school campus off limits. The plan should name school and/or district spokespersons. At the same time, a tone of cooperation can be set by arranging mutually convenient locations and times to meet and provide journalists with useful information. The media can be a useful resource for disseminating helpful, reassuring information to the community. Chapter 14 explores ways of sharing information with news reporters.

Team Debriefings for Planning During Response

During the first response briefing, team leaders should plan for a mid-day or after school debriefing that includes all members of the blended school and district teams, school administrators, and other key staff members. The focus of all debriefings is to share information learned during the response and to plan interventions to address perceived needs.

The time and location (often where the initial briefing took place) of debriefings is disseminated with multiple reminders. Debriefings are generally planned for times when students can be occupied and monitored, such as lunch period, but may need to be deferred until after school. Debriefings also provide time for responders to take a deep breath, relax, and eat.

Purpose of team debriefings for planning

- Share information about the response process among all responders and school administrators.
- Discuss counseling and response themes to sense needs and plan the next round of interventions.
- Share and document names, status, and needs of students and staff who have received attention, and identify school team members to monitor those at risk.
- Brainstorm a to-do list, prioritizing tasks for responders and school administrators, including status of letters for parents/guardians, contacting the bereaved family, determining information to be shared with staff, and if another staff meeting is necessary.
- Determine when the next team debriefing will take place, taking care not to conflict with a school staff meeting.

- Attend to the well-being and needs of caregivers.

Constructive Action, Creative Expression

Crisis responders actively support students through anticipated phases of grief, while constantly monitoring for those at risk. They respect the students' need for reassurance, to be together, to be left alone, to express feelings, to find meaning. They recognize students' need for power and constructive action. Often, empowerment means involving students in supporting each other and the bereaved family. Materials can be provided for creative expression such as compiling a memory book for the family. An advisory committee planning a memorial may be comprised of students and staff. In the case of a death by suicide, the expression of grief can be accepted, while the possibility of contagion may be reduced by distancing students from identifying with or glorifying the act. Instead, students can learn about depression, suicide prevention, and engage in constructive, life affirming activities (Hart, 2012; Reeves et al., 2010; Zibulsky, 2012) (PREPaRE Model: Providing Opportunities to Take Action).

Disengagement and Demobilization

Final Phase of Response

The crisis team should begin initiating disengagement when the school staff is sufficiently stable to care for students making progress toward normal routine and recovery. Responders should gradually encourage return to routine with support as needed, from the beginning stages of the response. Teachers should be helped to understand that a return to class does not necessarily mean that all students will be ready to concentrate fully on academics. Demobilization should involve planning for follow-up. Staff should continue to monitor students, including those most at risk for stress reactions, and refer if further attention appears needed. Err on the side of caution. Continue to support families of the most affected students. Informal and clinical interviews, evidence-based instruments, rating scales and a multi-tiered support network can help identify maladaptive reactions that indicate referral for more intensive care (Heath & Cole, 2012; Holland,

2012; Rossen & Cowan, 2013). Chapter 21 further describes disengagement and demobilization measures.

Acknowledgements and Appreciation

Thanking the school staff for supporting students and each other promotes the process of recovery. It is valuable to publicly recognize that families and the school community are working through a difficult time.

Anniversaries

Prepare for possible needs associated with the anniversary of a serious incident until affected students are no longer attending the school, and possibly longer. Chapter 21 discusses trauma anniversaries in more detail.

Debriefing for Crisis Team Closure

The benefits of team members engaging in post-incident examination cannot be overstated (PREPaRE Model: Examining the Effectiveness of Crisis Prevention, Preparedness, Response, and Recovery). The closure debriefing for the crisis team is generally conducted at the end of the last day of response or several days to a week afterward. The purpose is to experience peer support, process response effectiveness, facilitate stress management, and mitigate stress reactions. Chapters 19 and 21 further discuss debriefing for closure.

Essential Reminders for Crisis Response

- Try to brief prior to intervention. At that briefing:
  √ Gather and share information.
  √ Plan triage, evaluation of psychological trauma, and intervention as needed.
  √ Plan locations for individual, group, and classroom interventions.
  √ Plan for sensitivity to developmental and cultural diversity.
  √ Plan staff meeting: stabilize, inform, and educate to support students.
- Provide appropriate information to faculty and staff. Com-

municate with all stakeholders throughout the crisis, and establish ongoing contact with the family of the injured, ill, or deceased person.

- Plan debriefing sessions—share information, sense needs, get names of affected students and staff, plan follow-up and next set of interventions.

- During response and disengagement, plan to monitor and refer those presenting risk for severe stress reactions or life-threatening behavior.

- Think systemically—keep families, district, and other schools in the loop—consider the needs of siblings, friends, relatives, community members.

- Encourage and involve school staff and students whenever possible. Administrators, psychologists, counselors, social workers, nurses, and teachers can play leadership roles, helping students replace despair with hope, constructive and cooperative action.

- Care for the caregivers—monitor need for nutrition, rest, counseling, stress management. Be prepared to make refer-rals for severe stress reactions.

- Provide a comfortable space for group and individual crisis counseling and creative expression.

- Engage in acts of kindness. Expressions of empathy can be conveyed in both direct and indirect, overt and subtle ways.

9

Coping with a Drowning

Abstract

After the drowning death of a third grader, school and district leaders cooperated in an effective way, blending resources. A school counselor communicated sensitively with the children while the school response team contributed meaningful support for the father and counseling for students. Sample letters and memos are included. *Themes are: 1) reaffirming children's safety and security; 2) effective principal leadership and school resources; 3) school counselor informing and reassuring children; 4) supporting the family.*

INTRODUCTION

It was a quiet Friday in December at a small elementary school. The calm suddenly gave way to disbelief and shock late that afternoon when the mother of a third grader phoned the office secretary saying her daughter had drowned in the bathtub. The little girl was new to the school, having entered the previous September. Her parents were engaged in a custody battle. The girl's father called next, seeking information. The school counselor, Laura Becker, recalls seeing police and paramedics rush toward the apartment complex.

The children returned home from school that Friday with nothing said about the death of the child. There was little to say, only emotions to be stirred without resources or time to meaningfully resolve them. School officials did not see or hear from the mother again and she did not attend the funeral. The father became the contact person for the school.

The media phoned the school, but there were few facts to share, except that support would be needed for students and staff. The media speculated whether the mysterious death was accidental. In time, the girl's death was ruled an accident.

PREVENTION/MITIGATION

A caring school community nurtures student resilience (PRE-PaRE Model: Developing Resilience and School Connectedness). Many classrooms in the elementary school began their day with a Responsive Classroom style "magic circle" in which teachers facilitate and affirm their students' sense of belonging, security, and expression of feelings (Charney, 1992; Charney & Wood, 1981). The familiar structure of the magic circle was the source of needed reassurance and support each morning in the classroom affected by the loss of their classmate. While the school provided effective resources as the response unfolded, the unexpected nature of a sudden death presents daunting challenges. The students' early emotional and cognitive development placed them at elevated risk for emotional trauma (Jimerson et al., 2012a, 2012b).

PREPAREDNESS

Late Friday afternoon, I received a phone call from fellow team coordinator, Marty Tracy, telling me what happened and that there would be a meeting at the school late Sunday afternoon to prepare for crisis response on Monday. It was still relatively early in the experience of our recently established district crisis team. The PREPaRE Model emphasizes that the response level should match the degree of need determined by crisis event variables (Brock et al., 2009; Reeves et al., 2011). While the sudden, off-campus death of a third grader was clearly traumatic, she was new to the school and had no siblings. We anticipated that those most affected would be from her classroom and the neighborhood. We decided that a limited number of district level responders would join the competent building level team to plan and carry out the response. Regardless of resources, it is exceedingly difficult to prepare for a sudden death (Jimerson et al., 2012b).

I pulled into the school parking lot for the Sunday planning meeting. The place appeared deserted. Late afternoon sunlight and shadow splashed against the building. I entered through an unlocked front door and went to the principal's office. Principal Ann Kappel welcomed the planners. While there was an undercurrent of sadness, she created an atmosphere that was business-like and task-oriented. The school counselor, Laura Becker was present along with the school nurse, and four members of the district crisis team: the school psychologist JoLinda DiSanto, Elliot Davis, Marty Tracy, and me.

Effective Leadership and Skilled Resources

It quickly became obvious that the school had effective leadership and skilled resources to serve the needs of its students and staff (PREPaRE Model: School Incident Command Structure). School counselor Laura Becker led the intervention with students. School psychologist JoLinda DiSanto had experience as a member of the district team. Principal Ann Kappel reviewed what we knew and led brainstorming on what needed to happen.

Several members of the district crisis team supplemented the school team, which led the response. Other district responders were alerted to be on call, and to mobilize if necessary (PREPaRE Model: Levels of School Crisis Response: Building/District). Ann Kappel wrote a letter to parents and guardians. Sent home with students, it included tips for discussing death with children and addressing possible grief reactions (PREPaRE Model: Psychological Education: Informational Documents). We discussed crisis counseling for the third grade classroom teacher, including substitute relief if needed. Laura Becker and JoLinda DiSanto would intervene with those students throughout the day and follow up with those who need extra attention.

We anticipated that students who lived in the apartment complex and neighborhood would be affected, and that some may have witnessed the emergency response. We would usher these students from their bus to the library where Laura Becker would speak to them.

Principal Ann Kappel emailed faculty while a phone tree also alerted faculty to meet in the library before the start of school. All crisis resource people would attend that meeting, and teachers would receive handouts on children's reactions to death and grief.

RESPONSE

Staff Meeting

During the staff meeting, the principal, Ann Kappel, and the school counselor, Laura Becker, provided information about the death, introduced district team members, and talked with the teachers about responding to their students, recognizing various reactions, and monitoring the need for more intensive support (PREP<u>a</u>RE Model: Caregiver Training). Most teachers said they felt comfortable talking with their students about the event. The initial identification of students needing more support, *primary triage,* focused on those most closely affected—classmates and children from her neighborhood (PREP<u>a</u>RE Model: Primary Triage: Evaluating Psychological Trauma). However, staff was briefed that children who didn't know the deceased girl might also be affected by her death—especially those who had been coping with death, separation, or divorce in their families. The staff was reminded to "Please be vigilant for children who may need individual attention."

School Counselor Informs and Reassures

Laura Becker addressed the students from the apartment complex and neighborhood in the school library soon after they left their school bus. Her tone was calm and caring. She spoke with them clearly, using words they could understand. Addressing the children was difficult, but her words flowed. She focused not on her own sadness or stress, but on the children's needs.

She told the neighborhood children that she understood some of them knew the sad news, while others may not have known.

She acknowledged that some had seen the medical personnel, police, and television camera crews. The school counselor confirmed the death, but added that the circumstances were unclear. "This is a sad time. It's okay to feel sad. It's okay to talk about what happened and how you feel."

"You may have questions. We will try to answer them, but we don't have all the answers. We don't know exactly what happened."

Laura Becker reassured, "It is very unusual for a child to die. Your parents and families and teachers care about you and will take care to make sure you are safe." (PREPaRE Model: Reaffirm Physical Health and Perceptions of Safety and Security)

She told them the responders care about their feelings. "There are lots of people here who understand feelings and it's okay to talk with them. If you want to talk, they will listen to your stories. They are friends, people we know and trust. Ask your teachers if you may talk with the helpers."

Since the children were cautious and taught not to talk with strangers, the school counselor reassured them it was all right to talk with the "helpers."

"There are also parents and other adults at home and in school who are there to listen to you and keep you safe. You may hear different rumors and stories, but we don't know exactly what happened. You can talk about what you hear and how you feel with your families, teachers, and with the helpers in school."

During the response, Laura Becker's work was reminiscent of another elementary school counselor who worked almost non-stop after the death of siblings in a house fire. Like that counselor, she worked hard for the next several days, heeding reminders to eat, take breaks, and take care of herself.

Reaffirming Safety and Security

Interventions continued in the classroom of the deceased girl, and to a lesser extent in other classrooms (PREPaRE Model: Provide Interventions and Respond to Psychological Needs). Small groups, and occasionally individuals, were seen in the school library. Safety was a big issue. Newspapers and other media reported news of a drowning death in the bathtub. Some of the "witnesses" talked about blood and rumors that their classmate had been killed. We listened, but stuck with the information we knew at the time, that it was a very unusual accident. There were many discussions about ways to be safe in the bathtub. The children needed reassurance and specific safety strategies.

"It is extremely rare and unusual for a child to die in the bathtub."

"Children never go down the drain with the bath water."

They talked, made drawings, received caring attention. They needed to hear the mantra of reassurance repeated. This kind of accident does not usually happen. Adults care about them and were there to keep them safe at home and in school. They can do things to help themselves stay safe (PREPaRE Model: Reaffirm Physical Health and Safety).

$\sim$

In the affected classroom, every morning began, as usual, with circle time. This afforded Laura Becker and JoLinda DiSanto an opportunity to sit in and support the students and their young teacher for several days. It also provided an opportunity to conduct *secondary triage* – to identify students needing more attention during the course of response interventions (PREPaRE Model: Secondary Triage: Evaluating Psychological Trauma).

On the first day, the school counselor addressed children who lived in the girl's immediate neighborhood; teachers spoke with students in their classrooms; counselors intervened in the affected classroom; and district team members made themselves available for small group and individual counseling. The principal sent information home to parents and phone calls were made to parents/guardians of students who needed monitoring and possible counseling follow-up. The combined school and district crisis teams debriefed at the end of the first day and met periodically throughout the response.

After the first day, there was not much activity beyond the affected classroom. On the second and third days, the classmates decorated a box and filled it with cards, drawings, and memories.

Some of the little girl's belongings from her desk were included in the box. Filling the box for the family became a focus of constructive activity for the students. The art teacher was a great source of materials (PREPaRE Model: Ensure Perceptions of Safety and Security: Provide Opportunities to Take Action).

RECOVERY

A Father's Resolution

The distraught father surprised the school with a visit before the funeral. He brought back some of his daughter's books. He also seemed to want to take away memories, some connection with his daughter. The principal, nurse, and counselor brought him into the principal's office. He cried, a big man reduced to profound grief. He needed to talk with people who had last seen his daughter. His daughter's teacher, who joined the supportive group, recounted fond stories about the little girl. The scene was emotional and meaningful.

∽

The principal, counselor, and school nurse attended the funeral in Philadelphia and presented the father with the decorated box containing memorial artifacts. No children attended. The district crisis team covered the school.

Brock et al. (2009) observe that during the recovery phase, toward the conclusion of a response, it is important that collaborating responders conduct *tertiary triage* to review students served throughout the intervention, discuss specific services provided, and identify students needing ongoing support and follow-up (PREPaRE Model: Tertiary Triage: Evaluating Psychological Trauma). The information and support provided for teachers and the immediate reassurance and interventions provided for the students created an atmosphere in which the affected classroom was able to return comfortably to normalcy and learning.

∽

After Laura Becker, the school counselor, had worked intensely for days, members of the team tried to talk her out of taking lunch duty. We wanted to care for her, thought she might be exhausted, and would benefit from a break. She refused to give up lunch duty, explaining, "I need to be in there with the third grade lunch like always. It's the normal thing to do."

She was able. She was right.

Lessons Learned: Reflection and Discussion

1. When a school has sufficient and able resources to deal with a crisis, district response should be limited to supplemental or "on call" capacity, and logistical support. *How and why do we assess a school's level of need, and respond without bringing in more responders than necessary?*

2. The school administration, staff, and students can play a meaningful role in supporting a grieving family and if able, the family can keep the school informed of funeral arrangements. *How can a family's wishes regarding public or private funeral be respected, while meeting student needs to acknowledge the death?*

3. Without minimizing the need *to care for the caregiver,* reestablishing normal routine for students remains a priority for crisis responders such as the school counselor in the present case study, if able to continue functioning in a healthy, effective manner. *How can responders balance the needs of students with care for the caregiver?*

Letter to Parents and Memos to Staff
District / School Letterhead

Dear Parents,

It is with a great deal of sadness that I share with you that one of our third grade students, _____, unexpectedly and tragically died last week. Our deepest sympathy is extended to her family at this very difficult time.

Today, the staff implemented a plan for responding to this situation and helping our students and their families cope with this tragic death.

Our school counselor, school psychologist, and other district counselors and personnel have met with classes, as well as individual students, to discuss the death and help students talk about their feelings, recognizing that the most important thing we can do is to be supportive and encourage discussion about this unfortunate situation and the feelings it gives rise to.

Both the building and District staff will continue to work closely to identify children who may need individual attention, and parents will be contacted if that is necessary. If you feel your child is experiencing any concerns or anxiety, please call _____, our school counselor. With this letter, I'm enclosing some material that may be useful in understanding how your child may be feeling and reactions you could possibly see in your child.

We know you join us in our concern, support, and sympathy for those affected by this unfortunate incident. We very much appreciate your understanding and concern.

Sincerely,

Principal

~

Memo to Staff

Talking to Children in the Classroom about _____'s Death

As you may know, _____, a student in _____ class, has died. We do not know, at this point, all the facts nor do we know the cause of death. Many of our children have heard about it from the news. We hope most parents have discussed her death with their children. Your children will certainly have questions about death and a classroom discussion is necessary and appropriate. If you are uncomfortable handling this alone, please let us know. Do not feel that you must do this alone. A list follows on do's and don'ts when talking to your class.

- Tell the children what happened in a quiet and direct manner. Do not compare death to sleep. It is important to share facts about death without unnecessary or frightening details, and to address their fears.

- Allow the children an opportunity to express their feelings. Recognize and validate these feelings, which can range from sadness, to anger, to fear and may change moment to moment. All of this is normal. It is important to remember that not all children express emotions in a similar way. Some children become very quiet while others become extremely silly. This is also normal.
- Some children may need to share their own experiences about death. Be patient and listen. Allow them to do this. You do not need to share your own experiences.
- Do not cut the children off or move on with the rest of your day until the children have finished talking/sharing.
- Do not get involved in long discussions about rumors. Simply tell the children that we do not know everything yet, particularly if discussion speculates about circumstances of the death.
- There will be many new faces in our building today and possibly over the next few days. Explain to the children that these people work in the school district and have come to help us. It may help them to know that they are people that [counselor] and [principal] know and have asked to come to our school.
- Watch closely for vulnerable children, those who seem particularly upset, withdrawn or are having difficulty coping with the news. These children may have experienced other recent deaths or are involved in difficult custody battles.
- Classroom activities for the rest of the morning should be structured. Allowing the children time to draw or write may be appropriate. This is not a good day to introduce new concepts.

- Remember, we are all in this together and we will do our very best to provide all the support you need.

∽

District / School Letterhead

Dear Staff,

Thank you for all of your support and concern as we have worked through the tragic death of _____.

It has been a difficult time for the children and for all of us, but it is also gratifying to work with staff members who really have been supportive and helpful in every way. I have the highest praise for our school's crisis group, which is comprised of _____, _____, _____, and _____, as well as the District counselors, psychologists, and administrative personnel.

Yesterday, _____'s father came to visit us. _[counselor]__, _[nurse]___, _[teacher]__, and I met with him, and, as you can understand, his grief was palpable. We suggested making a monetary contribution in _____'s memory to the church, and he agreed. If you would like to contribute, please give the money to _____. If you have any thoughts or suggestions about anything else we should do, please let _[counselor]__or me know. The funeral is _____. A group of us will attend to represent our school.

Please remain vigilant for any concerns that children exhibit in the days ahead. The counselor will remain available.

Thank you.

Sincerely,

Principal

10

Triage—Casting a Broad Net

Reflections

M y first experience with triage came in the Air Force while stationed at a large hospital in England. We had a massive night drill in which I was assigned the role of an emotionally traumatized airman running around the perimeter of an incident with many injuries, trying to elude the crisis responders.

When the responders recognized my frenzied role, they apprehended and restrained me. According to triage, as a non-medical emergency I was immobilized between two stretchers lashed together, and placed into an ambulance. However, they were much too gentle in binding my restraint, which provided the opportunity to wriggle free and disappear into the East Anglia night. I gleefully watched the scurrying figures from the darkness at the edge of the drill.

It took awhile for the responders to realize that their unstable casualty had escaped from bondage in the ambulance. They were busy dealing with more severely injured persons. I watched, dancing behind trees surrounding the scene, eventually becoming bored. After thinking about hitching a ride to Cambridge, I re-entered the lights of the drill and placed myself in peril of re-capture.

I slowly walked up to a group of medics as they worked on a drill 'victim' and silently admired their work. After what seemed like a long time, one of them spotted me. I was again apprehended, but this time, had forfeited gentle treatment. They were a bit angry I hadn't gone along with the program and stayed put the first time. I knew I was in some trouble when one of them said, "You won't get away this time, you jerk," lashing together the stretcher sandwich much more tightly, with me, the meat in between. "Ow" I said, "That's enough. I'm not moving."

My fellow airmen restrained me far more effectively the second time, mercifully allowing just enough slack to breathe. The next day I was surprised to learn I had become a hero to the officers who planned the drill, but was less than a legend among my fellow airmen.

The Complexity of Psychological Triage

Medical triage is more immediate and straightforward than psychological triage following a traumatic incident. Both forms of triage assess the severity of physical or psychological injury and prioritize the order and extent of treatment needed.

Psychological triage is more complex and multifaceted, especially in a school setting where the impact of traumatic incidents may be minimal, or may encompass an extended community with networks of meaningful relationships. Planning interventions must take into account diverse reactions and needs, hierarchies of leadership, academic priorities, routines and schedules that are unique and challenging. During the period when multifaceted student triage is in progress, a parallel, interrelated system of teacher, staff and caregiver triage is at work too. Rossen and Cowan (2013) point out that "schools play a crucial and unique role in mitigating the effects of adversity, stress, and trauma on students."

Triage must consider categories of susceptible students, including those having identified *risk factors* or *warning signs*, those having identified *special needs* (i.e. learning, physical, emotional or intellectual disabilities; anxiety, depression), or those having a *history of trauma, loss, bullying or aggression*. Attention to students prone to aggressive behavior, who may act out in a stressful situation, should strive to protect grieving students, who are especially vulnerable (Brock et al., 2009; Reeves et al., 2010).

The space for conducting direct triage with students should be large enough to accommodate large and small groups, and individuals. The school library, with adjoining rooms for privacy, is often useful for triage and interventions. There should be a plan to safely escort students needing attention to the triage location from buses and hallways as they arrive, or when referred from classrooms. When designing interventions, the triage process helps form homogeneous groups having similar stress reactions. Grouping individuals having similar levels of crisis exposure helps prevent vicarious traumatization and possible contagion. Basic needs for safety, food, shelter and clothing are priorities during triage (Barenbaum et al., 2004; Brown & Bobrow, 2004). Fresh water, fruit, tissues, writing and art materials are staples to have available.

A Model of Psychological Triage

School Crisis Prevention and Intervention: The PREPaRE Model (Brock et al., 2009) provides a model for the practice of psychological triage that includes evaluation at multiple phases—primary, secondary, and tertiary.

Primary evaluation utilizes risk factors and early warning signs for psychological trauma to make initial decisions about the extent of crisis intervention needed for individuals and it establishes treatment priorities in the school community.

Secondary evaluation takes place during the response, as interventions are provided. Responders identify those having more severe perceptions of threat and "more durable crisis reactions." Observations of warning signs by responders, teachers, and other caregivers are important in refining treatment priorities and monitoring those who may need referral for therapeutic treatment.

Tertiary evaluation during disengagement from the response evaluates crisis facts, risk factors, and stress reactions for more enduring warning signs to determine those, usually a minority, needing continued monitoring, counseling, and/or referral for outside psychotherapy (Brock et al., 2009; Heath & Cole, 2012; Holland, 2012; Jaycox, 2004; Jellinek & Okoli, 2012; Nickerson et al., 2009; Smallwood et al., 2006).

Multiple Resources for Identification of Need

Triage often begins at the initial response briefing, with brainstorming to generate the names of potentially vulnerable students such as those known to have a close relationship with an injured or deceased student, or those who were in close physical proximity to the incident (PREPaRE Model: Primary Triage: Evaluating Psychological Trauma). During early triage, it became routine for our team to contact other schools having relatives, friends or neighbors who might be affected, and to speak with the administrative or counseling staff.

Teachers, counselors, and administrators are valuable resources during triage. At briefings, faculty meetings, and through email memos early in the process, they are asked to monitor their students' emotional status. Staff should be given information and handouts describing common stress reactions and warning signs of more severe reactions that indicate the need for referral (PREPaRE Model: Psychoeducation: Caregiver Training). Teachers are reminded to care for one another, and to seek help from available resources, if needed.

Triage frequently expands with the cooperation of grieving students who name peers they believe are hurting, including those absent from school. Another source of triage information during interventions is the writing and drawing of sympathy cards, memory books, paper murals, and other artifacts. These activities should be supervised, and the products monitored, because they give a sense of students' emotional status, including red flags that require attention.

During psychological first aid and crisis interventions, responders document the names and pertinent information of students receiving support, including those who need follow-up (PREPaRE Model: Secondary Triage: Evaluating Psychological Trauma). The documentation can be written on forms or specially designed 4 x 6 cards outlining specific information to be obtained (Brock et al., 2009). When team debriefing sessions are held throughout the response, crisis counselors share the names of students who need follow-up. Often the school counselors, social worker and psychologist assigned to the impacted school, are responsible for monitoring a specific list of students. Follow-up may include regularly checking in with the student for a flexible period of time, brief counseling with the permission of the parent/guardian, and/or referral to an outside agency for therapeutic treatment (PREPaRE Model: Tertiary Triage: Evaluating Psychological Trauma).

Contacting Families of Most Affected Students

During team debriefing sessions, responders develop lists of identified students' parents/guardians to be contacted as soon as possible. Often, the couselors or other staff members monitoring the most affected students' progress contact their parents/guardians to inform them about common stress reactions, stress management, and red flags that signal more severe reactions and the need for immediate referral (Nickerson et al., 2009).

One of the strengths of having a skilled team is *division of labor* for multiple phone contacts and other necessary tasks. However, this requires effective coordination to be certain that responders are aware of their responsibilities and document completion of assigned tasks (Brock et al., 2009).

Identifying Degree of Need: Intervening Without Imposing

The process of triage requires responders to cast a broad net, but to draw in the net with deliberation and care. After a traumatic incident, most students generally recover naturally, using existing support systems with minimal or no intervention. To impose a psychological intervention designed for more severely affected students on a minimally involved student, risks more trauma exposure and possible harm. As the response unfolds, using specific vulnerability criteria, screening forms, observation and clinical judgment to assess the degree of need, helps identify those at risk for acute or post-traumatic stress, and other severe reactions requiring more intensive treatment. (Brock, 2002c; Brock et al., 2009; Brymer et al., 2012a; Conolly-Wilson, 2008; DiRaddo & Brock, 2012; Everly, 1999; Heath & Cole, 2012; Holland, 2012; Nickerson et al., 2009; Reeves et al., 2010; Ritchie & Hamilton, 2004; Sandoval & Brock, 2009).

Effective psychological triage during the primary and secondary evaluation phases can have implications for the course of later emotional distress or wellness. Early, universal interventions such as psychological first aid, emotional stabilization of school staff and students, reestablishing social support systems and psychoeducation can mitigate more severe traumatic stress reactions requiring treatment after tertiary evaluation. While recognizing the benefits of early intervention for those in need, it is necessary to remember the importance of not intervening for those, typically the majority, coping effectively without structured intervention (Sandoval & Brock, 2009).

Evaluating Risk for Psychological Trauma

Factors to consider while assessing the risk for psychological trauma (Brock et al., 2009):

- *Predictability, intensity,* and *consequences* of the event, and *duration* of exposure to the traumatic incident.

Variables interacting with the nature and circumstances of the traumatic incident are personal risk factors such as:

- *Physical proximity* to the event—witnesses or first responders
- *Emotional proximity*—having a close relationship with the victim (family, friends, classmates, teachers, and teammates)
- *Internal personal vulnerability*—having difficulty with emotional regulation or a previous history of trauma or mental health issues
- *External personal vulnerability*—having minimal family and social support systems
- *Perception of threat*—perceiving continued risk.

During the crisis, responders must be vigilant for:

- *Early and enduring warning signs* of psychological trauma—including symptoms of maladaptive coping, significant depression, dissociation or psychosis, or post-traumatic stress reactions. These factors indicate individuals most likely to need intervention and possibly therapeutic treatment (Brock, 2002a; Brock, 2002b; Brock, 2002c; Brock, 2012; Brock et al., 2009; DiRaddo & Brock, 2012; Reeves et al., 2010; Reeves et al., 2012) (PREPaRE Model: Evaluating Psychological Trauma).

- In a catastrophic incident, multiple groups of students, staff, and community may be severely affected. Risk factors must be considered throughout the school community (Brock et al., 2009; Poland & Rosenberg, 2011). Who has a recent history of dealing with death? Who has experienced previous depression or suicidal ideation/threat? Who is perceiving the present incident as an ongoing threat? Who does not appear to have a family, community, or peer support system? The aim is to match the level of intervention with the degree of need (Brock, 2002b; Brock et al., 2009; DiRaddo & Brock, 2012; Everly, 1999; Nickerson et al., 2009; Reeves et al., 2010; Saltzman et al., 2001).

Graphic organizers can also be useful for identifying individuals and groups at greatest risk after a traumatic event. Death by suicide or a suicide attempt creates circles of students who are at risk. *Mapping* concentric circles with people near the center being in closest *physical* or *psychosocial (emotional) proximity* to the event or victim helps to identify a *population at risk*. The various groups identified by mapping constitute overlapping *circles of vulnerability,* with those most severely impacted at the center (Brock et al., 2009; Poland & Rosenberg, 2011).

Necessary actions that may seem obvious, can elude an overwhelmed crisis team in the chaos of a disaster. A well organized, coordinated model for psychological triage offers the best chance for those needing attention to be identified. It is important, throughout the triage process, including primary, secondary, and tertiary evaluations, to monitor and provide follow-up for those who are most vulnerable. Treatment for those at high risk can save lives.

11

Death
of a Kindergarten Teacher

Abstract

When a beloved kindergarten teacher dies, fellow teachers and staff, students, and parents—many of whom she had taught, grieved for her. The school and district community came together for a memorial assembly to celebrate her inspirational life. This chapter includes sample letters and memos informing and preparing parents and teachers of her impending death, and responding to community needs. *Themes are: 1) preparing for a death; 2) grieving a loved teacher; 3) explaining death to children; 4) reaffirming children's safety and security; 5) bibliotherapy; 6) support for family and for school staff.*

INTRODUCTION

Some of the most difficult and complicated responses over the years follow the death of teachers. Sometimes the death is sudden. More often, it is the result of a long illness. Some teachers had been on leave for many months, while others worked until weeks or even days before death. These teachers had often endeared themselves to both students and staff. Death sometimes touched students and their parents across grades and schools. While it is important to inform people across schools, it is not always clear how far to inform across a district.

A kindergarten teacher revered at the elementary school

105

where she taught for over thirty years died after a long fight with cancer. She began teaching at a young age, and with characteristic determination, she taught until several weeks before her death.

PREVENTION/MITIGATION

News of her passing occurred at an elementary school with a caring, mostly veteran teaching staff dedicated to the students and to each other. The school climate was positive. Counselor Helen Lareau had implemented a school-wide conflict resolution and anti-bullying program (PREPaRE Model: Developing Resilience and School Connectedness). With the support of Principal David Moore, the counselor embraced the task of mitigating the impact of the teacher's imminent death by providing ongoing information, training, and group discussions for teachers, who would need sufficient emotional stability to care for themselves and their students (PREPaRE Model: Exercising School Crisis Plans). David kept the staff apprised of their colleague's struggle and of ways to support her family. In consultation with the district, Helen provided psychoeducational materials and preparation for teachers and families about the grieving process, children's reactions to death, how to reaffirm a sense of security, when to refer for more support, and how to use creative activities to facilitate self-expression (PREPaRE Model: Informational Documents/ Caregiver Training).

PREPAREDNESS

While the teacher's death was anticipated, it was still a shock when she died. The resources provided by the principal, counselor, teachers, and staff were extraordinary. Working through their sadness, they supported their students and each other. After educating themselves about how to talk with young children about impending death, they used age-appropriate language to keep students informed of the teacher's struggle. They prepared to sensitively share the sad news about the teacher who had taught many current students and also many of their parents. They planned ways to help the students remember the teacher and the lessons she had taught them. She taught a valuable lesson about how to live life. She loved her work and courageously continued teaching for as long as she could.

RESPONSE

Limited District Level Response

Principal David Moore invited a limited number of district responders familiar to the school staff to assist the building level response (PREPaRE Model: Matching Level of Response with Crisis Event Variables). A primary responder task was to support teachers needing assistance in their classrooms. At the faculty briefing, I reminded teachers they needed to take care of themselves to be able to take care of the students. They didn't need to "tough it out." There was crisis counseling for faculty and students. The teachers were used to being honest with their students and were reassured that "It is okay to answer questions honestly—on a level the students can understand. It is also okay to say, 'I don't know.' It is okay for the kids to see you sad."

Substitutes were available for teachers who needed to take a break or to get crisis counseling. While the degree of preparation for teachers and students was remarkable, some needed more support.

A caring teacher tearfully invited me to her first grade classroom because she believed she could not discuss the death of her colleague on her own. The students all knew the kindergarten teacher and most had been in her class the previous year. We talked about our sadness. We listened as the children expressed their thoughts and feelings. We talked about missing her. We reassured them that this kind of illness and death usually happens to older people (PREPaRE Model: Reaffirm Physical Health and Perceptions of Safety and Security). We began talking about pleasant memories and lessons learned from the teacher. The conversation expanded as the children shared stories about the deaths of relatives and pets. This afforded a *secondary triage* opportunity to identify students who had recently experienced a death and might benefit from follow-up (Brock et al., 2009).

The visit included bibliotherapy—a reading of *The Tenth Good Thing About Barney* (Viorst, 1972) —a comforting story about coping with the death of a pet cat as part of the cycle of life. In the book, the family expresses fond memories of Barney. One student asked about going to heaven. I acknowledged that many people believe that people and pets go to heaven after they die. Others understood the meaning of death in different ways. The children were encouraged to talk more with their parents and families about what they believe. They were reminded that there were people in school they could talk to—their teacher and other grown-ups who care and who understand their feelings. When I left the room, the teacher managed a smile through her sorrow.

RECOVERY

Memorial

The school planned and presented a beautiful memorial assembly for the school and district community (PREPaRE Model: Special Considerations When Memorializing an Incident). It was an upbeat celebration of a life—an inspiration to lead good lives, reflecting the lessons so many of us began learning in kindergarten.

Lessons Learned: Reflection and Discussion

1. In situations when there is a protracted terminal illness, there is opportunity for beneficial preparation of staff and students. *What are some specific ways that students and staff can prepare for the death of a teacher or student?*

2. Classroom teachers can be prepared to work with students coping with death, but can also benefit from the option of requesting in-class support from an experienced responder. *As a responder, how might you engage a teacher requesting in-class support in conversation about ways to best provide support?*

3. Bibliotherapy—reading developmentally appropriate books on topics relevant to the crisis—can be a useful tool for educating and comforting students, and encouraging discussion. *When*

might bibliotherapy be useful, and what are some ideas for selecting an appropriate book?

The following are sample templates of letters that kept a school community informed through this difficult time.

∽

District / School Letterhead

Dear Parents:

I learned yesterday from Mrs. _____ that she had made the difficult decision to remain home for the rest of the school year. As she rests and adjusts to new medication, she anticipates a rebuilding of her energy and strength. She wanted me to be sure to let you know she is facing the coming weeks with a "positive attitude" and hopes to visit the school in the spring.

Our counselor, Mrs._____ and I will meet with the children tomorrow to let them know Mrs._____'s illness required her to take medicine that makes her very tired. As a result, she must stay home now to rest. We will let the children know Mrs._____will not be returning to school.

In seeking a substitute for Mrs._____, our priority is finding someone particularly sensitive to the needs and questions of our children as they cope with the absence of this most special and important person in their lives. I am hopeful someone can be hired in time to start on Monday and will let you know if that is the case.

For the understanding and support I know you will provide Mrs._____, your children, and our school family, I thank you.

Please feel free to call me.

Sincerely,

Principal

P.S. Should you care to send notes or cards to Mrs. _____, simply send them to school and we will make sure she receives them.

~

To: All Staff

From: [School Counselor]

Re: Information that was relayed to our Kindergarten students today about Mrs. _____. I think you may also get some questions from your students.

[Principal] and I are telling the children that Mrs. _____ is sick and that she will not be coming back to school. We are explaining that she is taking new medicine that makes her very tired and that she needs to get a lot of rest. Make sure they understand that good doctors are caring for her.

We will tell the children their new teacher is going to be Ms._____.

If you get a question re: her having cancer, I would answer honestly that she does have cancer, but that not all cancers are the same. Mrs. _____is taking the right medicine for cancer and is resting and taking good care of herself. Tell the children that cancer is not contagious so no one can catch it.

Please watch for signs of distress from the children and call me if you need to.

Thanks.

School Counselor

~

Memo

To: All Staff

From: [School Counselor]

Re: Card Making Session, [Date]

Here are some facts we need to relay to the children during the card-making activity. They need to know that one of our teachers, Mrs. _____, is sick and that she is not coming back to school. She has cancer and is taking a new medicine that makes her tired. She needs lots of rest. She is being cared for by excellent doctors.

It is important for the children to know that not all cancer is the same. There are many different kinds. There are some kinds that are completely cured after the person takes a special medicine. With other kinds, people do not get completely well again. Mrs. _____ is taking the right kind of medicine for her illness.

Will she die? We don't know. Just remember she is taking her medicine and listening to her doctors.

Some children may relate an experience their family has had with cancer.

Watch for signs of distress among your children. Please let me know of any children who are distressed and call me if you need to.

Then have the children make cards. Be sure to read each card to make sure it is appropriate. It is okay if a child prefers not to make a card.

~

District / School Letterhead

Dear Parents:

Today, all of our students were given an opportunity to make cards of greeting and encouragement for a teacher many of them had as they began their school experience in kindergarten, Mrs. _____. For those of you who may not know, Mrs. _____ decided last week that dealing with the cancer she has faced for the past two years was making teaching too difficult to continue. In describing this situation to their classes, teachers identified the cause of Mrs. _____'s illness and, with great care, honesty and sensitivity, addressed questions and comments raised by the children. The important need to openly express different emotions, feelings, and remembrances was recognized in each room as I'm sure it will be in your homes.

At this time in our school family, your understanding, support, and prayers are deeply valued.

Sincerely,
Principal

To: All Staff
From: [School Counselor]
Re: Process for informing students

If the notification of death comes during the school day, there will be a letter sent home with the students telling the parents what has happened and asking them to inform their children. No announcement to the faculty will be made until after the children leave, when the teachers will be asked to attend a short faculty meeting. Letters for the children to take home will be distributed on the buses.

If notification comes after school hours, we will let staff know by way of the phone tree. We will let parents know the next school day also via a phone tree. The parents will be told what has happened and that we have talked with the children. They will need to talk further with their children especially in terms of religious beliefs.

A 7:30 am faculty meeting will be a time of sharing for ourselves and to prepare for the day.

Regardless of when we receive notification, classroom sessions will be conducted with these goals:

- Help the children understand what has happened or inform them about what has happened.
- Express their feelings.
- Have their feelings recognized and validated.
- Begin normal routine with flexibility.
- Be watchful for vulnerable students.

I am including information to help us handle this situation. Please read the attached pages and note any questions you may have.

We can help ourselves prepare by remembering while helping the children understand what happened that we need to take care of our own feelings. I am suggesting that two adults (classroom teacher and additional support person) be present for the individual classroom discussions. Do not be afraid to ask for support at any time; we are making arrangements now to help with release time/class coverage.

It is important to share the facts about death, to address children's fears and fantasies, and to support their grief through the expression of their feelings. Some children may be less affected, while others will need to tell you about their experiences with death. Be patient and listen; you do not need to tell them about your experiences. Help them put their feelings into words and let them know you understand what they are saying by "reflecting back" to them what you have heard. Let the children know that all feelings are okay; try to help them remember "special things" about Mrs._____. Feelings can range from sadness, to anger, to fear of abandonment, just as expressions can be sad one moment and joyous (running out to play) the next. All of this is normal. Be prepared to have the subject come up later.

For relief after the classroom sessions, I recommend that the children be permitted to go out for an extra recess.

‿

District / School Letterhead

Dear Parents:

We learned today that Mrs. _____ died last evening. For the past several years, she fought with great courage to overcome cancer and only two weeks ago made the decision to stop doing that which she did with unique and superior skill, teaching her kindergarten classes.

Tomorrow morning our teachers will discuss with each class this loss to our school family. Our counselor, psychologist, and other staff members will provide additional emotional support to children who need it for as long as necessary in the days ahead.

The viewing is at 7 pm tomorrow evening at _____Funeral Home at _____. The service is at noon Thursday.

To both honor and celebrate Mrs. _____'s commitment to providing almost 1500 [School] students with a remarkably strong and loving start to their formal schooling, our school will be closed __[Day]_[Date]_____ afternoon. Students will be dismissed at 11 am [Date]_____.

Thank you for your sensitivity and thoughtfulness in this time of sadness for all of us.

Sincerely,

Principal

P.S. Attached is information prepared by [School Counselor] to assist you in addressing this situation at home.

$\sim$

District / School Letterhead

Dear Parents:

As you now know, our school and community have lost a treasured family member. As we try to help our children cope with this death, here are a few ideas that may help in talking to your child.

In addition to the need for information that is clear and understandable, it is necessary for your child to be able to express his/her feelings and have them recognized. Encourage your child to talk with the assurance that all feelings are okay; help your child feel supported by listening carefully and answering questions honestly. When we hear of another's death, our own feelings about death often surface. Like adults, children think of their own experiences and feelings about death. Remember that these feelings may focus on the person who has recently died, someone who died previously, an impending death, or anxiety about death in general. You may wish to talk about your religious beliefs and explain death in those terms; in that way, the loss may make more sense and be more acceptable to your child.

When faced with the death of someone close to them, children may go through four stages of grief: 1) numbness 2) disorganization that may show itself with crying, loss of sleep or appetite, irritability, or apathy; 3) grieving in which the child may express fear, sadness, fear of abandonment, or anger; 4) acceptance. Do not be afraid to express your feelings of sadness. Encourage your child to reminisce about his/her experiences with Mrs. _____.

Possible questions

"What is death?"

<u>Do</u> say: "Death is when the body totally stops breathing."

<u>Do not</u> say: "Death is when you go to sleep."

Announcing the death

Do say: "She died."

Do not say:

a) "We lost _____" (Children can get lost.)

b) "She expired." (Library cards expire.)

c) "It is when you pass away, pass on, or are buried six feet under."

"What happens after the body stops working?"

You can explain these possibilities: "Some people believe the soul or spirit lives in another place (e.g. heaven) or the person who died lives on in your memories." This is the ideal time to explain your religious beliefs.

"Why do people die?"

Dying is a natural part of life. All living things—plants, animals, people—die.

"What is going to happen at school?"

You will have a class meeting to discuss what happened. You will have a chance to talk about your feelings.

Please feel free to contact me for further information. Thank you very much.

Sincerely,

School Counselor

∽

Dear Parents:

We trust the following information will help you and your children prepare for coming events related to the death of Mrs. _____. Many of you have addressed with your families what has happened, answered questions about it and discussed values and ways of dealing with these difficult circumstances. We have also taken time this morning, in each homeroom, to speak with students and give them an opportunity to share their feelings, thoughts, and remembrances of Mrs. _____.

Tomorrow's schedule is somewhat different from what we indicated in yesterday's letter in that the funeral service will take place at 10:30. We still plan to dismiss at 11 am. A number of our teachers will leave at 10 to attend the service, but we have made plans for classroom supervision in their absence. Since we are expected to provide a meal to children before they leave, we ask that you prepare a bag lunch for eating in the classroom. (Beverages will still be available as will the regular school lunch.) We would greatly appreciate if homeroom mothers come in around 10 to help.

Promptness in picking up children at dismissal is important.

Attending a viewing and/or funeral service is a significant experience for young children and the decision is one that you as parents will carefully consider.

We would like you to know a memorial celebration of Mrs. _____'s gifted teaching and influence on young lives is planned for an evening next week, most likely [Day] or [Day]. This will be a family event at which children and adults may share special times, poems or pictures in remembering this wonderful human being. A Kindergarten Fund is organized to accept contributions that will be used for students. We will send details in the next few days.

Please call with any questions or thoughts. Your support keeps our school family close.

Sincerely,

Principal

Should you care to send a note or card of condolence to the _____ family, the address is: _____.

McDonald's Night, which was to be tonight, is postponed.

12

Engaging Children to Work Through Grief

Reflections

While encouraging a child to work through grief, the crisis responder evaluates the degree of psychological trauma and risk for stress reactions, which determines the type and extent of intervention needed to facilitate recovery (Brock et al., 2009; DiRaddo & Brock, 2012) (PREPaRE Model: Evaluating Psychological Trauma). Like grief, recovery is a process that takes time. Healing does not proceed in a constant, linear progression. Rather, it is a gradual journey, with ups, downs, and occasional setbacks on the road to a better place.

Most approaches to engaging children to cope with traumatic incidents, including death, involve perceptive listening and learning about their needs. This facilitates developmentally appropriate movement toward self-expression, support systems, stress management, problem solving, and recovery (Brymer et al., 2006; Brymer et al., 2012a, 2012b; Dugger & Carlson, 2007; La Greca et al., 2002; Osofsky, 2011; Webber & Mascari, 2010; Wolfelt, 2004; Worden, 2009).

Promoting Prevention and Resilience

Preparation for engaging children begins before a traumatic incident or death occurs. It starts with a supportive school climate responsive to the needs and feelings of students and staff (Bear, 2010; Brock et al., 2009; Charney, 1992; Charney & Wood,

1981; Doll et al., 2014; Durlak et al., 2011; Reeves et al., 2010; Ristuccia, 2013).

The PREPaRE Model encourages a school climate that promotes safety, prevention, and student resilience. The resilient child is better able to cope with and recover from traumatic events. Variables that foster resiliency can be taught proactively and used during crises when opportunities for learning and the need for resilience are heightened. *Internal resilience variables* promote active coping styles and self-esteem; they teach emotional regulation, problem-solving skills, and internal locus of control; and they validate the importance of faith and belief systems. *External resilience variables* support families, facilitate peer relationships, and provide access to positive adult role models and prosocial institutions. PREPaRE emphasizes reestablishing social support systems and reuniting students with their families, peers, teachers, community, and familiar environments and routines (Brock, 2011; Brock et al., 2009; Reeves et al., 2011).

When we engage children and adolescents in working through emotional trauma and death, we can model, practice, and teach the principles of resilience. We can teach about the grieving process to normalize fearful reactions. We can model personal qualities and facilitate strategies that manage stress, promote recovery, and encourage connecting with families and other social support systems (Demaria & Schonfeld, 2014).

We can model leadership that engenders resilience and facilitates the natural tendency toward healing. We join with schools to foster a positive, responsive climate that encourages a culture of resilience. (Everly, 2011; Everly & Brown, 2009; Thompson, 2006).

The following aims at helping schools encourage the constructive expression of thoughts and feelings.

Setting the Stage for Engagement at School
- Prepare kits with handouts and brochures for parents, guardians, and teachers. (Suggested handout: Helping Children Cope with Loss, Death, and Grief: Tips for Teachers and Parents, National Association of School Psychologists

(2003) www.nasponline.org)

- Prepare kits for students with creative art materials (writing, drawing paper, crayons, markers) that are developmentally and culturally appropriate.
- Maintain library books about death, loss, hope, and resilience. (Bibliotherapy)
- Train school and district crisis teams with coordinated intervention plans.
- Train administrators and teachers to be familiar with helpful roles, discussion topics and activities for working with grieving students, children's grief reactions, and when to refer students or themselves for support.

Through Children's Eyes

Looking at death and trauma through children's eyes may expose a shattered sense of security and trust. Their world has changed. It is scarier, less safe, less certain than it was before. We try to understand each child's perceptions and unique ways of coping. Developmental and cultural considerations, previous experience, and exposure to an earlier traumatic incident influence each child's understanding, grief reactions, and ability to bounce back (Brooks & Goldstein, 2001; Everly & Brown, 2009; Jimerson et al., 2012a; Pfohl et al., 2002; Seligman, 2007).

Many factors influence the way we discuss death with a child and how we offer support. A continuous source of comfort that transcends age, experience, and culture is the opportunity to demonstrate that when bad things happen, the child is not alone. Through words and actions, discussion, art and play, we invite, but do not force children to share their stories and to express their thoughts, feelings, and reactions. They show us their concerns and needs, where they are in the grieving process, and how we can support their recovery.

Interpreting the Expression of Feelings

Children sometimes do not directly tell the story of a traumatic experience depending on developmental stage, cultural norms, or conscious or subconscious emotions such as fear, anger, or guilt. Instead, they may express themselves indirectly, talking around the experience and their feelings. They may describe related thoughts or fantasies, enacting what is troubling them through play, or illustrating problems through creative expression, such as in writing, drawing, or story telling. Crisis responders and caregivers should be observant for affective, behavioral, and developmental signs of trauma in young children. *Psychoeducation* for parents, guardians, teachers, and other caregivers will increase awareness of both subtle and overt signs of trauma in children (Garro et al., 2011; Wolfelt, 2004). The parent, teacher, or responder may need to become an interpreter of the child's actions and conversation, listening with a therapeutic 'third ear' to understand the meaning and emotional concerns behind the child's words (Fraiberg, 1959).

Careful Approach to Evaluating Need

Brymer et al. (2012a) suggest approaching affected students carefully. Responders should introduce themselves, offer assistance without interrupting, and respect those who decline help, while letting them know where help is available. They should not proceed based on *assumptions* about how children should react. Careful observation of the children's actions, statements and feelings provides cues on when and how to engage and what themes to explore. Not everyone exposed to trauma wants or needs intervention (Brymer et al., 2012a, 2012b; McNally et al., 2003; Rossen & Cowan, 2013). Crisis intervention that is not needed, or does not match the individual's degree of need can cause harm (Brock et al., 2009; Everly, 1999; Nickerson et al., 2009).

Recognizing Psychological Trauma

Make decisions about the intervention level after carefully evaluating the need. The PREPaRE Model describes predictive factors useful in recognizing and assessing the degree of risk for psychological trauma. (Chapter 10 explores risk factors in depth.) Screening instruments, rating scales, observation, structured and unstructured interviews, and clinical judgment help responders evaluate children experiencing complicated grief, maladaptive stress reactions, and to assess severity and treatment needs (Heath & Cole, 2012; Holland, 2012; Reeves et al., 2010; Reeves et al., 2012) (PREPaRE Model: Evaluating Psychological Trauma).

The parent, teacher, or responder must be alert for both overt and subtle signs of traumatic stress in very young children. When the signs are subtle, it is sometimes difficult to recognize that young children are psychologically traumatized. The symptoms of post-traumatic stress disorder (PTSD) in children may be different from, and less obvious than symptoms in adults. A child's reactions to a traumatic incident may go unrecognized or be misdiagnosed as a disorder unrelated to the incident (Carrion et al., 2002). A child can be traumatized without witnessing the incident. After hearing or reading about an event, a child's imagination or experiences with media or game portrayals of violence, may fill in the blanks, vividly constructing an incident that was not directly observed.

A Model of Interventions

Stephen Brock and his colleagues adapted a three-tiered intervention model (Gordon, 1983) in which Tier 1 *universal interventions* encompass individuals at low, moderate, and high risk for traumatic stress reactions. Tier 2 includes *selected interventions* targeting those at moderate and high risk. Tier 3 includes *indicated interventions* appropriate only for those at high risk. Crisis responders should use the lowest tier level appropriate for meeting needs, avoid excessive intervention, and respect natural movement toward recovery (Brock et al., 2009).

The PREPaRE Model offers detailed descriptions of the purposes of various interventions, along with how and when to implement them (Brock et al., 2009).

Tier 1 universal interventions

- Prevention of psychological trauma
- Reaffirmation of physical health
- Ensure perceptions of security and safety
- Evaluation of psychological trauma
- Reestablish social support systems

- Psychoeducation, including informational bulletins, flyers and handouts, classroom meetings, and caregiver trainings.

Tier 2 selected interventions

- Student psychoeducational groups
- Classroom–Based Crisis Intervention (CBI)
- Individual Crisis Intervention (ICI)

Tier 3 indicated interventions include therapeutic treatment, using such methods as Cognitive-Behavioral Therapy (CBT), which provides promising treatments for anxiety and post-traumatic stress disorder (PTSD) (Christner et al., 2007; Jaycox, 2004; Kendall, 2011; Mennuti et al., 2006; Nickerson et al., 2009). Kennedy-Paine et al. (2014) suggest de-stigmatizing the need for mental health services prior to crises to enhance the willingness to seek help.

Engaging Children After a Traumatic Incident

While most students experiencing traumatic stress are eventually able to calm themselves, some have such intense, persistent reactions that the ability to function is compromised. The provider of psychological first aid should be ready to engage emotionally overwhelmed students manifesting extreme reactions. Simple grounding techniques such as orienting questions, breathing relaxation strategies, or guided imagery may be useful for calming. Active listening and assisting students with problem-solving strategies can help them identify and clarify immediate needs, and develop a plan to meet those needs (Brymer et al., 2012a, 2012b).

Many of the suggestions and guidelines in this section about engaging children and working through their grief reactions are based upon useful *generalizations* about individuals and groups after traumatic incidents. These points do not apply to the grief experience of every child or group.

Guidelines: Psychological First Aid for Students

- Initiate contact without intruding or interrupting.
- Offer practical assistance, such as water and food, which translates to physical and emotional comfort.

- Do not make assumptions about student needs. Ask simple, respectful questions about what they need.
- Be present in a supportive way while understanding that not all of those affected want or need to talk with you. Young people will either avoid you or flood you with contact.
- Calm and orient those who are upset.
- Speak calmly and slowly with patience, responsiveness, and sensitivity.
- Listen carefully, trying to understand what they want to communicate and how you can help. Young children may express needs through behavior such as play.
- Reinforce personal strengths and coping strategies. Provide opportunities for constructive action.
- Give accurate, age-appropriate information that addresses their immediate goals and helps them connect with support networks.

Source: Brymer et al., 2012a.

Helping Children Cope

Share developmentally and culturally appropriate information. Answer questions clearly and honestly, avoiding unnecessary, upsetting details.

- Develop understanding of normal reactions to death and ways of expressing feelings. Explaining the grief process to children can help them better understand their feelings.
- Without forcing, provide opportunity to talk about what happened and to express thoughts, feelings, and questions. This may involve overcoming the fear that speaking about the recent event may cause another bad event to happen.
- Provide opportunity to express feelings in a variety of constructive and creative ways that can include talking, crying, playing, drawing, role-playing, sharing memories, and making memory books. Convey that "It's okay to play and feel good, even when you are grieving."
- Address immediate personal concerns and needs such as the fear of being abandoned and the need for reassurance

of security. "Most of us live long, healthy lives. There are many grown-ups to take care of you."

- Provide opportunity to reunite with social support systems, especially family, friends, meaningful school and community affiliations. Children should sense that adults empathize with their experience and care about them.
- Reestablish when ready, school routines with support as needed. Reestablish life routines with referral for therapeutic support when needed.
- Help children develop a plan that includes specific coping strategies, stress management, and a network of support. Encourage developmentally appropriate problem solving to constructively address concerns.
- It's normal to sometimes feel guilty. Be alert for magical thinking. "You may worry about a time when you were so angry you wished the person would go away. You may wonder if something you did caused the death. Everyone gets angry sometimes. The death was not your fault." Listen for statements containing hidden questions: "We had a fight," implies "Am I to blame?"
- Provide opportunity to participate in rituals such as funerals or memorials to structure grieving, vent emotions, support coping, and further a sense of closure. Developmentally appropriate, culturally sensitive preparation for rituals can increase the likelihood of benefit. "Talking about the person who died helps us remember and celebrate the person's life."

Source: Adapted from Grollman, 1967; Molaison, 2003.

Helping Parents Help Children to Cope

- Set aside a talking time to hear thoughts and reactions your child wishes to share. Make sure you understand your child's perspective to correct false beliefs.
- Explain in a direct, age-appropriate way what happened. Answer questions honestly. Avoid disturbing details. Assure reasonably that you will be there to care for your child.

- Be prepared to discuss difficult subjects if your child raises them. Look to your child for cues indicating the need to be reassured and better understand. Your child may need to talk about some details and feelings repeatedly. It is okay to let your child know there are some things we don't know or understand.
- Be aware that you and your child may be in different places in the way you are each dealing with the traumatic event. For example, you may reach a stage of anger or acceptance, while your child remains in a state of grief and sorrow.
- Correct false assumptions your child may have about a death, such as guilt or magical thinking that his/her thoughts or actions caused it. Correct any misunderstanding clearly and directly.
- Be prepared to address the topic of death whenever your child brings it up. Continue to be available and reassuring to your child over a long period.
- Do not let your child watch disturbing pictures on television. Spend time with your child away from the television.
- Reestablish routines in your child's daily schedule, especially in relation to bedtime.
- Family religious or spiritual beliefs can be integrated into thoughts, discussions, reactions, and ways of finding meaning and coping with traumatic events.
- Encourage your child to make a drawing, write a letter, or in some way express sympathy for those grieving the death of loved ones. Older children may find comfort in writing their thoughts and feelings about what happened. Teenagers often benefit from peer support, or engaging in constructive, life-affirming activities.
- Expect increased need for physical contact and support, reactions reflecting fear that something will happen to you or to other loved ones. Expect more 'childish' behavior, sadness, anger, playfulness and other feelings.
- Grief reactions are normal, but if your child continues to experience severe distress or has difficulty with normal

functioning, seek help from professional resources in the school or the community.

Source: Adapted from Raundalen & Dyregrov, 2004.

Trauma and Grief of Adolescents

Adolescents may present the misleading image of a 'cool' or strong facade, which could mask feelings of pain and grief, causing them to go unnoticed. The effects of submerged reactions can appear long after the traumatic event.

Helping Parents Help Teenagers to Cope

- Be a listener. Reflect genuine concern without giving advice.
- Communicate that grieving may last longer than expected, although the intensity usually subsides over time. Encourage and allow healthy expression of grief.
- Do not avoid talking about the person who died or the event for fear it might re-awaken the pain. Usually, teenagers want to talk, although it may be in a manner and time they select. Follow their lead.
- Times of grief are not times to make changes or important decisions. Try to keep the situation as normal as possible.
- Watch for trouble signs in adolescents. The need to appear competent may prevent teenagers from reaching out to others for assistance.
- While most grief reactions to trauma are both normal and temporary, seek immediate help for any sign of suicidal thinking.
- Referral should be considered if trouble signs are especially severe and intense over an extended period, or represent striking changes in usual behavior. Trouble signs may include:

    1. Withdrawal and isolation
    2. Physical complaints (headache, stomach pain) emotional concerns (depression, sadness, tension, suicidal thoughts, confusion)

3. Anti-social behavior (stealing, acting out, aggression, substance abuse)

4. School problems (avoidance, disruptive behavior, academic failure.)

- The power of the peer group is apparent in dealing with teenage grief. Adolescents often form networks of support, leaning on each other during difficult times. Encourage helpful, cooperative, life-affirming activities.

- Less frequently, the peer group can be a catalyst for further tragedy. After a suicide, caregivers must be vigilant to prevent suicide clusters, contagion, or pacts that signal the danger of further suicides among those most at risk.

- While most teens support each other moving toward recovery, some may succomb to contagion, which can breed copycats. This underscores the need for triage, psychoeducation, open discussion, constructive actions to empower, and when necessary, referral for more intensive treatment.

Source: Adapted from *Responding to Critical Incidents: A Resource Guide for Schools*. British Columbia Ministry of Education (1998).

Preventive Measures to Minimize Contagion

- Do not announce a death by suicide over the public address system or in an assembly. It is better to inform students through a written statement in the classroom where staff can intervene as needed.

- Using the principles of triage, help affected students express feelings about the deceased student and the suicide. Intervene with anyone experiencing suicidal ideation. Monitor and refer for closer assessment and outside treatment as needed (Brent et al., 2013; Erbacher et al., 2015; Jellinek & Okoli, 2012).

- Give students an opportunity to express a broad range of feelings and educate for understanding. Let them know it is normal to feel a variety of emotions, which may include sadness, anger, confusion and guilt. Accept the expression of anger toward the deceased for the suicide.

- Provide multiple opportunities for students to receive counseling. Observe and contact students who are unusually withdrawn or who are sad or aggressive. Be alert for misdirected blame or anger that could result in self-harm or violence toward others (Jellinek & Okoli, 2012).
- Notify parents of any student who appears to be at risk. Emphasize the need to monitor the child and to anticipate grief reactions. Discuss ways to be supportive, and when and how to seek professional support (Brent et al., 2013).
- Identify students who appear to be at risk based on their creative expression while writing and drawing, or in statements they make, including posts on social media, or in concerns expressed by their fellow students (PREPaRE Model: Secondary Triage).
- Students can be helped to understand that it is okay to grieve, remember, and say goodbye to the deceased student, but to distance themselves from the act of suicide and from glorifying or memorializing it. Any memorial event should have voluntary attendance. It should **not** be permanent, and should focus on remembering the individual, not the fatal act. Trained staff or crisis responders should attend memorials and the funeral to identify those who appear to be at risk.
- Strengthen protective factors such as caring relationships with family and adults, and meaningful connections at school. Emphasize self-esteem and coping skills, treatment for emotional or substance problems, and cultural or religious beliefs that value preserving life (Brent et al., 2013).
- Plan to monitor and attend to student needs and feelings with the approach of anniversary dates. It is okay to talk about but not to ignore it.
- Encourage life-affirming activities and goal setting.

Feelings and Conflict Resolution

The expression of anger coupled with a threat of violence by a student led to an important teachable moment, which may have prevented serious trouble. I was co-facilitating a small group of middle school students grieving the accidental death of a student hit by a truck. A boy in the group remarked about a student he observed smiling and laughing earlier that day. Resenting the laughter, which he believed was disrespectful, he threatened to 'beat up' the student who laughed. The co-facilitator and I expressed understanding of his angry feelings, but emphasized that it was totally unacceptable to physically attack another student. We talked with him and the group about the variety of feelings, including laughter that could be expressed after a death. We reminded the boy that the student who laughed may not have been friends with the deceased student, or may not have known him at all. He may have been joking about something very different, or the laughter may have been an expression of anxiety about the death. No matter what the reason, 'beating up' the boy would be a destructive, rather than constructive expression of anger. It would not honor the memory of his friend.

After a death, anger is a normal grief reaction, but we must understand and channel it constructively (Jellinek & Okoli, 2012). *Off-target anger* can be destructive. The angry middle school student was supported in thinking of alternatives to violence. He could help others who were genuinely grieving. He could choose to confront the laughing student with his feelings rather than his fists, but only in the presence of a school counselor or administrator. We established a contract with the student stating he agreed not to 'beat up' or touch the other student. Finally, we told him we needed to inform the school administration so they could monitor the situation and follow-up with him to be supportive. We let the student know we appreciated his feelings, the dialogue, and his assurance he would not engage in any violent acts.

When engaging students in working through trauma and grief, there is an important distinction between necessary, helpful intervention and unnecessary, harmful imposition. The responder should strive to facilitate, or simply not to obstruct the natural tendency toward recovery (Brymer et al., 2012a; Levine & Kline, 2007). Out of tragic circumstances can come amazing opportunities to find hope, resilience, compassion, and appreciation for self and others. These opportunities often begin with the crisis responder carefully engaging and serving those in need.

13

Cultural Competence When a Teacher Dies

Abstract

When an instructional aide, respected in the Latino community, suddenly dies at home, crisis response is needed at multiple locations with different age groups, all requiring cultural and developmental sensitivity. This case study emphasizes the importance of getting to know the various ethnic groups in the school community. The district team becomes a mobile crisis unit, traveling from school to school, blending with building teams and meeting with groups of grieving students. This chapter includes a sample bilingual letter to parents. *Themes are: 1) cultural competence: a source of comfort, 2) crisis response at multiple locations, 3) response in the primary language, 4) developmentally appropriate response.*

INTRODUCTION

Mobilization Across School District and Culture

Early morning phone calls summoned the district's crisis response team to an elementary school after an instructional aide choked to death while eating at home. We soon learned that the deceased instructor had been a revered leader in the Latino community. He and his wife were internationally acclaimed ballet dancers. They taught dance and conducted an after-school tutoring program. The couple's two sons were students at a district high school. We immediately contacted the high school to discuss support for the sons and their family.

Students throughout the school district were emotionally touched by this sudden death. Our response centered on an elementary, middle, and high school. For most of the affected students, Spanish was the primary language, and many spoke little English. Inclusion of a Spanish language interpreter was a unique aspect of the response along with serving multiple locations and ages.

PREVENTION/MITIGATION

Cultural Competence and Connections

A Source of Comfort

Schools reflect our multicultural society and crisis responders can demonstrate cultural sensitivity in various ways (PREPaRE Model: Cultural Variations). School and district crisis teams should familiarize themselves with the diverse customs and needs of racial and ethnic minorities they serve. Kemple et al. (2006) suggest that schools conduct a multicultural needs assessment to identify barriers such as a lack of translators, and address them in their crisis plans. The capacity to communicate in the primary language of grieving students is essential. If not enough members of the crisis team speak the primary language, interpreters must be recruited or hired, and if necessary, trained in the skills of effective interpreting.

Our response emphasized the importance of establishing partnerships with ethnic and cultural groups in the school community. As the response unfolded, we realized we could have done more to establish cultural connections. Silva (2004) suggested getting to know the "cultural brokers"—leaders who can be resources for connecting with and understanding the community and its grief. In this case, the community was mourning one such leader.

132

More subtle expressions of cultural sensitivity are demonstrated by understanding culture-specific reactions and rituals associated with death. When gestures of understanding and acceptance are expressed toward members of a cultural minority, they may experience a significant sense of comfort and support. An expanding body of research and case studies provide evidence of the challenges and benefits of cultural competence when planning and implementing crisis response (Athey & Moody-Williams, 2003; Heath et al., 2005; Ortiz & Voutsinas, 2012; Pederson, 2003; Rabalais et al., 2002; Sandoval & Lewis, 2002; Silva & Klotz, 2006; Sue & Sue, 2003; Vasquez & Janvier, 1991; Young, 1997).

PREPAREDNESS

Understanding Norms

Responding in Primary Language

Preparedness does not begin and end with a trained crisis team. Each response has unique challenges and the present one was no exception. Being prepared means being ready to think through the details of the particular situation, solve problems, and spontaneously, to meet unanticipated needs.

Different cultures have different attitudes, norms, and ways of dealing with trauma. Each can have unique rituals to come to grips with death. Some cultures show dramatic, animated reactions. Others present a more stoic façade, expressing little external reaction. Internally, an individual may be torn by grief or in contrast, calm and peaceful. In either case, the person's feelings are mediated by cultural beliefs and customs. Understanding culturally mediated reactions is especially relevant when evaluating the degree of psychological trauma (Ortiz & Voutsinas, 2012).

Cultural competence becomes more complex since cultural norms and even language can significantly vary within groups often thought of as homogeneous. "Latino" can mean Mexican, Puerto Rican, Cuban, El Salvadoran, Dominican and more.

Reactions within each of these communities can be very different. Spanish as a primary language can also vary, depending on the dialect. When possible, it is beneficial to have an interpreter who uses the dialect most prevalent among those affected by the incident.

We had a trained district crisis team, but no member was fluent in Spanish. Recruiting from the school staff, we selected an instructional aide to be the lead interpreter. The Latino community held her in high esteem. Though saddened by the tragedy, she was sensitive to student needs and ably controlled her emotions. She functioned effectively interpreting for all age groups. We discussed with her the challenges and requirements of being an interpreter: communicating the meaning of each speaker as accurately as possible, without changing the content or tone of what is said. Beyond the basic communication of language, she was invaluable for keeping her hand on the pulse of the students and briefing the team on perceived issues and feelings of the young people (Vasquez & Janvier, 1991).

RESPONSE

School level crisis teams consisting of administrators, counselors, and school psychologists were mobilized in each of the three schools most affected, creating systems of support (PRE-PaRE Model: Provide Interventions and Respond to Psychological Needs). The district level team essentially became a mobile crisis unit, beginning at the elementary school, where the Instructional Aide was known through his work in the community. The team traveled to the middle school where he was assigned, and finally to the high school where students knew him through his community work. Each school had a group of twenty to thirty students who appeared to need attention. *Primary* and *secondary triage* was happening at each school, with staff and students collaborating to identify the most affected students (PREPaRE Model: Evaluating Psychological Trauma).

With our new interpreter, the team met with student groups throughout the day. Each group was older than the previous one. We began the interventions in early morning and saw the final group by late afternoon. Having an interpreter was critical, since communicating in Spanish was necessary to include all students. Reflecting on the process, I believe that all of the students, regardless of age or bilingual proficiency, felt more cared for, comforted, and respected because we communicated with them in their primary language. In a sense, the repetition of words in translation slowed the interpretive process, allowing more time to consider everyone's words, reflect on thoughts and feelings, and create a more peaceful, comforting atmosphere.

Developmentally Appropriate Response

We spoke about death in a manner consistent with the needs of the three separate, grieving age groups (Jimerson et al., 2012a; Pfohl et al., 2002) (PREPaRE Model: Developmental Variations). The youngest group hardly understood the concept of death, but many of the children, kindergarten through third grade, cried loudly, expressing emotional pain. With the younger students we spoke about the sudden, accidental death and repeatedly reassured them that choking death is rare and that adults care for you and will continue to provide for your safety (PREPaRE Model: Reaffirm Physical Health and Perceptions of Safety and Security). We chose our words carefully and read comforting books (bibliotherapy) that helped the children understand. We provided drawing materials and creative projects to help them express their feelings. In all of the age groups, we were careful not to use phrases like "passed away," "rest in peace," or "eternal sleep." Especially for the younger children, confusing "death" with "sleep" could cause anxiety and sleep disturbance.

Many students, especially in the middle and high school, had taken initiative before the tragedy, to form a network of support emanating from their connections in the community (PREPaRE Model: Reestablish Social Support Systems). Many had bonded as a minority group coping with the dominant Anglo culture, language, and school community. They had formed friendships, often through activities organized by their teacher who had now died.

With both middle and high schoolers, we listened and discussed the meaning of the man's life, his aspirations, and hopes for them. The high schoolers understood the concept of death. I am not sure how demonstrative they had been with their school crisis team earlier in the day, but by the time we joined them, their emotions were subdued, with some quiet sobbing and tears. Consistent with a previously observed pattern when popular high school teachers died, older students took initiative, comforted each other, and formed a network of support—especially when given the opportunity, space, and materials to be creative (PREPaRE Model: Reestablish Social Support Systems/ Providing Opportunities to Take Action).

We carefully avoided telling any group, "I know how you feel." We could imagine their feelings, listen, and empathize when they expressed their grief. We talked especially to the older students about the process of grieving and coping. When they sought meaning, we encouraged them to express themselves, and to find comfort in their family or faith, and to begin healing. We contacted families of students who needed monitoring or referral (PREPaRE Model: Tertiary Triage: Evaluating Psychological Trauma).

Hearing anecdotes and memories the high school students shared about this valued community leader, I had an uncanny feeling, almost like knowing this man whom I'd never met. I learned to appreciate him and to sense what he meant to the students. I decided to take a risk and make a personal statement, "I didn't have the pleasure of knowing your teacher, Señor _____, but I have heard what you are saying about him. It sounds like he was a very good man who you appreciated and will miss very much." Spanish translation followed, and then some smiles.

RECOVERY

The PREPaRE Model emphasizes the importance of examining all phases of a response as an opportunity for a crisis team to learn valuable lessons (Brock et al., 2009). This self-analysis can identify a school community's immediate and long-term needs (PREPaRE Model: Examine Effectiveness of Crisis Prevention and Intervention). Examining the present response, it is clear that more outreach was needed with the Latino community and other cultural minorities, including the development of interpreter services in Spanish and other languages.

The day was long. We supported building crisis teams in multiple schools. We enlisted and trained an interpreter so we could listen to students in their primary language. Every crisis response has unique challenges, but this one seemed to have more than most. The degree of collaboration, cultural, and developmental understanding in response to this sad event made the day satisfying in terms of what our extended bilingual team accomplished in support of grieving students.

Lessons Learned: Reflection and Discussion

1. Culturally competent crisis response is one of the most powerful ways to express genuine respect and empathy for students from diverse racial and ethnic groups. *What are some ways we can educate ourselves as responders, and express cultural sensitivity during a response?*

2. It is essential to plan for available interpreters in order to conduct crisis response in the primary language of affected students. *How would you, as a responder, prepare a volunteer who fluently speaks the students' primary language, but has no experience as an interpreter?*

3. Circumstances may require that selected members of the district crisis team travel to more than one school to support and supplement school teams. This could mean working with students at different developmental stages in one day. *What are some ways to plan for this type of multiple response?*

4. Cultural norms and even language can vary within ethnic groups generally thought of as homogeneous. For example, "Latino" can include people from many different countries of ancestry (or origin) with widely different traditions. *How might your crisis team conduct a "cultural needs assessment"?* A *needs assessment* is used "to identify areas to be addressed, so that plans and strategies may be developed..." (Brock et al., 2009).

Letters to parents, written in both Spanish and English, edited for confidentiality follow:

District / School Letterhead

Estimados miembros denuestra comunidad:

Nos entristecimos recientemente en nuestra comunidad escolar por la muerte repentina del Sr. _____, maestro doe "EST" (Ingles como Segunda Lengua). Como una comunidad escolar, les damos nuestro pesame a los familiares y amigos del Sr. _____.

A menudo, cuando oimos de la muerte de otra persona, empezamos a preocuparnos de nuestros propios sentimientos sobre la muerte. Los adolescentes, como adultos, empiezan a pensar en sus priopias experiencias con la muerte, y muchose experimentan muchas sensaciones y emociones normales. Estas sensaciones se pueden enfocar en la persona quien ha muerto, otra persona quien ha muerto, una muerte inminente, o ansiedades sobre la muerte en general.

Nosotros hemos informado a los estudiantes que no tenemos todas las respuestas. Les recomendamos que escuchen cuidadosamente a su hijo y contesten sus preguntas honesta y sinceramente.

El personal de [Escuela] quisiera dar apoyo y ser sensible a todos nuestros estudiantes y sus familias y ayudarles a hacer frente a esta perdida. Hoy, [Escuela], tenia consejeros adicionales, psicologos, y trabajadores sociales de nuestro "District Crisis Response Team" (Equipo de la Respuesta de la Crisis del Distrito) disponibles para ayudar a cualquier estudiante que necesita sus servicios.

Si piensan que su hijo necesita apoyo adicional, favor de llamar a nuestros consejeros al: _____ o a _____, trabajadora social, al _____.

Sinceramente,
Director

District / School Letterhead

Dear Parents:

We are saddened by the sudden death of Senor _____, an English as a Second Language tutor at [School name] Middle School. As a community, we express our condolences to the family and friends of Senor _____.

Often, when we hear of another's death, our own feelings about death surface. Teenagers, like adults, begin to think of their own experiences with death, and many normal feelings surface. These feelings may focus on the person who has died, or another who has died, someone who is near death, or anxiety about death in general.

As school staff, we have let students know we don't have all the answers. We encourage you to listen carefully to your young adult, answering questions openly and honestly.

The [School name] staff wishes to be supportive and sensitive to all of our students and their families in helping them cope with this loss. Today, [School name] has additional counselors, psychologists, and social workers from our District Office Crisis Response Team available to interact with any student or staff needing these services.

If you feel your child needs additional support, please call our counseling office at [phone number], or District Social Worker, ____ at [phone number].

Sincerely,
Principal

Section 3

Team Development: Building Skills, Caring for Clients, and for Ourselves

14

Media Message: Mutual Benefit or Added Trauma?

Reflections

School crisis response teams can develop skills and a plan for working with the media. A cooperative, mutually beneficial relationship will support the crisis team in caring for those affected by traumatic events (Brock et al., 2009; Reeves et al., 2010).

Managing the Impact of Words and Images

When a crisis team responds to media requests, it helps to remember that journalists have a demanding job. While protecting a grieving community, adopting a cooperative approach discourages reporters from pushing beyond reasonable boundaries of student and staff privacy. In rare circumstances, they may need to be asked to show restraint in pursuit of a story so as not to sensationalize tragedy. Establishing a mutually beneficial relationship can present opportunities to encourage moderation in the media's use of words and pictures.

With its powerful visuals, television news seeks to inform the public with minimal censorship, but must balance that objective with the public's need to be protected from objectionable images. Schools can help students cope with disturbing visuals by honest reassurance of safety, explaining how people are working to improve the situation, and by educating them about how to manage viewing news coverage. Since children are sensitive to repeated portrayals of violence, their access to reports and images should be monitored and limited (Eth, 2002; Singer et al., 2004). Caregivers should similarly be aware of potential harm from children's access to social media.

For example, when images of the space shuttle Challenger exploding in the sky, or airplanes crashing into the World Trade Center were shown repeatedly on afternoon television, children perceived each exposure as terrifying. When the incoherent rage of a psychotic mass murderer on the Virginia Tech campus was shown repeatedly on television, the images could have inspired psychopaths, or other unstable viewers to copy horrific acts. Repeated harmful images can further traumatize vulnerable young people or expose others to threats. The interest of a crisis responder is to minimize additional trauma (PREPaRE Model: Ensure Perceptions of Safety and Security: Minimizing Crisis Exposure).

Establish Media Boundaries During a Crisis

Do not permit members of the media to enter the school building or the campus to interview, film, or photograph students or staff.

Encourage staff to refer media to the district spokesperson.

Establish an off-campus location and times for press conferences where district representatives share information.

A media liaison is named by the district administration, with primary responsibilities to:
- Dispel rumors
- Provide accurate information consistent with the public's right to know
- Set realistic expectations for the outcome of the crisis
- Provide the public with information about resources available to assist individuals and families.

Source: Adapted from Brock et al., 1996; Petersen & Staub, 1992.

The Media Can Help

The media can play a helpful role in the aftermath of a traumatic incident (PREPaRE Model: Collaborating With the Media). When information about safety, prevention, intervention, and recovery must be disseminated quickly, the media can help. When crisis responders have a positive working relationship with the media, reporters can let the public know what measures to take to assure safety, and they can convey when safety has been reestablished. The media can reassure the community that those in need of physical or psychological first aid are receiving care. Information can be provided about the needs of traumatized individuals and specific ways that family, friends, and community can support recovery efforts. Information about constructive action is especially critical during disasters where there are mass casualties. For example, "Here are suggestions about reassuring children who are experiencing fear for their safety" or "Here are suggestions about measures to reestablish a safe environment for our children."

Planning for Media Collaboration

Advance planning and quick, prudent action can make a real difference in constructively working with media. Beyond restricting media from the school building and campus, plan to direct media trucks, cars, and equipment to a specified area off campus—for example, across the street rather than on the same side as the school. With the cooperation of police or state troopers, safe corridors can be established along key routes to keep them clear for emergency vehicles and to shield students walking to and from school. The plan should include directives to school staff, students, and families, encouraging and supporting their right to decline interviews. Planning ahead can shield students and families from media attention during school arrival, dismissal, at bus stops and while walking to and from school.

Provide the media with ongoing information about the crisis. Specify an off-campus location where school representatives can meet with the media. Scheduling news conferences away from the school helps to protect student, staff, and family privacy. The principal or superintendent, media liaison, law enforcement, and medical personnel can provide information at news conferences.

Communicating with the Media

1. Establish a communications center for the media at district office or other off campus site. (Be sure it is large enough. Certain events attract nationwide attention.)

2. Prepare a brief written statement, such as:

"The safety of our students and staff is our first priority. We have implemented emergency procedures. (Name of district media liaison) will provide you with additional information as soon as possible" or "This was an unexpected event/tragedy which saddens us all. We are not aware of all the details at this time. We have implemented support services to provide for the safety and well being of our students and staff."

3. Be specific about plans for press conferences.

Example: "The superintendent will address the press in (location) at 10 a.m. for 30 minutes, followed by a 15-minute question and answer session. At this time, no students or faculty will be available for interviews and no one will be admitted beyond (set limits of access)."

4. All information releases should be approved by district administration. Official spokespersons may be designated by police, firefighters, and medical authorities. These individuals should work together closely to plan release of information.

5. Communication tips to remember:

- Put the students and staff and their safety first, as an ongoing theme.
- Be succinct and careful with what you say—less may be better.
- Be honest. Acknowledge the incident.
- Provide brief, factual information describing the crisis.
- Provide information about the school's plans to address the situation.
- Avoid speculation, prediction, or accusation.
- Avoid exaggerating, sensationalizing, or romanticizing what occurred.

- Do not provide information that could enable copying the incident.
- Use qualifiers: "Our initial information states..." "It appears that..."
- Respect the privacy of individuals, including victims and their families. Do not release names or identifiable information, unless it is public knowledge and next of kin have been notified.
- Report who was involved in general terms, respecting confidentiality (number, gender, grade in school).
- Convey your belief that a sense of order will prevail.
- Report what the school district has done, is doing and will do to help students, staff and community recover from the event.
- Display calm and professionalism.
- Avoid jargon and acronyms.
- Do not argue, or become defensive.
- Never say, "No comment." An appropriate response might be, "I do not have that information at this time. I will share that information with you when it is available" or "I cannot answer that question at this time" or "We are still evaluating that. I'll get back to you." Refer to another source, if appropriate.
- There is no such thing as "off the record."
- If appropriate, use media to inform parents and guardians when, how and where they can pick up their children, obtain additional information, or access community resources for dealing with the event.
- Update media representatives on a regular basis. They can be helpful disseminating necessary information to the community.
- When feasible, provide copies of media statements to district staff.
- Maintain a record of communications and news releases. If possible, videotape conferences.

Source: Adapted from Brandywine School District Crisis Response Manual.

Further Information

The National Association of School Psychologists developed tips for teachers, parents, and adolescents to cope with traumatic events. These are available at www.nasponline.org/crisis.

See relevant NASP (2006) handout, "Responsible Media Coverage of Crisis Events Impacting Children." www.nasponline. org/resources/crisis_safety/Media%20Guidelines.pdf

15

Severe Psychological Trauma: Death in the Classroom

Abstract

This case study describes what happened after a middle school student collapsed and died in a classroom. Teachers, students, administrators and the school nurse were either witnesses or first responders. Unanticipated events include a student confronting crisis team members about planning a memorial service and intrusion by media. *Themes are: 1) traumatic incident; 2) school-wide triage; 3) media intrusion; 4) funeral and memorial issues; 5) care for the caregiver: outside help.*

INTRODUCTION

While I didn't want to lose the day in my schools, something told me I should attend the workshop titled, "Hearts Behind the Badge: First State CISM Team."

I learned about Jeffrey Mitchell's Critical Incident Stress Management (CISM) model and how it could help mitigate stress reactions among traumatized first responders (Everly & Mitchell, 2003, 2010; Mitchell, 1993; Mitchell & Everly, 1998).

A Severely Traumatic Incident

We did not have cell phones at that time. During the presentation, I heard my beeper and saw that it indicated 9-1-1 and the phone number of our office's lead secretary. I left the presentation to call the secretary who told me a student had collapsed and died in one of our middle schools. I could feel the color drain from my face. I returned to the workshop to say a couple of quick good-byes and ran to my car. I remember nothing of the drive upstate to the scene of the sudden death.

PREVENTION/MITIGATION

Traumatic events are often sudden and cannot be prevented. Recovery after an unexpected tragedy frequently depends on a combination of factors, such as the school climate and the extent to which students feel cared for and have a sense of belonging. The extent to which students feel they have a role in the recovery process is also relevant (PREPaRE Model: Developing Resilience and School Connectedness). The capacity of school and district crisis teams to intervene is also a mitigating factor. The incident occurred some years before the evidence-based PREPaRE Model (Brock et al., 2009) was developed, though its concepts are relevant and applied to this incident. Jimerson et al. (2012b) point out that while prevention may not be possible, a comprehensive crisis plan that is flexible and includes preparation for a wide range of unusual events such as sudden death on campus can mitigate emotional trauma. The plan can also support coping and it can instruct caregivers.

PREPAREDNESS

Reeves et al. (2012) suggest that a key element of crisis preparedness involves conducting a *vulnerability assessment* to determine potential environmental risks. This assessment reviews preventive measures and potential hazards inside and outside of the school building, strengths and needs relating to students' physical and psychological safety, and review of the school's emergency communication procedures. Following the assessment, planning can encompass universal prevention programs as well as targeted, incident-specific preparedness and response protocols (Reeves et al., 2010; Reeves et al., 2011) (PREPaRE Model: School Building Vulnerability Assessment).

After the crisis teams are trained, the teachers and support staff can be taught constructive ways to react to crises and to respond to grief reactions with developmentally and culturally appropriate interventions to facilitate coping (PREPaRE Model: Psychological Education: Caregiver Training). Systems can be developed to assess and address student needs during the response (PREPaRE Model: Evaluating Psychological Trauma). This includes teaching parents to help their children to cope, and coordinating with community agencies and professionals. Crisis response planners can be flexible in evaluating the varying effects of sudden death on students and staff, and they can include long-term follow-up (Jellinek & Okoli, 2012; Jimerson et al., 2012b).

Preparedness after a vulnerability assessment often involves the planning and implementation of appropriate drills or exercises (PREPaRE Model: Exercising School Crisis Plans). When drills are properly conceived and carried out, they enhance student knowledge and skills on ways to respond to emergencies without increasing anxiety (Zhe & Nickerson, 2007). Much less frequent events, such as the sudden death of a student or teacher on campus, may not lend themselves to drills that require student involvement. These types of severely traumatic incidents may be thought out and practiced through discussion-based exercises such as tabletop drills and workshops (Reeves et al., 2010).

Our district crisis team had been gaining experience with higher incidence events such as the off-campus death of students, teachers, and parents, but never the sudden, incomprehensible death of a student in a classroom in the presence of his peers. We had not conceived, drilled, or practiced response to such a severely traumatic incident. There were no protocols in place. Our inexperience and lack of practice led to some mistakes during the response, and some lessons learned.

RESPONSE

As I made my way back to school from the workshop, members of the district crisis team joined the school team in providing psychological first aid to students. School had been dismissed by the time I arrived. Here's what happened. Shortly after lunch, the thirteen-year-old had gone to his math class and remarked to the student in front of him, "I feel funny." He collapsed. His classmates' laughter at his presumed prank turned into horror when they realized he had lapsed into unconsciousness. Hearing the commotion, eighth grade teachers rushed to join the shocked math teacher and her students. The school nurse was summoned and CPR performed but the student was not revived.

The principal, the nurse, and district responder Marty Tracy joined the family at the hospital where the boy was pronounced dead. Weeks later, we learned that the death resulted from a previously undetected heart defect. In their grief, the family kept the principal informed of funeral arrangements.

The boy was popular, a likeable student with an endearing manner and a ready sense of humor. His death was grieved throughout the school. For our team, this was a uniquely challenging experience due to the severity of emotional trauma and exposure to student witnesses, their teacher, and the first responders—other teachers, counselors, the school nurse and administrators. *Primary triage*, which identified student and staff witnesses, was obvious although the task of working with these traumatized individuals was exceedingly difficult (PREPaRE Model: Primary Triage: Evaluating Psychological Trauma).

Jimerson et al. (2012b) observe that following a sudden, unexpected death there is greater risk for psychological trauma among those who witnessed the event, relatives or friends of the deceased, and those with early developmental levels, mental illness, or limited social support (Brock & Davis, 2008). Brymer et al. (2012a, 2012b) suggest that psychological first aid providers prepare to attend to "individuals whose reactions are so intense and persistent that they affect the students' ability to function or be oriented to their current environment." Strategies such as minimizing exposure to the traumatic incident (PREPaRE Model: Emergency Procedures that Minimize Exposure), simple grounding techniques, or breathing relaxation exercises can help calm students who witness a devastating event (Brymer et al., 2012a, 2012b).

Crisis Counseling, Debriefing, Faculty Meeting

Crisis counseling began immediately in the school library and in smaller adjacent rooms with student witnesses to the tragedy (PREPaRE Model: Provide Interventions and Respond to Psychological Needs). The blended school and district crisis teams provided psychological first aid, identifying students who appeared most affected and needing further intervention. Counseling was also available for the affected teachers, but the focus was on the students.

After school, we debriefed as a blended team, joining the school administration and counseling staff to plan our response. The principal composed a letter to the entire school community and a separate letter to parents and guardians of students in the affected classroom. Counselor Leslie Carlson proved especially able and assumed a leadership role. She later joined the district team, and eventually became one of its coordinators.

Before leaving on the first day, we triaged further, reviewing the names of all students who had been counseled, discussing those who appeared to need small group or individual follow-up the next day. We divided their names among crisis team members for parent/guardian telephone contact (PREPaRE Model: Secondary Triage: Evaluating Psychological Trauma).

We held a faculty meeting—with coffee—before school the next morning and shared what was happening, what resources were available for student and staff counseling, how to be supportive of students and each other, and when and how to refer students needing more attention (PREPaRE Model: Caregiver Training). The superintendent provided floating substitutes who were available if teachers needed relief.

We distributed to staff information about grief reactions and a handout on talking with students about death and grief. We advised about escorting distressed students to the library where crisis team members would be available all day. Teachers were reminded to monitor students not only for the most obvious grief reactions such as sadness and crying, but also for other changes in behavior such as being unusually quiet, withdrawn, angry, or acting out. Plans were made for school counselors familiar to the

153

students, reinforced by district responders, to follow the deceased youngster's schedule to support students and teachers throughout the day.

After the faculty meeting, the team stationed members at strategic locations such as buses, hallways, faculty lounge, and library to escort students and to offer continued crisis counseling. Some counselors were assigned to facilitate small groups while other counselors met with individuals. Everyone continued documenting names of students seen and their emotional status. Responders were assigned to the affected teaching team's corridor in the event that extra support was spontaneously needed.

Each class offered opportunities for structured discussion and for monitoring the emotional status of students and staff who witnessed the student collapse in the classroom. The PREPaRE Model (Brock et al., 2009) offers structured group and individual interventions, including some especially useful for an affected classroom. "Student Psychoeducational Groups" provide an opportunity to answer student questions and dispel rumors before focusing on instruction about common crisis reactions and plans for stress management. As part of a comprehensive intervention program, "Classroom-Based Crisis Intervention" (CCI) offers a longer, more intensive session for students who are exposed to the same traumatic event. It is recommended that participation be voluntary and by parental consent. CCI provides an opportunity for similarly affected students (homogeneous groups) to share their stories, identify and normalize common reactions, and to identify maladaptive reactions requiring follow-up. A key to CCI is to arm participants with coping strategies, information and individualized plans for stress management, and to follow-up with parents and caregivers with information about how they can support coping. Finally, for distressed students in need of individual attention, PREPaRE offers a structured "Individual Crisis Intervention" (ICI), which reestablishes coping, provides support, identifies crisis-generated problems, and begins adaptive coping and problem solving. ICI affords an opportunity to assess the student's level of risk for stress reactions or potential self-harm.

Throughout the first two days after their friend's death, students had an opportunity to express their grief. They shared thoughts and feelings about the incident and how it was affecting them. They were exposed to many caring adults who actively listened, empathized, and taught about the grief process and stress management strategies. They were encouraged to talk with their families, who continued to be contacted with information about their children's status and ways to support them (PREPaRE Model: Reestablish Social Support Systems/ Caregiver Training). Students appearing most at risk for psychological trauma were referred for outside treatment.

Eventually, students receiving crisis counseling began sharing pleasant memories of their classmate, and began writing anecdotes and drawing pictures for inclusion in a memory book to be presented to his family. As in previous crises, the art teacher provided plenty of materials. There was also a paper mural taped to the wall in an accessible, easily monitored hall location where students could express thoughts in prose, poetry, and drawings. Students contributed to murals that were given to the grieving family. Creative expression helped students feel a sense of control, working individually or in groups (PREPaRE Model: Providing Opportunities to Take Action). Gradually, they returned to their regular class schedule. More and more, the normal routine was reestablished.

Media Boundaries: Intrusion

A number of incidents, some inconsequential, some not, were unique to this tragedy. We awaited word of the funeral while diligently seeking a return to normal routine. While I monitored the cafeteria during eighth grade lunch, an upsetting incident involved a news photographer who accompanied the district superintendent who had been well meaning and supportive, except on this occasion. The *News Journal* photographer snapped photos of students as they ate lunch. The scene took on a surreal quality, an intrusion far from normal routine.

I felt anger and confusion approaching the superintendent. I said, "What is this newspaper photographer doing here?"

His response in the noisy cafeteria was a quizzical look and a shrug.

I felt powerless to pursue the matter. As the district authority, he had his reasons.

I momentarily lost my ability to reason, because I proceeded to approach and bargain with the photo journalist. "I wish you weren't in here doing this," I said to him.

"What's the problem?" he asked.

"We are trying to establish a normal routine for these students and you are in here taking photos," I said.

I thought surely he realizes it is not normal routine for his large, obtrusive camera and tripod to be reminding these kids about what happened while they are at lunch.

Maybe I was being too sensitive. I wanted to leave the cafeteria. It felt so intrusive, so lacking in respect. If there was an agreement with the media, trading photos to establish broader boundaries, I did not know about it and gave up speculating (PREPaRE Model: Media Relations Protocols/ Collaborating with the Media).

Funeral Plans

As the family liaison, the principal received information about the funeral. Our position was to respect the wishes of the family regarding whether the service would be private or open to the public, including students. The family decided to welcome the public. The district provided substitutes for teachers attending the funeral. We sent letters home with details and asked that responsible adults accompany students who planned to attend and to stay with them for the rest of the day rather than return them to school. Before the funeral, we offered counseling to students attending the funeral and addressed any cultural or religious differences they might experience.

District and school staff would disperse throughout the crowd at the church, to be in proximity to the students. We anticipated that some students would attend without parents or guardians. On the morning of the funeral, we got word that a well-meaning bus driver had offered to pick up students at school bus stops and deliver them to the church. He was told not to proceed, that his kind offer was counter to the school's wish that responsible family members accompany the young mourners. In response to team concerns that students might be waiting at the neighborhood bus stops, team member Elliot Davis and I circled to every stop on the route several times, checking for students. None was waiting. We drove past the church where a crowd filled the steps and spilled onto the entire block. I learned from those who attended that the service seemed to provide comfort for the family, students, and staff. There would be an opportunity for students to talk about the funeral and their feelings at school the next day.

RECOVERY

Memorial versus Return to Normalcy

An incident unique to this crisis provided a source of learning. Students from a classroom near the one where the student collapsed, wanted to have a large memorial in the gymnasium soon after the funeral. During debriefing, the crisis team discussed the situation with the school administration and reached consensus that the nature and timing of the proposed memorial might interrupt the emotional healing that began at the funeral and might interfere with the timely return to normal routine. While not all students attended the funeral, the service did signal a degree of closure. Individual and small group counseling, on or off campus, continued for those "at risk" but the team feared that a large memorial ceremony after the funeral might cause the school's grieving process to regress. The team decided that a memorial toward the end of the school year could be planned with student input. Though it was a difficult decision, we believed it was best from our perspective at the time (PREPaRE Model: Special Considerations When Memorializing an Incident).

As I walked along the main corridor, beginning to feel a sense of relief with disengagement imminent, I was approached by an eighth grader. She walked toward me quickly, purposefully, and with a serious demeanor. A few feet away she said, "Are you a leader of the response team?"

"Yes," I smiled weakly, preparing to go into counseling mode. Her voice had a mixture of assertiveness, anger, and tremor. I sensed she was near tears.

"You should let us make a memorial for our classmate. He was our friend. This is *our* school."

I was taken by surprise. My immediate reaction was to be as non-defensive as possible, realizing that her strong feelings needed to be respected, even though we did not agree. It took courage for her to approach an authority figure and stranger.

"I appreciate that you are telling me about your feelings. That is not easy and it takes courage. We are not saying there will be no memorial. We just feel the timing might not be good right after the funeral. There will be a memorial planned for later in the school year."

She walked away, dissatisfied. I wondered if we were doing the right thing.

Stating guidelines for delivering psychological first aid in schools, Brymer et al. (2012a) emphasize the importance of listening carefully when students, parents, and staff want to talk, and understanding what they tell you and how you can help. At that point, I focused on listening, and then went to the team.

Through discussion with a fellow coordinator, social worker Kitty Rehrig, who had also been confronted in protest, it appeared that one of the eighth grade teachers resented the actions of the crisis team. She was apparently expressing her anger toward us through her students. Perhaps she felt we were overstepping boundaries by controlling a process that should have been left to the teachers and students. Perhaps her resentment was legitimate. We tried to keep teachers informed, but did not always seek teacher or student input for decisions that directly affected them. I recalled the "free floating" anger that often accompanies traumatic incidents. Whether the teacher was expressing a desire for more control, or other emotional needs, her anger was real and directed toward the team. Initially, we were annoyed that she was "stirring up her students." If she had complaints, why not come to us directly?

158

While we resented the teacher's apparent efforts to sabotage our good work, we needed to get over our own feelings and try to understand what was happening (PREPaRE Model: Examine Effectiveness of Crisis Prevention and Intervention). Problem solving mode was needed. We were there to do psychological first aid, not psychotherapy, but as crisis responders dealing with severe emotional trauma, we sometimes needed to analyze reactions in therapeutic terms. When clients are expressing anger, fear, or powerlessness toward us, we need to recognize our feelings, perhaps debrief, and then explore our clients' feelings. Their feelings might provide a clue that helps us figure out and address their needs. Brymer et al. (2012a) point out the importance of "practical assistance" including problem-solving strategies to identify and clarify immediate needs, and to develop and implement an action plan to address those needs. There are times when the crisis team must solve problems and clarify difficulties arising out of its own response in order to understand how to help those who are affected.

An immediate issue we needed to explore was finding ways to empower the students and teachers. Providing them with information was important, but we also needed to seek more input when decisions affected them. The school administrator was in the best position to make some decisions, with consultative input from the blended crisis team. Students and staff could provide input or decide memorial plans within parameters set by the building administration. A faculty-student advisory committee could plan a memorial. While this was a good solution to the immediate problem, another level of exploration and understanding remained necessary.

Was the teacher's anger and need for control also a cry for help—an expression of traumatic stress? Was she fixated on anger that a young student died in class? Was she replaying the powerlessness of running into a classroom where he lay unconscious and could not be revived? The students who witnessed the incident were receiving lots of care and counseling. The adults, especially the teaching team and first responders had received far less support. They appeared at risk for post-traumatic stress reactions.

159

We needed to offer the angry teacher and the other adult responders more support.

A Valuable Resource

I thought back to the downstate workshop for police and firefighters on Critical Incident Stress Management (CISM) that I had to quickly leave after learning I was needed at the middle school. I had learned that the CISM team was on call to travel regionally to help those at risk for stress reactions. They were trained to provide Critical Incident Stress Debriefing (CISD) to mitigate the symptoms of post-traumatic stress disorder (PTSD). I spoke with the school administrators, school nurse and counseling staff about the CISM team and the work that they do. The reaction was quick and unanimous. They asked that we invite them to offer a voluntary session with the teaching team, school administrators, counselors, school psychologist, and nurse—about fourteen people in all. Nearly all would participate, including the "angry" teacher. The session was limited to staff who were on the scene of the incident, witnesses, first responders—the most vulnerable adults.

I contacted the leader of the CISM team and she responded as if she'd been waiting for my call. "You looked upset when you left the workshop. We worried about you."

Her welcoming response made it easy to set a date and time. The CISM team of four trained individuals arrived shortly after the end of school on the appointed day. I had set up a quiet space in a room adjoining the library and arranged a circle of comfortable chairs and a table with water and healthy snacks, compliments of food service. Boxes of tissues were available. I welcomed the CISM team and left the school.

I was told that the work done that afternoon was a help for those involved (PREPaRE Model: Caring for the Caregiver). Several days later, I was told by one of the two school secretaries that they resented not being included in the session. They had been very involved in the event, had made and received crucial phone calls. Should they have been included in this "homogeneous" group of witnesses and first responders? Was it an oversight not to include them? Perhaps another mistake and lesson learned. Perhaps not.

Lessons Learned: Reflection and Discussion

1. Attend workshops to enhance your knowledge and to network with others. What you learn may have an immediate positive impact on your morale and practice. *How might you develop a professional development plan that addresses personal and district needs?*

2. Sudden, severely traumatic incidents can place unique, extraordinary challenges on a crisis team and school. *In what ways can a team prepare for rare, catastrophic incidents, as well as the difficult, more frequently confronted events?*

3. Always address the emotional needs of teachers, administrators and staff, who must be stabilized in order to care for the students. *How can triage be planned and conducted to meet the psychological needs of the entire system—students, staff and community?*

4. Staff who are monitoring students for reactions that warrant referral must be aware of obvious signs of sorrow, such as crying, and less obvious behaviors such as being unusually withdrawn, angry, or aggressive. *What are some ways to educate staff to recognize trauma and grief reactions?*

5. Regardless of the most proactive plans for working with the media, expect the unexpected, and be prepared to cope with it. *What are some ways to establish and enforce media boundaries?*

6. In developmentally and situationally appropriate ways, student input, including service on an advisory committee, may be helpful when planning a memorial event. *What are some ways to engage students when planning a memorial?*

7. Planning for a funeral, including preparation of students for cultural and religious differences, and requiring responsible adult supervision, does not mean all will go as planned. *How can advance planning address community needs, such as of those*

who are —and are not attending the funeral, and of those who need adult supervision?

8. When faculty or students struggle with misdirected anger and other emotions, responders can view such emotions as diagnostic. Responders can devise ways to understand and resolve underlying needs and conflicts. *During a crisis, what are ways that responders can diagnose and plan helpful interventions to address evolving needs?*

9. Consider who may need outside help, including teachers and support staff. *How might the crisis team take inventory and contact community agencies, law enforcement, and crisis management service groups that could be called if necessary?*

16

Memorials
and Funerals

Reflections

During my involvement in school crisis response, I rarely
attended funerals, choosing instead to remain at a
school or outside the service. Once when I worked as a
recreational therapist at a children's hospital, the mother of an
eleven-year-old girl who died of cystic fibrosis asked me to serve
as a pall bearer. I was joined by respiratory therapists, nurses,
and other hospital personnel in carrying the casket to her grave.
We were meaningful to this girl and her family—more than I had
realized. We were there when her condition required repeated
admissions to the hospital. We saw the resilience of her spirit. She
was one of the feisty ones. We saw her battle, suffer, and decline.
It was exceedingly difficult to say goodbye.

Reeves et al. (2010) discuss guidelines for dealing with death
and memorials, reminding us that children's understanding of
death depends upon their age and cognitive development. Very
young children do not comprehend the permanency of death, and
may engage in "magical thinking"— possibly feeling guilt that
they caused the death. Children are literal in their interpreta-
tion of language, so using the euphemisms "sleep" or "rest" for
death, could result in fear of sleeping. Between the ages of 6 and
11 years, children begin to view death as permanent, and eventually as part of their own life cycle. In early adolescence, age 12 to
13, they understand that death is final and are curious as to its

nature. Their understanding of its permanence may still be influenced by exposure to the media and to video games. Reeves et al. (2010) point out that crisis interventions, including how memorials are planned and implemented, may actually serve as "prevention efforts for future negative events, as they can build additional coping skills and resiliency variables to protect students from the emotional impact of any future event."

According to Molaison (2003) "Memorializing rituals help students to begin the healing process and are a safe, structured vehicle for expressing strong emotions. Rituals provide comfort in times of stress; they bond members of a community and provide order during chaotic times. They allow us to reaffirm meaning, and support us in facing questions about life and death."

Poland and McCormick (1999) emphasize that knowledge of developmental differences helps the counselor preparing children for memorials and funerals. They also suggest school districts set parameters, assuring equity in planning the extent of memorials, and appropriate memorials for suicide or high-risk behavior to avoid contagion. While the specific circumstance of the death, i.e. accident or suicide, may indicate very different ways of remembering the student, there should be some consistency for each type of circumstance (Vaillancourt & Gibson, 2014) (PREPaRE Model: Special Considerations When Memorializing an Incident).

Preparing Schools for Funeral Services

- Respect the wishes of the family for a public or private funeral.
- If the public is invited, inform students, their parents and guardians of options, including the family's wishes regarding attendance at the service.
- Do not use school resources such as buses for a memorial or funeral (Hart, 2012).
- Inform students, parents and guardians of "in school" alternatives, when students are not invited to the funeral service or choose not to attend.
- If the public is invited, children who attend must be accompanied by a responsible adult, ideally a

parent or guardian.

- Prepare students who will attend a funeral for the sights, sounds, and rituals they may experience—especially if there are ethnic and cultural differences.
- Ask staff and faculty who attend to disperse themselves among the children in the chapel. Trained staff and crisis responders can monitor students at risk for stress reactions.
- Ask students attending the funeral not to return to school that day, but to remain in the care of a family member.
- Plan to provide opportunity for individual and small-group processing if students do return to school on the day of the funeral.
- Assign crisis responders or counselors to the school on the day of the funeral to care for students who need attention.
- Assign crisis responders or counselors to the school the day after the funeral for students who want to talk about the funeral.

The funeral ritual can facilitate closure for the initial phase of grief. Processing afterward should acknowledge feelings, recognize the possible need for follow-up support, but continue returning students to normal school routine as soon as possible (Heath et al., 2008).

Help Children Understand a Funeral

- What the ritual will be like
- Whether they will see the body
- What the body will feel, smell, and look like
- What people will be doing (crying, wailing, or perhaps even giggling because they're anxious)
- What is likely to be said, and what a eulogy is
- What the hearse looks like
- How the cars form a procession with lights on.

Source: Brooks & Siegel (1996).

These suggestions can be adapted to the age of the children, cultural differences, and specific funeral plans.

Planning and Presenting School Memorials

Written school or district policies are helpful in planning appropriate memorials for each type of incident. Policy guidelines should ensure equity in the scope of observance.

Allow memorial rituals for *all* deaths of students or staff, including those that occur during summer months, and those associated with suicide or drugs. This practice sends the consistent message that we value life (Molaison, 2003). However, in the case of stigmatized death the *act* must not be celebrated or glorified.

A memorial advisory committee with representative stakeholders, including interested students with adult supervision, can ensure that decisions are consistent with policies. Having a menu with options can support various forms of expression in planning a meaningful memorial. Students have an opportunity to take ownership and be empowered by taking constructive action.

Encourage students to participate in constructive, life-affirming activities such as writing letters and poems, developing a memory book for the grieving family, and supporting mental health and wellness organizations.

Memorial services provide an opportunity to identify and monitor students at risk. They should be developmentally appropriate in content and duration. The range of activity can be broad, depending on circumstances—anything from a moment of silence to an assembly to other acts of remembrance can be appropriate. While a menu of options is useful, creative ideas can enhance the memorial. Emphasize good judgment consistent with school policy. While students can be invited to a memorial, the event should be structured such that students can easily choose not to attend.

Set time-length guidelines for how long short-term memorials such as bulletin boards, paper murals, or decorated lockers may stay up. Set guidelines too for their removal (Molaison, 2003).

Consider a timeline for memorial events that does not rush

grief work or cause re-traumatization. Encourage return to normal routine. The best memorials are life affirming and they foster hope and resilience (Heath et al., 2008; Johnson, 2006).

Exercise sensitivity to diversity and cultural differences in rituals, traditions, and practices (Ungar, 2008).

Teachers, school administrators, and staff are in positions to model healthy grieving for students, including expression of feelings.

Teachers should be offered counseling support and information to help care for their students and each other (PREPaRE Model: Psychoeducation: Caregiver Training). If the deceased is a staff member, substitutes should provide teachers the opportunity to attend the funeral.

It is useful to set guidelines for long term memorials such as tree planting, plaques, scholarships, and gifts to the library (Molaison, 2003). Permanent memorials should not be placed directly in front of the school, but in an accessible location that allows the choice to visit.

Consider the appropriateness of a voluntary remembrance activity on the anniversary of a traumatic incident. The type and severity of the incident may indicate whether an event should be planned. When appropriate, schools may create environments that support healing through reflection and discussion. Regardless of formal recognition, staff should be vigilant around anniversary dates for the emotional needs of vulnerable students (Zibulsky, 2012).

Planning Memorials after a Death by Suicide

Use caution when counseling students and memorializing a death by suicide, using best practices to avoid contagion (Erbacher et al., 2015; Hart, 2012; Jellinek & Okoli, 2012; Ruof & Harris, 1988; Zenere, 2009a). A best-practice intervention acknowledges the memory of the deceased individual while distancing students from the self-destructive act.

Continuously monitor the memorial and identify students who appear at risk—depressed, withdrawn, friends of the deceased, those in proximity to the act, or having suicidal ideation. Consider referral for more intensive support when needed (PREPaRE Model: Evaluating Psychological Trauma).

In the event of a death by suicide, high-risk behavior, or criminal conduct, provide an opportunity to grieve and remember the deceased without glorifying the suicidal or stigmatized act. Clearly and unambiguously encourage students to distance themselves from the act, which can be characterized as an irreversible, bad decision.

No permanent memorials should be established to honor someone who died by suicide, or as a result of criminal or reckless conduct. While the needs of grieving students should be addressed regardless of circumstances, in the event of a stigmatized death consider brief, limited observance such as a moment of silence, voluntary funeral attendance, or a constructive act such as donating to a charity or participating in a prevention/wellness organization (Hart, 2012).

In the case of death by suicide or high-risk behavior such as driving under the influence or substance abuse, use teachable moments as part of the grief process to provide education and constructive action. Relevant endeavors include suicide prevention, explaining how to understand depression and bipolar disorder, and participating in organizations such as Students Against Drunk Driving (S.A.D.D.) (PREPaRE Model: Providing Opportunities to Take Action).

Pay special attention to anniversary dates of a suicide, not for a formal recognition, but to acknowledge a difficult time for affected students. Be especially vigilant monitoring students identified at risk for imitative behaviors or contagion (Erbacher et al., 2015; Hart, 2012; Jellinek & Okoli, 2012; Ruof & Harris, 1988; Zenere, 2009a). It may be prudent to approach at risk students individually, to evaluate their emotional status, offer support, and address their needs when necessary.

During many years of crisis response, I recall only a couple of instances of clear deaths by suicide, although other deaths followed high risk-behavior or suspicious circumstances. When death resulted from behavior such as climbing a high voltage electrical tower or speeding a car into a tree, we proceeded with caution. We treated the incident as a postvention—an intervention after a suicide with the goal of supporting the bereaved family, friends, peers, and colleagues. We were aware during counseling and at memorials that we needed to support the grieving process, but distance students from identifying with the victim or glorifying the act. We tried to adhere to interventions and memorials consistent with "best practices" to avoid contagion (Erbacher et al., 2015; Hart, 2012; Jellinek & Okoli, 2012; Ruof & Harris, 1988; Zenere, 2009a).

17

Being Present:
In the Skin of the Responder

Reflections

Here's what I learned from my work in a hospital with patients who knew they would die at a young age. When a person is experiencing emotional pain, sometimes just being there, being fully present for the person can be comforting. I learned this from a young adult with cystic fibrosis. He did not want to be greeted always with a comment or inquiry about his illness. He did not want sympathetic statements. He preferred when someone cared enough to be present, friendly, and ready to talk about a topic as light as sports or as heavy as love or death. When he felt comfortable, the conversation he initiated ranged in subject matter from light to heavy, depending on what he wanted to discuss. He instructed us about his wishes. He was a good teacher who died when he was twenty-one.

The lessons that young man taught are helpful to know when responders are strangers entering a crisis with no knowledge or history of serving those affected by a traumatic incident. Responders must be open to being present and finding comfort in an uncomfortable situation. Comfort while being fully present without feeling they *must* say something immediately to make things better. Responders communicate care and empathy with an expression, a gesture, a word or a phrase. A lecture or sermon is unhelpful. Making contact, being friendly, establishing rapport, communicating quickly, yet patiently, that 'I am here to listen when you are ready to tell your story. That eventually, I can help you cope and find meaning in an incident that seems random, meaningless, and incredibly painful. That eventually, I can help you find some degree of power and control, when powerlessness, loss of control, and loss of hope are overwhelming.' Brymer et al. (2012a) caution that we should not assume that all students or staff want to talk with us. The calm, supportive presence of a responder often helps people experiencing distress feel safer and better able to cope.

Those responding to crises in school settings usually have not had the time nor opportunity to establish relationships with grieving people in need of psychological first aid. Responders often enter the scene as strangers to the individuals affected by a traumatic event. Rapport must be established quickly in a stressful environment where the helping relationship is unique. Trust normally means that one person can depend on another to follow through with expected behavior or support, especially in difficult times. Trust means the helping person will be understanding, respectful, and caring of another's feelings. Under normal circumstances, trusting relationships are established with quality interactions occurring not just once, but over time.

The crisis responder usually does not have the luxury of a previously established relationship. What does it mean to enter a crisis as a stranger and to be fully present for those affected? The impression must be immediate that the responder is stable, dependable, caring, and trustworthy. A few factors help make this possible. First, an extreme situation has created intense need for support. Second, a responder is explicitly identified as part of a team available to provide that support. Third, the responder has chosen to be there and has the personal qualities, training and skills needed to quickly establish rapport. 'As a responder, I am comfortable with my role respecting your feelings, focused on your needs, and ready to establish a helping relationship.'

Beyond preparation and training, the crisis responder is strengthened by perceptiveness, self-reflection, and a desire to serve. The responder must develop the ability to remain reasonably calm and flexible during stressful conditions.

Qualities and Skills of the Crisis Responder

- Having the ability to be with people who are suffering emotionally without making them feel better right away;
- Having the comfort and courage to see and deal with strong feelings under difficult circumstances;
- Having the ability to establish rapport quickly, but the restraint not to impose on those not wanting help;
- Having the comfort and courage to recognize and deal with conflict under difficult circumstances;
- Having the ability to focus attention, be creative, and solve problems in a crisis;
- Having the ability to feel and express empathy, but maintain emotional boundaries so as not to be immobilized by intense feelings;
- Having the insight to know your own issues so you don't confuse them with other people's issues;
- Having knowledge, comfort, and sensitivity to work with developmental and cultural differences;
- Understanding that different people cope differently with challenging situations;
- Understanding that crises present opportunities for people to understand themselves and others, resolve conflict, and reaffirm meaningful goals.

The Art of Listening

A basic, essential skill often used by the crisis responder is the art of listening. It is a skill that allows us to be present, show empathy, and connect in a meaningful way with those who grieve. Skilled listening is one of the ways we perceive the cues of people affected by trauma. They tell us where they are emotionally and what they need. They tell us with their words, or by not saying a word. They tell us with body language, facial expression, intonation, and actions. Sometimes, we listen to silence.

Wachtel (2011) describes a sensitive form of listening that attends to what is not conscious, what is muted, what is experienced with unexpected affect or does not seem consonant with the person's behavior or present experience. Sometimes we look and listen with our clinical "third" eye and ear. There may be significant meaning hidden *behind* the spoken words. This means being fully present and observant, with heightened perceptiveness on many levels. It means using our senses, clinical judgment, and intuition. Seeing and hearing needs and feelings that are not obvious or overtly expressed. Seeing interactions — the dynamics of the group. There is so much happening during a crisis that our own perceptions may be insufficient. Being present often means relying on the presence of fellow team members to check observations and perceptions with them. Leaning on them, and listening to each other for ideas and support.

Say Something that Invites Reactions

While it is clearly important not to feel compelled to direct a salvo of words at traumatized individuals, it is also important to recognize there are times when the responder should *say something*. Regardless of whether words come easily or feel awkward, the responder should generally make at least a brief statement of introduction — who I am and what I offer, with an invitation to those affected to tell their stories, or talk about their reactions. Otherwise, those experiencing trauma might feel that expressing themselves is not acceptable. The openness of responders to listen and discuss the incident can encourage others to voluntarily share, rather than withhold information or emotions (Demaria & Schonfeld, 2014).

Part of being present is constantly reaffirming a sense of safety and being ready to intervene to mitigate further psychological trauma. The interventions of caring responders after the traumatic event also provide opportunities to perform *secondary triage* — to evaluate the degree of psychological risk and possible need for further treatment.

Active and Reflective Listening

Our ability to communicate is challenged during crises when the need for effective communication is magnified by chaos, noise, fear and profound sorrow. Under any circumstance, the quality of communication can foster feelings of powerlessness or empowerment. Effective communication skills can be learned and they can be developed. Some years ago, after drilling and practicing "I-statements," paraphrasing, clarifying, summarizing and more, an overwhelmed graduate student protested to me, "I used to *talk*, now I *communicate*."

It is true. When we are new at using effective communication skills, it often feels awkward or uncomfortable. It is important to remember that skills are not substitutes for being genuine and for genuinely caring. Over time, they begin to feel more natural as they become part of us, and can help us be fully present during crises.

Active listening is the tool that aids being present when interacting with anyone experiencing a traumatic incident. It requires that the listener help the speaker clarify and elaborate the story being told. The listener is empathic and attentive to the speaker's thoughts and feelings. It is a useful communication skill when people begin talking personally about how they were affected by the incident. Active listening is supported by key skills that enable empathic understanding—*encouraging, paraphrasing*, and *summarizing* (Ivey et al., 2010).

Encouraging involves the active listener expressing brief verbal and nonverbal cues that signal acceptance of what is being said, including graphic or depressing details of a traumatic incident. The speaker is comforted and encouraged to continue talking. *Paraphrasing* occurs when the listener repeats back to the speaker the essence of what was said. It tells the speaker that the listener heard the content with an opportunity to clarify meaning and check for accurate understanding. *Summarizing* helps the speaker feel heard and clarifies complex issues during the course of discussion. When the listener summarizes, it helps to integrate and organize expressed ideas and feelings, and to transition between topics or to end the session (Ivey et al., 2010).

Reflective listening happens when the listener identifies and repeats back the essence of the *feelings* behind the speaker's words and nonverbal behaviors. It tells the speaker that the listener heard the emotions and empathizes with them. It can clarify complex feelings, encourage the speaker to elaborate and to express emotions in more depth, or to correct an inaccurately reflected emotion. Reflective listening is like paraphrasing feelings rather than words. It is often helpful when the acknowledgment of feelings is brief, or combined with paraphrasing or summarizing.

When the reflective listener feeds back such phrases as "You sound really worried/sad/confused/or frustrated" or "Sounds like you are feeling angry" or "That must have been scary," the effect can be supportive. Reflective listening can be especially helpful when the speaker's words carry strong feelings and the feelings are not easily stated. Individuals who have experienced traumatic events may find it easier to tell the story of what happened without overtly expressing feelings about it. Reflective listening allows the speaker to feel an emotional connection with the listener that can reduce tension, stress, and the weight of disturbing feelings (Ivey et al., 2010).

Once feelings are recognized, it may be easier to work with them toward constructive outcomes. However, since not everyone welcomes reflection of their feelings, it is generally more helpful after rapport is established and when the reflected feeling is accurate. The responder should never impose discussion of the incident or associated feelings upon any affected individual or group. Discussion of difficult events and emotions should always be voluntary, and the option should be clearly stated. Being present means allowing affected individuals to tell where they need to be, rather than the responder presuming where they should be.

Remaining Present in the Presence of Suffering

The pain witnessed by responders can be intense in the extreme. Movement toward client recovery can be painfully slow (Jellinek & Okoli, 2012; Johnson, 2006; Levine & Kline, 2007). Responders generally enter the scene with defenses down, and with senses taking in suffering in order to understand, empathize, and plan appropriate interventions. They must proceed with caution and not immerse themselves emotionally to the extent that they become immobilized and unable to be fully present for those who are traumatized. It is *their* tragedy. It is *their* friend or peer or teacher who has died. It is *their* grief, and the responder is there to help them cope.

A sense of humor helps us manage many aspects of life, although generally not during crisis response. Perhaps the situation is too intense or sad, and the need to stay focused trumps the use of humor. More often, relief comes from fascination with some of the unexpected turns in human interaction, or appreciation for the thoughtful, supportive acts of students, school staff and members of the crisis team. It is true that *crisis* and *opportunity* are often intertwined. During a response, there are inevitable teachable moments when students can be helped to understand their feelings, the feelings of others, their struggle with powerlessness and despair, and their ultimate power and resilience.

Appreciation for Caregivers

Angela Aiello (2010) explores the expression of gratitude as an aspect of self-care. Remembering to appreciate survivors, team colleagues, and yourself can be a powerful, renewing force in the midst of and in the aftermath of a crisis. It takes only a moment to extend a word of acknowledgment to a team member or to write a note of appreciation to a school counselor or administrator. I was generally surprised to get notes of thanks, but also felt recognized and appreciated. Appreciation helps fuel resilience and the ability to remain "fully present" for those experiencing emotional trauma. Such notes helped keep me energized. Otherwise, I would not have kept the following notes of thanks that convey the meaning of crisis response.

Notes

"I can't begin to thank you enough for all you have done in the past weeks. Your steady presence, your focus on the kids' needs, your untiring effort and your ability to lead us in the direction of what needed to be done was so supportive and helpful. You lead without coercion and facilitate group cohesion. Thank you so much for being here."

∽

"I want to express my appreciation for you and the crisis team. You did a great job of leading and focusing the group and you seemed to know just when to intervene and when to listen."

∽

"Thanks so much for your help and support in the classroom on Wednesday. I could not have made it through class without you! You did a really wonderful job with the kids and I just wanted to let you know how much I appreciate all you did!"

∽

"Thank you so much for all of your help during our recent crisis. The addition of all of the wonderful people who assisted our students and us over the week made the situation go much more smoothly. You are a group of caring and talented people. Thanks again for your efforts and support."

∽

"Thank you for your endless patience and support in the last weeks. Our every need was answered. Thank you also for letting me "vent" my frustrations. I pray that we never need to come together in a tragedy like this again, but find it comforting to know so much support is there when needed."

∽

"Dear Colleagues, Many thanks for your support and expertise yesterday. We appreciate your quick response and your sensitivity during a very unsettling time. I was greatly reassured by your involvement and I think that feeling spread to all of our kids. I understand _____ may join us for lunch tomorrow and is eager to see his friends.

Thank you for helping us to smooth the way for this dear little boy!"

⌒

"Thank You!! From the Education Association Leadership Team. We want to extend our thanks and appreciation for the time and effort you have given in the past few weeks to our colleagues. Know that your efforts to 'raise up a saddened and wounded soul' help strengthen our hopes during a troubling time."

⌒

"Jeff and Marty, I wanted to let you know how impressed I was with your leadership last week. Your ability to see the big picture while organizing so many different aspects of a crisis is amazing. Seeking input from a team before putting ideas into place is the mark of true leadership. I commend you both."

⌒

I came to appreciate many fellow responders over the years and some have become friends for life. Among team members, it is natural that some gravitate toward one another for support during and after an incident. Having a partner can really help. Someone you can spill your guts to. Someone with whom you can express your frustration or just talk about what you see happening. Someone who can help translate your perceptions into planning to meet the most recent needs of those affected. Sometimes the team as a whole served as the "sidekick" for the responders. We briefed and debriefed, examining our response effectiveness (PREPaRE Model: Examine Effectiveness). After particularly traumatic responses, designated facilitators took us through telling our stories, including our most challenging moments, how we coped and continue to cope and be present.

⌒

Through the years, colleague Marty Tracy served on the

team. He'd spent many summers saving lives as a lifeguard with the Atlantic City Beach Patrol. Perhaps those experiences helped Marty keep a cool head through school crises. His ideas and practical judgment were always on target. He could think and move under stress. His usual work in the school district was to coordinate health and physical education, school nurses, and driver education. His character, demeanor, and experience as a teacher and a lifeguard made him a knowledgeable responder. He was dependable, calm under stress, and someone who could be leaned on. Marty viewed himself as a support person, and not a crisis counselor. Although he felt that counseling was a role for others, his talents really did extend to counseling—certainly for team members, administrators and teachers, but at times also for students who needed someone to listen. They all felt comfortable with him. Marty never recognized his ability in this area, but we did. He could primarily be described in PREPaRE Model parlance as a "Getter"— one who took care of logistics. He could run to district office, when necessary, and get things done. He would return to the scene with assurance of substitute teachers, district administrators to secure the school perimeter, or with stacks of letters and handouts for parents, still warm from the graphics department printers. I'm not sure Marty realized how much we valued his contributions in crises and as a friend.

Post Script: "I Should Be There"

Soon after my retirement from the school district, a highway car crash took the lives of a father, mother, and son. Their daughter, a high school student, survived with minimal physical injury. The crisis response team was mobilized, focusing on the middle school of the deceased boy and the high school of the surviving girl. I remember thinking, "I should be there." But the team was in good hands, under effective new leadership. They were well educated through training and experience. I no longer belonged with them during a response. Perhaps afterward, if they wanted to talk, they know I am here for them.

18

Betrayal of Trust

Abstract

The most disturbing and emotionally debilitating response in my experience followed repeated rapes of a sixth grader by a teacher. With criminal acts, she victimized the student and betrayed the trust of the entire school community. This case study describes the planning and implementation of system-wide interventions focused on students, staff, and community. We did not anticipate the extent of need for creative problem solving, conflict resolution, and care for the caregivers. A sample meeting agenda is included. *Themes are: 1) systems thinking: multiple interventions; 2) reestablishing trust; 3) leadership and authority; 4) media management; 5) conflict resolution.*

INTRODUCTION

The crisis team was mobilized early one evening late in the school year. The calls, which originated with the phone tree at the district office, asked us to report the next morning before students arrived to an elementary school for an early morning briefing and emergency faculty meeting. A sixth-grade teacher had been charged with multiple counts of raping a student. Details in the local newspaper were compelling. Based on court records, the *News Journal* reported the alleged perpetrator acknowledged having sexual intercourse with the student on multiple occasions.

PREVENTION/MITIGATION

Could this betrayal of trust been prevented? Painstaking and necessary procedures, including criminal background checks, are required in an effort to ensure that predators do not find their way into schools. The accused teacher apparently had no previous record of molesting children. Schools establish universal programs to create a positive, caring climate that supports students and enhances learning. Schools develop comprehensive plans for student and teacher safety, crisis prevention, and effective preparation and response to traumatic incidents (Reeves et al., 2010). Generally, they do not have universal programs, exercises, or response plans for times when a teacher molests a student. Such acts are unusual and so far beyond comprehension that subtle warning signs of inappropriate teacher behavior might be interpreted with denial of nefarious intent. Still, having a comprehensive response framework that is flexible and adaptable for unexpected traumatic incidents proved beneficial in planning and implementing the present response (Jimerson et al., 2012b).

During the primary grades, many students are presented with programs by parents, school counselors, and organizations that discuss *good touch / bad touch*, recognizing when a stranger or a person in your life is not respecting private physical or emotional boundaries, and what to do about such an intrusion. Since these formal efforts to prevent child sexual abuse often involve discussion of body parts and of inappropriate touching or behavior, parents may choose to opt out, or to educate their children privately (Ortiz & Voutsinas, 2012). In this case, these were not options. The sexual terms and behaviors reported in the media offended the entire school community. Because teachers are trusted, warnings about inappropriate behavior are rarely directed toward them as potential predators. In fact, the overwhelming majority of teachers have earned a place of trust and respect. When a rare incident occurs, it is an abuse of authority and a devastating betrayal of the entire community.

PREPAREDNESS

I lay awake the night before and awoke early the next morning contemplating the work of the crisis team and anticipating chaos at school. I expected that our intervention would need to be system-wide. We had often dealt with the profound grief associated with death but death does not encompass manipulative malevolence designed by a teacher. This incident shook the sense of safety and security that is the foundation of learning. I anticipated that our intervention would need to address three major groups—the *students*, the *staff* and the *school community*. I did not anticipate how deeply all three were affected. As we learned more about what the teacher had done, we learned that multiple and varied interventions were needed.

I arrived at the school at 6:20 a.m. and entered the long, rectangular disciplinary room where our team briefing would take place. Approaching a large blackboard at the far end of the room, I wrote three words in large, upper case letters across the top. The words were "**STUDENTS**," "**STAFF**," and "**COMMUNITY**." They represented columns under which the team would develop interventions. I filled in some of the major tasks under each heading. We would provide the affected children with *psychological triage* and offer crisis counseling in the library. Smaller rooms adjoining the library could serve as space for small group and individual interventions. A similar process of triage would focus on the teaching staff (PREPaRE Model: Primary Triage: Evaluating Psychological Trauma).

RESPONSE

I arranged several long tables and as many chairs as could fit the perimeter. Bottled water and fresh fruit were brought in as team members and school administrators entered the room. I sat in front of the blackboard. The principal ducked in and out of the briefing room while handling many difficult issues. Key school staff members were part of the district crisis team, including an assistant to the principal, the school psychologist, and a social worker, all highly skilled and caring individuals. They were clearly affected by the news but able to function effectively and share a leadership role. This made it easier to blend the school and district teams to identify needs and design interventions. We were not yet aware of the PREP<u>a</u>RE Model (Brock et al., 2009) and had no formal Incident Command System. We did apply concepts such as *division of labor* to the many tasks, and *span of control* as leadership arose within small groups addressing a variety of response functions.

Discussing psychological first aid in schools, Brymer et al. (2012a) emphasize the importance of recognizing and engaging a school's *internal support systems*. The skilled, effective leadership of those who worked within the building—and also district level responders—was a significant benefit, especially when *conflict resolution* was needed. One school counselor was an effective response partner, but another, who had formed a professional relationship with the accused teacher, was distraught to the point where she needed support and a break from crisis-related duties.

During this crisis, I took a more directive, authoritative leadership role than I recall in earlier incidents. There was a critical need to maintain open communication among team members, including discussion of information at scheduled debriefings to help sense needs. The sharing of facts, feelings, and perceived issues in the school *and* on the team, was necessary to plan interventions. My role included facilitating discussion and planning, and providing a secure structure to support the team so we could do our job. The tension was beyond description. I monitored myself and tried to do the right thing for the team. I also monitored the team's demeanor—the verbal and nonverbal feedback that gave cues when we were on the right track or confused and needing to "back up" and re-evaluate.

Initial Briefing Session

During the initial briefing session, I asked the administrator to share facts and to anticipate the impact, feelings, issues, and needs within the school. The three focus areas on the blackboard formed the framework for brainstorming plans for intervention. We anticipated themes to discuss with students. We needed to hear their stories, understand, empathize, respond to their questions and confusion, and provide reassurance that most adults in school can be trusted (PREP<u>a</u>RE Model: Reaffirm Physical Health and Perceptions of Safety and Security). We wanted to convey the message that what this teacher did is rare. We discussed empowering the students, when appropriate, by providing developmentally suitable information about personal boundaries for "good" and "bad" touching and for protecting themselves from sexual advances by either strangers or people they know.

The district superintendent joined our briefing and we prepared for the faculty meeting that followed. There, the principal took the lead, providing her staff with tips on what to say and not say to students. She spoke of crisis counseling and support available for students and staff; she gave tips on how to address student and parental needs. Extra substitute teachers were available to relieve faculty when needed. Members of the alleged perpetrator's teaching team were particularly upset. We addressed feelings that ranged from disbelief and denial to extreme sadness and anger.

Media was outside as the story had gone national. News reporters and trucks with satellite dishes lined the road in front of the school. Media was prohibited from entering school grounds and were directed instead to the district spokesperson. There would be opportunities to speak with the principal (PREP<u>a</u>RE Model: Media Relations Protocols/ Collaborating With the Media).

∼

We did not know the extent of the damage until we began crisis counseling with students and teachers (PREP<u>a</u>RE Model: Provide Interventions and Respond to Psychological Needs). Layers of victimization were beyond what anyone imagined. The perpetrator had nearly a full school year to manipulate students and create an unusual, dysfunctional classroom situation. The sexual acts had occurred off campus in her apartment and often involved a second boy, who observed.

In her classroom, she had "favorites," including the two boys she had preyed upon off campus, and the girlfriend of the victim.

She used nicknames for these favorites in class. At times, she sat on the young victim's lap in full view of his classmates. There were reports of inappropriate dancing in class. The errant teacher assigned "enforcers" and a "sergeant-at-arms"— students who forced classmates "to follow the rules" and not tell anyone outside the classroom what was happening. For her innocent pupils, class was often a lively, fun place. They had no idea it was in a sense, an extension of her crime scene. We learned that contrary to school policy, the class was often conducted behind a locked door, with windows covered. Noise sometimes brought complaints, but this fed into the "us" versus "them" mentality encouraged by the perpetrator. We were distressed to learn that she used this "divide and conquer" control tactic not only to bond with her students, but also with her teaching team. The effectiveness of her emotional manipulation became disturbingly clear as the crisis response unfolded.

Responding to Students

During crisis counseling, the team learned what had happened in the errant teacher's classroom. Children were confused and torn by feelings of affection for their teacher and feelings of denial or disgust at her actions. I recall a very unhappy youngster saying, "She's the best teacher I ever had." Through tears, he repeated, "She's the best teacher I ever had."

What does one say? Usually, we celebrate students holding a teacher in high regard. When this person was referred to as "best teacher," I felt revulsion.

"Your teacher is a pedophile," I thought, but did not say. Not then. I felt outrage toward the perpetrator, but did not show it. Nor the hatred I felt. Not then.

She had raped his classmate. Didn't he realize? I also felt a mixture of sadness and concern for her influence on this youngster's psyche. Circumstances had shattered his reality—his sense of trust. He must have felt utter confusion seeing someone he regarded so highly, charged with terrible crimes. He did not share any of the anger I felt—only a sense of sorrow and loss. He was saying, "She's the best teacher" in the present tense. How long would it take him to change his estimation? I listened. I empathized (PREPaRE Model: Individual Crisis Intervention Elements: Establishing Psychological Contact). I recognized that in the classroom, there were ways she seemed like the "best teacher." I tried gently to create some dissonance. It was my need in the moment—his need I felt, in the long run.

"It is very painful. It hurts a lot when you find out that someone you like has done very bad things. It takes time and it is hard to accept that someone you think a lot of, is not the person you thought she was. She did some things that were wrong. This is a sad time, but after awhile you will begin to understand it better and it won't hurt so much. There are family and people in school who care about you and will help you begin to feel better" (PREPaRE Model: Ensure Perceptions of Safety and Security: Providing Crisis Facts and Adaptive Interpretations).

We contacted parents and suggested ways to be supportive. In some cases, we recommended further counseling.

A disturbing theme arose during counseling with small groups of students. Some were from the perpetrator's homeroom, others had her for one or two subjects. Some students began blaming the victim. Others were silent—whether in tacit agreement that the victim was to blame, or disagreeing, but perhaps afraid to speak in his defense. We began hearing, "It was his fault." "He made her do it."

Did some silent students feel their teacher was wrong, but were scared to say it?

The situation was both twisted and complex. Some students stood in defense of an authority figure they had been taught to respect and obey. The scenario was further complicated by the victim's status as one of the teacher's "favorites." Talking freely about the favoritism, the classroom "pecking order," students may have resented the victim's status that went far beyond the boundaries of "teacher's pet." The perpetrator's manipulation had elevated her target's status in relation to her, while alienating and isolating him from his peers.

A division emerged between students who recognized that what their teacher did was unacceptable, and students who defended her and denied she was culpable. Still others were silent, fearful, confused. We grouped and intervened with students having similar beliefs (homogeneous groups) and with individuals to encourage open discussion of feelings with less concern about peers judging their perceptions. For those who blamed the victim, the response needed to be direct. The adult is **always** responsible and must always do the right thing regardless of the child's actions. Like a parent, a teacher has a special responsibility to keep students safe. Is it right for a teacher to have "favorites"? Is it right for a teacher to use her position of authority to corrupt the morals of children? Is it ever OK to take advantage of youth and innocence? The answer to each of these questions is a resounding, "NO."

Reestablishing Trust

In working with students, we needed to speak honestly about this teacher's corrupt behavior while reassuring them of the trustworthiness of other responsible adults, including teachers. Their world was torn by fear and mistrust. How is trust reestablished, along with a healthy dose of caution and good judgment? Listening. Information. Discussion. Education. We assured students that what this person did was abnormal, that most adults do not act that way. The vast majority of teachers and adults in positions of responsibility do the right thing on behalf of the well-being of young people. We discussed what a young person could do "if something doesn't seem right" relative to personal boundaries.

"If you are suspicious about someone's words, actions or intentions, talk with your parents, guardians, and other trustworthy adults."

"Communicate with those you feel you can trust. Ask them questions. Find answers. Find that you can trust again" (PRE-PaRE Model: Ensure Perceptions of Safety and Security).

Enlisting Support Systems for Student Safety

One of the many difficult aspects of crisis counseling was addressing the sexual terms students brought up. For instance, the newspaper had used the term "oral sex." There was a disparity of knowledge among the children. For many, terms like "sexual intercourse" and "rape" were foreign, and added to their confusion. They were children robbed of their innocence by circumstances set in motion by the sick and selfish acts of an adult entrusted with their care. This was one of the most frustrating conditions we experienced as crisis counselors. We felt that the children shouldn't be learning these terms in this way and in this context. It just wasn't fair. We wanted to keep the students safe, but felt powerless to prevent exposure to more trauma (PREP_aRE Model: Minimize Exposure to Trauma).

Never before had the provision of psychological first aid felt like a descent into hell. We found time during the day to vent, but mostly to debrief, share concerns and talk about the themes and structure of interventions with students. There was little time to grapple with our own feelings. With one of the school counselors taking the lead, we engaged in further *secondary triage*, generating names of students who were at moderate to high risk for traumatic stress reactions (PREP_aRE Model: Secondary Triage: Evaluating Psychological Trauma). Crisis team members shared the responsibility of contacting parents and guardians of these students by phone to discuss trauma reactions and ways to monitor and support their children. In some cases we referred for therapeutic treatment.

Throughout the response, it was essential to keep families informed, especially parents and guardians of students in the perpetrator's classroom. The principal sent letters home with all students, explaining the situation and the response, providing tips on how parents could be supportive, inviting them to contact the school with concerns, and informing them of referral for further support when needed. We planned and held meetings with parents at the school. Communication at every stage enlisted support, helped calm fears, created a spirit of collaboration, and increased goodwill (PREP_aRE Model: Reestablish Social Support Systems/ Caregiver Training).

Early on the first day, while planning for afternoon crisis counseling, the team discussed how to get students home safely through the gauntlet of media waiting outside. We called in district administrators and others to secure the school's perimeter and to create a buffer between students and the media. It was relatively easy to cover the boarding of school buses. The routes taken by those walking home from school and the various bus stops along the way were more difficult to shield. The large number of people that the district provided was invaluable. They were placed at strategic locations along the walking routes and at key bus stops. The crisis team appreciated this support in helping to keep students safe (PREPaRE Model: Prevent Trauma Exposure: Keep Students Safe).

Leadership and the Chair

The next morning, the team began pouring into our planning room. The school again provided juice, fruit, and water. I placed my paperwork at the head of the table in front of the chair where I sat throughout our initial briefing and debriefings the previous day. Additional crisis team members were summoned the second day. We anticipated more individual and small group counseling. One of the district social workers new to the response walked in and sat in the chair at the head of the table. My chair. What is the significance of a chair?

"That is the chair I have been using," I explained, asking her to please move. She complied by moving to the adjacent seat. This wasn't my style. In previous responses, I didn't care where I sat. Generally, I preferred when the school principal or counselor took the lead, or when members of the school crisis team functioned effectively in leadership roles. Empowerment was always one of our goals. Here, in this tense situation that chair, that symbol of leadership at the head of the table became important to me. Why? In the midst of the chaos we tried to navigate, I sensed that more than usual, steady, directive leadership was needed. Both crisis responders and school staff needed to feel stable and secure in order to focus on what needed to be done.

Responding to Staff

Layers of Victimization

Another factor added to the staff's pain and anger. The

perpetrator is white. The victim and the observer are African American. Some staff members recognized and discussed the racial issues in these crimes while others ignored it. As a crisis team working with multi-racial staff, there was limited discussion of the racial issue, but some African American staff members were especially upset. They expressed anger, and questioned how this abuse had happened. There was potential for more divisiveness among a staff already divided, as we would learn, by the accused teacher's manipulation. Administration and staff needed an opportunity to express and resolve feelings around the issue of race, but I'm not certain whether it happened during or after the immediate crisis, except for individual discussion and private complaint.

Conflict Resolution for Teaching Teams

Several members of the sixth grade team were deeply affected, but insisted on staying with their classrooms. Crisis counselors spoke with them individually, seeking emotional stabilization so they could work calmly with their students (PREPaRE Model: Ensure Perceptions of Safety and Security: The Effect of Adult Reactions and Behaviors). We supported other staff, including members of the fifth grade team that were affected in a different way. We were surprised to learn of animosity between some members of the fifth and sixth grade teams, with hard feelings traceable to manipulation by the perpetrator. The perpetrator employed an "us" versus "them" strategy to divide and control fellow teachers and students alike. Manipulation continued after the accused teacher was released on bail: she sent messages by phone and email to members of the sixth grade team.

We planned an intervention to meet separately with each group, first the fifth-grade team and then the sixth. Each was comprised of five or six teachers.

We planned the intervention to tackle the needs of the sixth grade team of teachers who were experiencing grief, loss, disbelief, confusion, and even protective feelings toward their colleague who, some felt, "could not have done this." The accused teacher was at the center of a tight social network that included

191

her team, but excluded others. Her priority was to have fun and, if necessary, bend school rules. Stretching the rules and relating to students as peers made it more difficult for other teachers to set limits. This was especially true of some fifth grade team members who were feeling anger, resentment, and concern for students they'd taught the previous year. They needed special intervention. Communication between teams seemed closed, except for complaints directed at the sixth grade team, causing them to band together defensively against outside threats. News of the rapes created a divisive situation. A wound festered among staff that would make healing from the emotional trauma more difficult.

I suggested group crisis interventions to include an element of *conflict resolution* for members of both teaching teams (PRE-PaRE Model: Psychoeducation). Skilled team members including school psychologist Phyllis Tallos and assistant principal Wilma Robinson facilitated the sessions, first with the fifth grade team and then with the sixth. We closed the sessions to responders not on the school's staff. Administrators planned the logistics and, for comfort, equipped the meeting room with water, fruit, and tissues.

The entire crisis team discussed the sessions' structure. The district's assistant superintendent sat in on the planning, listening attentively but silently. The teams needed an opportunity to tell their stories—how they learned about the alleged rapes, what they thought, how they felt. They were to be encouraged to describe the most difficult aspects of the event from their perspective. They would have an opportunity to hear thoughts and feelings they had in common—to see that their reactions and the unusual symptoms they might be experiencing were typical, given abnormal circumstances. Teachers would be encouraged to talk about ways to cope with the intense stress weighing on them. The facilitator would then summarize what was learned and remind the teachers about stress reduction strategies, networks of support, and the availability of individual counseling.

Finally, in separate meetings, each team would be encouraged to understand the perspective and struggle of the other. We hoped this part of the intervention would begin to heal the schism between the two teams of teachers. The sixth grade team struggled with grief, loss, and protective feelings that accompanied a sense of disbelief. They were likely feeling isolated, defensive, and vulnerable. The fifth grade team was feeling understandable anger, resentment, powerlessness, exclusion, and perhaps a degree of guilt for some of these feelings. The teams would likely share some similar feelings, especially an overwhelming concern for the students. They would also likely share similar stress reactions and suffering.

On the third day of the response, time passed slowly. As the time to begin the first session with teachers approached, the assistant superintendent confirmed her intention to observe the session. Assertively, I asked that she not sit in on the sessions with teachers.

I explained, "They need to meet as staff, facilitated by their colleagues, and without others observing. They need privacy and confidentiality to speak freely in a trusting atmosphere, without censoring their feelings, or fearing that what is said will be repeated outside the group."

She got on her cell phone. I assumed she was calling the superintendent for direction. What he said would determine whether she attended the sessions. To his credit and with my gratitude, he told her to stay out.

It was difficult not to participate in these staff counseling sessions, but it was the right thing to do. I checked in with Phyllis Tallos and Wilma Robinson after each session. Each went well, they believed. They thought the sessions were helpful, the teams receptive—even appreciative. After all, they all cared about the students and the students always come first. It was an honor to work with Phyllis and Wilma.

Responding to Community

The crisis team set about focusing on the third major part of the system—the community (PREPaRE Model: Caregiver Training). With school and district administration, we planned an evening meeting with the community in the school library where we had triaged and counseled many students. Rippling with tension and discomfort, the room was filled with parents, guardians, and others who were afraid, angry, and feeling anxious about their children. Many questions went unanswered either because we did not know the answers or needed to respect confidentiality. There were legitimate questions about some of the decisions made during the school year. The superintendent, the school principal, and the director of human resources spoke to the crowd. I don't recall much of what they said. I do recall that the father of a student tore into the superintendent with a verbal barrage of accusations and blame. During response to traumatic incidents, there can be free-floating anger, expressed indiscriminately and directed off-target, often toward an authority figure. Someone must be blamed. The perpetrator wasn't invited to the meeting. The superintendent was vulnerable, bearing the brunt of misdirected anger. The man's verbal assault was prolonged. The superintendent responded; the barrage continued and became repetitious. I remember thinking, "This does not feel like a safe atmosphere. Enough."

From the back of the room I loudly but calmly stated in the direction of the man who attacked, "Sir, you've had a chance to make your points. Let's give other people a chance to speak."

Brief silence. "Sorry," he said. The meeting moved on.

RECOVERY

The cathartic moment occurred during the community meeting when Phyllis Tallos, the school psychologist, expressed the extreme anger so many of us felt.

"I'm sure many of us would like to put our hands around the throat of that person and strangle her, but that wouldn't be lawful or the right thing to do," she said.

Reaction varied from stunned silence to uninhibited laughter. The collective response was tension release.

"What we can do is take care of our children and each other," she said while asking those gathered to read the prepared handout that was circulating. One of the parents, a psychiatrist, volunteered to speak about children's needs in this unusual situation and offered counseling for children in need through DuPont

Hospital for Children, where she worked.

⌒

The school and district crisis response team met for an extensive debriefing shortly after our work at the school was finished (PREP_a_RE Model: Caring for the Caregiver). We processed the response, shared feelings, vented, and talked about stress management. It helped, but was not enough. A year later, we met again to debrief and to exorcise residual trauma. Again, it helped, but was not enough. I believe many of us have come to terms with the fact that our attempts to care for each other were helpful, but could never be enough.

Having addressed a community's despair, I was left with the question, "How do we ascend from the depths of hell?" After some reflection, I believe we ascend on the shoulders of our determined colleagues—fellow responders and educators whose acts of kindness show children that there is still goodness in an imperfect world and that a measure of trust can be restored.

Lessons Learned: Reflection and Discussion

1. Depending on the severity and reach of a traumatic event, count on planning system-wide interventions. *Who are the system-wide stakeholders and what types of interventions might be needed?*

2. The leadership style to facilitate a response should be appropriate for the needs of the situation. While shared leadership and input are always relevant, styles may range from more democratic, consensus-driven decision making, to more authoritative, immediate decision making. Styles may require flexibility, varying with different tasks during the same response. *What are some leadership styles and decision-making processes, and when would they be most appropriate?*

3. Given the rare example of teacher misconduct and manipulation, the crisis counselor might work with students having high regard for the person who has committed reprehensible acts. *How are students' feelings respected while the counselor begins to create some dissonance in their view of the teacher, eventually enabling a more reality based and critical viewpoint?*

195

4. In situations where there is a perpetrator and a target, prepare for the possibility that the victim will be blamed, and the need to ascribe responsibility to the perpetrator. *What are some strategies for working with groups and individuals on a developmentally appropriate understanding of the dynamics of abuse?*

5. During certain types of crisis response, including sudden death and instances of physical or emotional violence, abuse or manipulation, there may be a need to conduct conflict resolution within or between student or staff subgroups. *What are some ways crisis teams can develop conflict resolution/mediation skills and recognize when their use is needed?*

6. Keeping the school staff and community informed and when appropriate, seeking feedback or allowing them to question and vent, can make the difference between people cooperating with the response or obstructing constructive efforts. *What are some ways to keep staff and parents/guardians informed, understanding, and supportive of recovery efforts?*

Here's a template for a letter sent to parents.

District / School Letterhead

Dear [School] Parents,

Earlier today, a teacher at [School name] Elementary School, Ms. _____, was arrested and charged with multiple counts of sexual misconduct with a student.

The District's first concern is to provide additional support for all students at the school. A district team of counselors, psychologists, and social workers are assigned to the school to support the [School name] counselors and staff as they address the needs of all students. If you have any questions or concerns about your child's reaction to this situation, please contact _____ , Assistant to the Principal, at [phone number].

In the best interest of students, the District has building substitute, Mrs. _____ assigned to Ms. _____'s classroom. The District will recruit a high quality teacher as soon as possible.

We know that you will join us in our concern and support for the students and staff.

Please direct media inquiries that you may receive to _____, District Information Officer at [phone number].

Sincerely,

_____ Superintendent

_____ Principal

Sample Agenda for Community Meeting

- Introductions and Agenda Overview
- Describe what happened, and the resolution (when appropriate).
- Describe steps taken to enhance safety and security at the school and for emotional support of students, families, and staff.
- Describe common reactions to this type of event.
- Describe ways adults can help their children cope.
- Describe indicators of need for referral for more intensive support.
- Describe services available at school and in the community, and how to access services.
- Question and answer period

Close with a statement of hope and compliments for the many strengths evident in the community and how the community is pulling together to help one another.

Throughout the meeting, recognize the anger or other feelings of the audience, but redirect the focus toward helping students return to school and to learning.

19

Care for the Caregiver: In the Eye of the Storm

Reflections

As a new school psychologist arriving in Delaware years ago, I collected resources for emergencies and for referrals. I noted the listing for the Mobile Crisis Unit and the contact person responsible for responding to individuals or families in acute emotional distress. Clients were often uncooperative, emotionally fragile, or volatile. Some were having suicidal ideation or intent. The job was demanding and stressful. When I tried to reach the young man responsible for the unit, I learned he had recently died by suicide. Feeling frustrated and powerless, I wished something could have been done to save his life. I knew about the concept of "burnout," but little about the extent of risk for those in the helping professions—particularly for those responding to traumatic situations. I was unfamiliar with the terms "vicarious trauma," "secondary trauma," or "compassion fatigue." I did not know about the importance of social support networks, coping strategies, debriefing, or stress management to mitigate potentially harmful effects on caregivers. The suicide of a young man dedicated to helping others struck me more as irony than a lesson in setting the priority to care for the caregiver. Through the years, we learned that caring for others also means caring for ourselves.

Team Development and the Need for Care

During a difficult crisis response, the school team focuses on the needs of students, staff, and community. From a systems perspective, the needs of the caregiver must be a priority as well. Whether caregivers are sufficiently cared for can determine whether the crisis team's development is enabled or blocked. Since school responders often experience a pull toward the demands of other responsibilities after a crisis, special attention is required to make certain they are getting the time and attention necessary for emotional recovery. Interventions for caregivers such as closure debriefings help assure their recovery and can save lives.

Challenge and Purpose of Emotional Regulation

How can crisis responders find the measure of quiet and tranquility necessary to function effectively? How can they regulate their emotions, process information, and sense needs in the midst of noise, chaos, and tragic situations? The ability to deliberate and to make clear decisions through individual reflection or collaborative problem solving is facilitated by finding a safe, quiet psychological or physical space to contemplate, if only for a few minutes at a time. Without this, the responder may feel like a leaf in the wind.

It is understandable that the normal inclination for a person surrounded by suffering, fear, and trauma is flight from the situation after a brief time. And yet, crisis responders frequently remain in challenging environments serving people's needs for extended shifts. While understanding the importance of being fully present to help, I sometimes experienced the detached feeling of "not being there." During a crisis, a fellow responder once said to me, "I really don't want to be here." Checking the statement with her, I confirmed that she was not asking to leave the scene. She was voicing the ambivalent thoughts many of us experience while enduring a response—realizing the vital need to be there, but wishing it was not happening. These are normal reactions— brief coping mechanisms to dissociate for a moment. However, if the brief escape turns into a more extended vacation, it is not helpful for the responder or those in need.

Self and peer monitoring helps responders regulate their emotions and remain fully present during a crisis. In general, the reactions of adults influence *perceived* safety and security, especially for young children (Dyregrov & Yule, 2006; Eksi et al., 2007). Since children often gauge the severity of an event by observing the reactions of caregivers, a calm and organized approach is crucial. Having an evidence-based, practical model of intervention supports a purposeful, coordinated, emotionally regulated, but caring response (Brock et al., 2009; Everly & Mitchell, 2010; Mitchell, 1993).

Eye of the Storm: The Metaphor

Metaphors illustrate thoughts and emotions that may be otherwise difficult to express. The vivid image of a natural disaster can describe the psychological atmosphere, the ecology of a landscape overcome by a traumatic event. The hurricane is an awe-inspiring natural phenomenon. The swirling, funnel-like storm system may be massive, powerful, and destructive. Around the perimeter, there is shattering noise, strong winds, debris, chaos. In stark contrast, at the center of the hurricane, the "eye of the storm," there is tranquility, a peaceful calm, quiet stillness surrounded by the raging torrent.

A hurricane, like a human crisis, may be mild or severe. It can arrive suddenly or with days' warning. The suddenness of a natural disaster or other traumatic event influences its perceived severity and our ability to prepare and intervene. A hurricane's severity is categorized just as we categorize other traumatic incidents. The degree of severity determines the nature and extent of response.

During the storm of crisis response, in the midst of chaos and noise, are times when responders find the *eye*—the calm and quiet place where the ability to think clearly and sense all aspects of the crisis enables coherent intervention planning. A psychiatric nurse on a hospital trauma unit discovered her own metaphor, a *comfort garden*—a peaceful place at work that helped her cope with a stream of traumatic events (Barkin, 2011) —a place where the caregiver can briefly reflect and renew.

Without minimizing the loss of life and property during hurricanes, they also provide *opportunity*. They are often catalysts to bring a community together, reaffirming hope and faith, and precipitating the rebuilding of property and lives. Crisis responders facilitate reaffirmation and rebuilding; they do their best to ride out storms, alternating between the swirling debris and the peaceful eye at the center, grasping for ways to help others cope and to move forward.

Risk to Crisis Responders

Arvay and Uhlemann (1996) found that stress levels among counselors working with trauma victims were similar to stress levels experienced by their clients. Sixteen percent of counselors working in trauma response reported emotional exhaustion and burnout, compared with only 2–6% burnout rate among counselors not working with trauma victims. Bolnik and Brock (2005) found that 90% of school psychologists reported at least one adverse physical, emotional, cognitive, behavioral, or work performance reaction to their interventions during school crises.

Crisis responders exposed to traumatized children are especially vulnerable to stress reactions (Figley, 1999). Kendall Johnson (1998) points out that addressing trauma in children's lives can be enormously stressful, tending to evoke unsettling feelings among professionals. Fear and helplessness at not being able to "fix" the pain are among the feelings. Responders may also feel anger and rage when adults victimize children, and guilt at not being able to protect the children.

Coping with Anger When Children Are Victims

1. Make a conscious effort to avoid displacing anger on others.
2. Find someone to talk with afterward to vent anger and to gain perspective.
Source: Johnson, 1998.

The breadth and depth of relationships among students and staff in schools creates one of the unique challenging aspects of school crisis response.

These relationships are often based upon mutual respect and

appreciation. Sometimes they are driven by anger and resentment. Schools provide opportunities for people to enjoy and annoy each other, to engage in and resolve conflict, to learn and grow together. When a traumatic incident strikes a school, many lives can be deeply affected. The responder is not immune from emotional devastation in the school community.

Risk Variables and Symptoms of Stress

Caregiver care begins with recognizing and understanding stress reactions and exacerbating variables that create greater vulnerability for the crisis responder.

Common Stress Reactions

- Change in levels of physical and social activity
- Substance use or abuse
- Difficulty sleeping
- Numbing, irritability, anger, or frustration
- *Vicarious trauma* manifested by shock, fear, helplessness or horror
- Confusion and difficulty concentrating or making decisions
- Symptoms of anxiety or depression.

Extreme Stress Reactions

- *Compassion stress* manifested by helplessness, confusion and isolation
- *Compassion fatigue* manifested by demoralization, rejection, and alienation
- Serious problems with interpersonal relations or domestic violence
- Flashbacks, or re-experiencing trauma
- Withdrawal and isolation
- Excessive need for control
- Substance abuse
- Extreme changes in sleep patterns
- Hopelessness and depression
- Risk-taking behaviors.

Sources: Brock et al., 2009; Brymer et al., 2006.

Variables That Place the Responder at Greater Risk

- Long shifts with heavy trauma caseload
- Extended time with traumatized children, either physically injured or abused
- Witnessing death
- Threat to physical well-being of self or loved one
- Discussing morbid details of trauma
- Recent loss
- Family difficulties
- Repeated exposure to trauma through the media.

Sources: Bride, 2007; Brock et al., 2009; Creamer and Liddle, 2005; Figley, 1995.

The work of crisis responders can be physically and emotionally exhausting. School crisis planners are wise to address ways to care for staff responders and any negative reactions they may feel following involvement in crisis response (Reeves et al., 2010). Assuring that responders have access to a peaceful physical or psychological space to reflect, recover, and plan, is a consequential step toward supporting caregivers.

Vicarious Trauma and Post-Traumatic Stress

Jeffrey Mitchell is a pioneer in recognizing stress reactions associated with first responders and crisis caregivers. He developed interventions designed to mitigate the effects of post-traumatic stress disorder (PTSD) (Everly & Mitchell, 2010; Mitchell, 1983; Mitchell & Everly, 1996, 2001). Witnessing, or being exposed to a traumatic incident can result in a constellation of debilitating, long-term stress reactions.

Symptoms of post-traumatic stress disorder can include:
- Repeated intrusive thoughts and images (flashbacks)
- Hyper-vigilance and exaggerated startle response
- Poor concentration
- Emotional numbing and avoidance
- Sleep disturbances
- Difficulty with interpersonal relationships that can include withdrawal, anger, or aggression.

During a crisis, it is normal to feel empathy for suffering people. The caveat is this: Responders who repeatedly witness traumatized people are at high risk for "vicarious trauma," also called "secondary traumatic stress disorder" (STSD) and "compassion fatigue" (Figley, 1995, 2002). Empathic caregivers can develop symptoms similar to those experienced by their clients. Responders must monitor their reactions to maintain control and focus on actions that serve the client. Reflecting deeply on the enormity of loss for a moment may evoke empathy, but dwelling on those reflections can result in loss of focus, immobilization, and stress reactions. Responders can reduce risk for traumatic stress by finding a peaceful space, sharing that space with colleagues, and practicing stress management and self-care.

Responsibility:
Care for Fellow Responders and Self

Those caring for others must first care for themselves. Flight attendants illustrate the point on commercial air flights, reminding passengers to secure their own oxygen masks before assisting others during an emergency. If you lose consciousness, you will be unable to help others. While helping others, crisis responders might ignore their own need to eat, rest, or sleep. Often, fellow responders must remind, jostle, or insist that colleagues attend to their own physical needs. We have also learned to care for the *emotional* needs of caregivers during and after a crisis.

Figley (1995, 2002) proposed standards of self-care for professionals working with traumatized clients, contending that *not* engaging in self-care is unethical. Self-care is necessary for responders to provide effective services and to avoid harming clients. Caregivers can learn to be aware of their own needs and monitor the needs of colleagues. Social support for caregiver self-care begins with the crisis team.

Preventive and treatment measures to avoid or mitigate stress reactions generally include individual and team approaches to renew caregivers (Creamer & Liddle, 2005; Feinberg et al., 2004; Figley, 1995, 2002; Stamm, 1999). Social supports, stress management, cognitive-behavioral and other strategies can help the

205

responder tolerate what happens in the aftermath of traumatic events (Jaycox, 2004; Mennuti et al., 2006; Tugade & Frederickson, 2004; Ungar, 2008; Zautra et al., 2010).

Strategies for Finding the Eye of the Storm

Crisis responders can find the eye of the storm in many ways. Internal and external resources can support the responder's physical and emotional health and enhance effectiveness during the crisis. Responders can develop *internal resources* to weather storms, including personal qualities, attitudes, behaviors, activities, and routines that serve the responder before, during, and after a crisis. *External resources* are developed in concert with others. They include social support systems, training and collaboration, and family and community involvement before, during, and after a crisis.

Internal Resources

Writing about her first crisis response as a school psychology intern, Angela Aiello (2010) described what she felt and what she learned.

> By the end of the day, I was so exhausted, physically and mentally, I could hardly move. In the next few days, my own reaction would surprise me. I felt irritable. I cried—a lot... I learned that in order to restore your well-being, you have to be able to recognize and separate your sadness from that of the people you have helped. Having patience and understanding that it will take some time to work through the emotions is important. In order to facilitate the process, remember to take time for yourself and to do the things that work for you in relieving stress. Get as much rest as you need, and don't feel guilty about it because enduring heartbreak can feel more exhausting than physical exertion. (p. 35)

Internal Resource Strategies

- Self-monitor for signs of stress, physical needs, and strengths, seeking relief when necessary.
- Get enough sleep and rest.
- Avoid long periods of response without colleagues or breaks.
- Ensure good nutrition throughout the response.
- Avoid or limit use of alcohol or tobacco.
- Exercise regularly.
- Use stress management techniques such as deep breathing, progressive relaxation, mindfulness, meditation, and guided imagery.
- Develop qualities and skills for assertiveness, resilience, cognitive reframing, time management, interpersonal communication, and conflict resolution.
- Practice religious faith, spirituality, or life-affirming beliefs.
- Engage in creative self-expression such as writing, drawing, painting, dancing, music, or teaching.
- Maintain fascination with the unexpected turns of human interaction, and appreciation for the thoughtful, kind acts of students, staff, and crisis team.
- Appreciate humor when you can, in as many aspects of your life as possible.
- Follow-up—self-monitor in the weeks and months following crisis response.
- If necessary, seek help with your own trauma history, which can make you vulnerable to vicarious trauma.
- If signs of vicarious trauma last longer than 2–3 weeks, seek a professional who is knowledgeable in treating trauma.

Sources: Brock et al., 2009; Brymer et al., 2006; Figley, 2002; Reeves et al., 2010.

External Resources

After a traumatic incident, reestablish and reconnect natural social support systems in schools and communities (Brock & Jimerson, 2004; Brock at el., 2009). Caplan (1964) recognized that interpersonal relationships affect psychological and social functioning, and they foster resiliency during difficult times. There is plenty of room in the eye of the storm to seek social support.

External Resource Strategies

- Prepare sufficient number of responders to address major intervention needs.

- Engage crisis team in training, drills, stress management strategies and team building activities.

- Encourage a buddy system in which responders partner, consult, and support each other.

- Encourage administration to support a culture in which staff can safely request help, ask for a break, say "no" when necessary, and monitor and remove a responder in need of relief.

- Limit responder shifts to a maximum of 12 hours.

- Rotate responder assignments from highest to lower impact stress levels.

- Include sufficient rotating "floaters" to relieve responders providing direct psychological first aid, as needed.

- Involve food service in providing nutritious food, snacks, and water.

- Learn to monitor fellow responders for those needing support—especially those who appear at risk.

- Engage in informational and planning briefing/debriefing sessions periodically throughout the response to monitor not only student and staff needs, but also needs of fellow responders.

208

- Engage in closure/stress debriefing at the conclusion of a response to examine team performance and responder needs.

- Closure planning can include strategies for stress management and, if needed, supportive interventions from colleagues.

- If needed, obtain supervision and support from administrator, team leader, or professional referral.

- Throughout crisis response, draw strength and support from appreciation of the team, cooperation, and common purpose.

- Plan for family and home safety such as fire drills and reunification plans.

- Plan for family and community support and recreation.

- Identify at least 5 people for social support including two dependable people at work.

- Engage in constructive pursuits such as volunteering for service organizations.

Sources: Brock et al., 2009; Brymer et al., 2006; Figley, 2002; Reeves et al., 2010.

Leadership and Resilience

Effective leadership fosters crisis team resiliency. A leader can be a catalyst for team cohesion, its sense of control and purpose, self-care, resilience, and enthusiasm for both mundane and meaningful tasks.

Crisis team leaders can support resilience and enable team members and affected persons in many ways. They can model resilience and appreciate the contributions of others. They can encourage efficacy and empathy while monitoring emotional needs of responders and themselves. Team leaders can plan debriefings for effective closure, stress management, and coping strategies. Team leadership is explored in more detail in Chapter 23.

Moving Forward After the Storm

Crisis team disengagement means leaving students in the hands of stabilized, recovering administrators, teachers, and support staff capable of caring for them. There should be a plan for all groups in the school community, including responders, to maintain movement toward recovery, resilience, and pre-crisis capacity. *The PREPaRE Model* (Brock et al., 2009) recommends debriefing with crisis responders, caring for the caregiver, and ongoing support for teachers and other staff until intervention is no longer needed.

Demobilization of the blended school and district crisis teams after a crisis should include plans for a timely closure debriefing. This is particularly important for the district team, since demobilization means relative isolation from the team support network. Team members will be returning to schools and families who can be supportive, but have not shared their experience. The district team needs to collectively examine its common experience, constructively evaluate its effectiveness and lessons learned, and determine the extent of psychological debriefing needed by the team. The need for debriefing should override the inclination of team members to leave immediately after the response to return to their regular school or district roles. While each team member is affected differently, all would benefit from peer support and a positive recovery plan that fits individual needs (Crepeau-Hobson & Kanan, 2014).

Like those they have helped, caregivers recover, realizing that finding a quiet place is no longer confined to the storm's eye. Sources of calm and support dramatically expand after confronting a crisis. It may take awhile, but life becomes more normal, more predictable, perhaps in some ways more meaningful. The experience and feelings of the response are integrated as a challenging part of the responder's life and it is possible to move forward.

The Strength to Continue

Crisis response takes a toll. Alcoholism, depression, and suicide are occupational hazards among responders. The strength to continue serving those experiencing psychological trauma comes from a variety of sources. For some it is religious and spiritual. For others it comes from training and skills. For some, it is the camaraderie of team and satisfaction in helping others. For most, the strength to continue comes from a combination of these qualities. Responders continue serving because it is their job and the career they chose. Whatever their motives, responders all need care, renewal, and help for giving so much of themselves.

20

Death of an English Teacher

Abstract

This case study describes the response to the imminent death of a beloved English teacher. It highlights the efforts of a young principal to support the teacher's family and to prepare his staff. An anecdote illustrates the balance between intervening when a student needs individual attention and imposing when a student does not. Sample letters are included. *Themes are: 1) preparing for a death; 2) school-wide triage; 3) grieving a teacher; 4) balance between intervening and imposing; 5) support for family and school staff.*

INTRODUCTION

An e-mail from the school psychologist let us know that a middle school English teacher was terminally ill with cancer. The principal took the lead in planning and contacted the district crisis team. I knew the teacher as she'd taught my daughter. She cared deeply about her students and inspired other teachers. She motivated her students to love learning and to love literature.

PREVENTION/MITIGATION

The middle school in this case study had a long history of supporting its students. The faculty generally cared about the students and each other. A program of Positive Behavior Support

(PBS) had been established and was functioning effectively (Sugai & Horner, 2002, 2006) (PREPaRE Model: Strategies/Programs to Improve Climate, Safety, and Resilience). The administration appeared flexible and open to communicating with staff and students about their concerns. The school had a trained crisis team in place (PREPaRE Model: School Crisis Teams).

PREPAREDNESS

The young, thoughtful, middle school principal characterized our dying colleague as "one of our beloved teachers." He was in touch with the family, who requested that the school community write memories and feelings about the teacher. Students and staff provided many such warm thoughts for the family's memory book. Since the teacher had been ill and away from school for months and students and staff were informed of her terminal illness, administration decided the response would be mainly building level, with limited district support (PREPaRE Model: Matching Level of Response with Crisis Event Variables).

The anticipated e-mail was sent to school staff on the morning the family sent word the teacher had died. The message included directions for teachers — the designated period, early in the day, when they would read a prepared statement informing students of the death, expressing the sadness of the school community, and inviting students to let their teachers know if they needed to talk with a counselor. The e-mail further instructed teachers to have the students complete a screening form giving them an opportunity to express feelings and request crisis counseling follow-up (PREPaRE Model: Evaluating Psychological Trauma). Teachers were encouraged to answer students' questions and send those needing intervention to the library at any time during the school day. The e-mail also included a description of various reactions that teachers might expect from their students. Finally, teachers were reminded of the dedicated phone number to call for classroom support or if they needed to leave their classroom. Substitute teachers stood ready. Every point in the message, including suggestions about how to listen and talk with grieving students, had been discussed at staff meetings in preparation for this day (PREP<u>a</u>RE Model: Caregiver Training).

RESPONSE

From the moment the statement was read to students, crisis responders were present to conduct *psychological triage* and to provide emotional first aid in the classrooms of the deceased teacher. "Classroom Meetings" described in the PREP<u>a</u>RE Model provide a useful structure for conducting discussion, getting cues from students regarding their concerns, and providing psychoeducation, including strategies to manage stress and cope with their reactions (Brock et al., 2009). Students from these classes and others throughout the school needing small group or individual crisis intervention were escorted to the library. Crisis responders were assigned to major hallway locations on each floor of the building to sweep and escort students in need. Responders in the library were assigned to individual and small group work (PREP<u>a</u>RE Model: Provide Interventions and Respond to Psychological Needs).

More students than anticipated sought help, some self-selecting small groups upon arriving at the library. After consultation with the school principal, a team leader contacted several "on call" district responders and asked them to report to the school. Selected responders were assigned to affected staff members. *Secondary triage* referrals for students and staff were generated during the response, as administrators, school counselors, teachers, and fellow students gave the names of those appearing to need individual attention (PREP<u>a</u>RE Model: Secondary Triage: Evaluating Psychological Trauma). Counseling with teachers occurred in their classrooms during breaks, or in private designated areas. The PREP<u>a</u>RE Model emphasizes attending to the emotional needs of the school staff so they may care for their students (Brock et al., 2009).

Balance Between Intervening and Imposing

Interventions in the library had been ongoing for several hours when fellow team member Nancy Carney and I were approached on behalf of a colleague. A classroom teacher asked that we remove a student resting at a desk in her classroom with his head cradled on his arms. He was not participating in the lesson and had refused suggestions that he leave to seek help in the library. We told the messenger we would investigate. We established that he was generally a cooperative student involved in class work, that withdrawn behavior was not normal for him, and that there had been a death in his family several months earlier.

When Nancy and I arrived at the second floor classroom, we observed through the window of the closed door that, as reported, the student's head rested on his arms stretched across his desk. The teacher conducted the class with no apparent disruption. Nancy and I reviewed the situation. The student had been informed that counseling or a safe, quiet space was available in the library. He refused to leave class to talk about his feelings and it seemed clear he wanted to stay in the classroom with his peers. It also appeared he preferred not to be disturbed. Avoidance coping in the early stages of a traumatic event is cause for concern, but not necessarily alarm. It may be an adaptive reaction (Brock et al., 2009). The fact that this student had recently experienced a familial death was a red flag indicating he should be monitored.

Nancy and I decided to avoid imposing ourselves, or embarrassing him in the middle of class. Instead, we would wait until the class ended before approaching the student. I tapped gently on the classroom door. When the teacher noticed us waiting in the hallway, she briefly left the room to greet us and was apprised of our plan, which she accepted. We thanked her for letting us know her student was upset and assured her we would follow through.

When the class ended, Nancy and I spoke briefly and unobtrusively with the student. We asked how he was doing. "Okay," he said. We encouraged him to take care of himself and to lean on others if he needed support. We reminded him that support was available in the library. He wanted to get to the cafeteria to eat lunch. This was good. He saw there were teachers and other adults who cared about him. Later, during the next team debriefing, his name was among those given to his school counselor for follow-up and monitoring (PREPaRE Model: Facilitate Normal/Adaptive Coping).

216

Brymer et al. (2012a, 2012b) suggest that psychological first aid is an *acute intervention* to reduce initial distress, to foster adaptive functioning, and to link affected people to services when needed. Responders are encouraged to provide "pragmatic support in a nonintrusive and compassionate manner" and not to force disclosure of traumatic details. They suggest that providers of psychological first aid circulate in areas where affected individuals gather, observing them in an interested manner. Without interrupting, responders can introduce themselves and offer assistance. The responder respects the wishes of those declining the offer, but indicates where help can be found.

Walk—Talk

We tried to meet student needs through a variety of interventions including an approach we called "walk—talk." Late one afternoon, we worked with ten students in the library, but we felt like we were stuck. The students seemed to have feelings to express, but said little. We took the students outside to the athletic track for a "walk—talk." The physical exercise and fresh air renewed all of us. The students found it easier to express thoughts and feelings while walking in a less formal, more relaxed setting.

∽

The work was intense throughout the first day, with little time for debriefing until after a faculty meeting at day's end. During the crisis team debriefing, we shared the names of students and staff who received counseling and those needing follow-up. The team divided responsibility for contacting parents of the most affected students by phone. An e-mail was sent to principals and counselors throughout the district, alerting them that former students of the deceased teacher might be affected. We made plans for the next day and listed a variety of ways students could contribute to the memory book. As in past responses, the art teacher was a helpful resource, providing materials for use in the library, and for a paper mural and monitored memory table in the main hallway. An informative letter from the principal was sent home with students to all families in the school community (PREPaRE Model: Reestablish Social Support Systems).

When we were finally about to leave the school, Nancy expressed appreciation to her fellow team members and to me personally, for our work. "You are really good at what you do. The team really does a great job." The praise took me by surprise. I think I deflected it, thanking her and praising her work and the team's effort. Nancy was a long-standing member of our team. For many years, she was also the lead elementary school counselor and volunteer at a community agency that provided grief counseling for young people and families. She was never afraid to ask hard questions or to speak her mind. She could be counted on to be in the most difficult situations with little notice. She had integrity and the respect of her peers. When she said something, she meant it. Nancy's kind words meant a lot to me.

RECOVERY

Normal routine was reestablished within a couple of days. The relatively quick recovery was likely facilitated by the positive school climate, preparation prior to the teacher's death, and effective response that stabilized and supported staff and students. At *tertiary triage* during the conclusion of the response, district and school teams reviewed names of students and staff that appeared to need follow-up. The responsibility for monitoring the students' progress was given to the school's counselors (PREPaRE Model: Tertiary Triage: Evaluating Psychological Trauma). The school staff honored the memory of their deceased colleague by re-dedicating themselves to the work she loved—educating and inspiring students.

These events happened some years ago. I recently read in the "Community News" that the middle school won an award for raising funds to fight cancer. While there were many reasons the school achieved that honor, I knew of one.

Lessons Learned: Reflection and Discussion

1. Death from a terminal illness, even when anticipated and planned for, can seriously affect students, staff, and even a school district. *What are some of the unexpected challenges and opportunities that can arise when responding to the death of a terminally ill teacher or student?*

2. Knowing when to intervene with a grieving student, and when not to impose when a student has the resources to cope with minimal or no intervention requires balance. *What are some ways to assess the level of necessary intervention and to determine when direct intervention is and is not necessary?*

∽

The following are memos, edited for confidentiality, sent by the principal to school staff and to district counselors as part of extended triage.

Memo

From: School Principal
To: [School Staff]
Subject: Update on [Teacher's Name]
Good Morning

I went to the hospital to drop off a card from all of us and to give [Teacher]'s daughter my contact information. [Teacher] is heavily sedated to alleviate the pain. Her daughter had many kind words for all of us. She didn't realize the extent of the relationship and kindness our staff has shown. As of [Day of the week], [Teacher] is at the _____Hospital. We do not know the exact cancer that [Teacher] has but we do know it is serious.

The family doesn't need any more food items. They ask you to write your thoughts, feelings, and memories of her. They want to be able to take out the letters at times to remember her and all of the wonderful relationships she's had with others. I have put together a notebook for anyone to add a letter. The mailbox marked LTP is on the far right of the mailboxes. A box of pocket sheet protectors is in the mailbox for your use with these memory items.

Each day, I will check the mailbox and add the items to the notebook, which we will present to the family at an appropriate time.

I will update you when we have more information.
Principal
[Name] Middle School

～

School Letterhead

Staff Statement to Students—during 2nd period

We just received word that eighth grade teacher, Mrs. [Teacher's Name], passed away after a battle with cancer. The [School] Community is saddened by this news. Everyone grieves differently. If you wish to speak with a counselor, please let me know.

Our thoughts and prayers are with Mrs. [Teacher's Name]'s family.

Instructions

1. Please read "Statement to Students" (above) at the beginning of the period.

2. Distribute the grieving information/screening form to students.

3. Answer any questions students may have.

4. Any student who wishes to talk with a counselor may go to the library any time of day—with appropriate escort.

5. Here's a list of expected behaviors to look for among students.

√ Appears unaffected.

√ Ask questions about the death repeatedly.

√ Is angry or aggressive.

√ Is withdrawn or moody.

√ Is sad or depressed.

√ Is afraid.

√ Has difficulty sleeping or eating.

6. Any teacher who needs support or needs to leave the classroom, please call the nurse. Floating substitutes are available.

7. Funeral arrangements will be shared when known.

～

District Letterhead

From: [District Secretary]
To: Counselors, District-wide
Cc: [Administrators, Principals]
Subject: Sad News

220

Counselors:

Sorry to inform you that English/Language Arts teacher [Teacher's Name] from [School Name] passed away today. Presently, the Crisis Team is at [School Name] providing support to students and staff. At this point, most students who previously attended [School Name] are unaware of the sad news. Please provide support and counseling to students who need it. For additional support, please contact Jeff Roth.

Section 4

Team Maintenance: Sharing Leadership, Expanding Knowledge, Ongoing Challenges

21

Disengagement and Demobilization

Reflections

The Imperative of Disengagement

As school crisis teams develop, they often continue to struggle with how to disengage from a response in a way that cares for their clients and achieves closure for themselves. Systems thinking is useful when planning disengagement, since it is helpful to consider interacting variables—groups, individuals, and issues that influence each other throughout an intervention. These variables can evolve in a way that adapts and orients toward recovery, or in a way that is maladaptive and disrupts recovery.

As in the initial stages of response, there is a tendency while disengaging, to focus exclusively on the students. However, the imperative of crisis team disengagement is to leave students in the hands of stabilized, recovering administrators, teachers, and support staff who are capable of caring for them. We must be certain that all subgroups—school personnel, families and community have a plan that maintains movement toward recovery and pre-crisis capacity (Brock et al., 2009).

Early in the response during team debriefings, it is useful to establish a tentative timeline for interventions and outcomes aimed at recovery and disengagement. The team collaborates to develop a specific plan to achieve both short and long term goals, with clear delineation of "who does what by when." The plan should always include focused interventions to minimize potential stress while providing support for teachers, administrators, staff, and team members. As part of disengagement, best practices calls for closure debriefing for crisis team members and first responders exposed to a severely traumatic incident.

Tertiary Triage and Ongoing Support Systems

Students differ in the degree to which they are affected and they vary in their need for intervention and follow-up. Ongoing triage throughout each response determines if students need intervention. For most, healing and recovery is a natural, spontaneous process with minimal support needed. For the typically small percentage most seriously affected by a traumatic incident or death—often family, friends, witnesses, first responders, and vulnerable populations—it is pivotal to monitor them after the event and as anniversary dates approach. Long-term follow-up is especially important after a severely traumatic or violent incident such as a school shooting or death by suicide.

The PREPaRE Model recommends *tertiary triage* during disengagement, which involves careful consideration of the possible need for continued monitoring or treatment, including psychotherapy for those most severely affected. Clinical judgment, risk factors, interviews, and evidence-based instruments help identify severe grief reactions indicating referral for more intensive treatment (Brent et al., 2013; Brock, 2011; Brock et al., 2009; Heath & Cole, 2012; Holland, 2012; Reeves et al., 2011). Mass disasters may require an instrument and support structure that can identify and track large numbers of the school community who need follow-up (Brock et al., 2009).

Demaria and Schonfeld (2014) suggest that the school community, including staff, parents and guardians, be educated to understand both short- and long-term reactions to traumatic incidents. As disengagement approaches, many needing follow-up can be monitored by a responsible crisis team or school staff member. Student support networks, including teachers, staff, parents, and peers can be established. Students can be provided options to participate with adults on empowering projects and voluntary advisory committees. Students can be educated about how to access ongoing sources of peer and adult support, counseling, and referral when needed.

Emphasizing the Need for Follow-up

When a traumatic incident occurs, there is a tendency during the first few days and weeks to concentrate many resources providing psychological first aid, triage, interventions, and attention to those most in need. After that initial response, in the weeks and months that follow, attention may be minimal, or non-existent. Even those most at risk may begin to feel that continuing to request help is an imposition—that they should "get over it" and move on. The reality is that for those severely affected by trauma, the need for monitoring and possibly therapeutic treatment could extend years beyond crisis response disengagement.

Anniversary dates of traumatic incidents and victims' birthdays deserve consideration and care. Do not act as though these events did not happen. Reactions may vary in the extreme, with some students re-experiencing intense feelings while others show little or no difficulty. The type and severity of a traumatic event as well as anticipated reactions should be considered when developing appropriate strategies to address the anniversary. A worthy goal is to create an environment that fosters healing rather than destructive aspects of grieving (Erbacher et al., 2015; Zibulsky, 2012).

Rossen and Cowan (2013) point out that crisis teams generally respond to acute incidents, facilitating return to normal routine without addressing "ongoing intervention and longer-term recovery for traumatized students." To prevent students from falling through the cracks during and after the event, they suggest an approach "to integrate the school crisis, safety, and mental health teams, all of whom have a student support role, within a multi-tiered support framework." They describe a "multi-tiered system of supports" (MTSS)—a continuum of services that coordinates student learning and mental health needs. Kennedy-Paine et al. (2014) suggest considering a "school-wide emotional wellness survey" approximately three months after a severe crisis.

The Right Time to Leave

When is the right time for a team to conclude a crisis response? While responding to the accidental death of a middle school student, I was approached in the hallway by a teacher who stunned me with these words: "When will you people leave?"

Her unsteady voice bore a mixture of anger and pain. "The children are milking it," she said. It felt like an insensitive but honest question from a usually sensitive teacher. I tried to explain that we needed to strike a balance, striving for return to normalcy while staying the course of the most overt grief, which has no set timetable.

I needed to respect this teacher, who was having such a difficult time. I was aware that people differ in their ability to tolerate exposure to grief situations. Perhaps she had made a valid point. I am sure that "milking" happens—feigning the need for nurturance to avoid going to class and resuming school work. I surveyed the situation. It was only the second morning of the response and as the teacher spoke, there were small groups of girls at the far end of the hallway, crying inconsolably. To leave the school at that moment would have obviously been premature. Decisions about when to disengage are not always easy, and the answer is often unclear. Respectful understanding and education of staff members helps prevent pressure for premature disengagement and assures better teacher cooperation for monitoring student needs.

In the concluding stages of a response, as normal routines are reestablished, emotions come under control, problem solving and adaptive coping are restored, there is an optimal time for team disengagement. That time is not always obvious. Responders may perceive students as still quite affected, while some teachers and administrators perceive them as "milking it." I have generally erred on the side of caution, giving students the benefit of the doubt. While the clear goal is return to normalcy as soon as feasible, students will successfully return to the normal routine only when they are ready.

Grief has its own timetable, and the process of healing is

generally a gradual journey with bumps and potholes in the road. We want to make certain there are strong guard rails to support movement in the desired direction and prevent the traveler from crashing. Complicating the issue further, one traveler may move at a very different pace than another. This requires an individually differentiated response.

When It's Time for Crisis Team to Leave

- The PREPaRE Model provides instruments to gauge the severity of a traumatic incident, and an effective model for triage. Response to crisis intervention provides indicators of movement toward recovery.
- Evidence-based assessment instruments and checklists can determine those most in need of attention, follow-up, and extended treatment after disengagement (*tertiary* triage).
- The training and experience of the team, in collaboration with affected administrators and staff, helps determine when school personnel are ready to assume the responsibility of caring for recovering students and staff.
- Prior to disengagement, the crisis team *gradually* encourages the most affected students to return to their normal routine for increasing periods of time, while maintaining support options as needed. Return to normalcy might begin with going to lunch and, over time, expand to more class time with teachers who understand the need for a gradual return to the demands of academic work.
- Responders learn about readiness to return to routine by observing how students interact with peers and adults, including what they say to responders and, more importantly, what they say to each other in the expression of emotion and needs.
- The PREPaRE Model provides "outcomes that reflect effectiveness," including criteria helpful in evaluating readiness for disengagement. These criteria are summarized later in this chapter under the section *Examining Outcomes for Effectiveness.*

We cannot expect all students to calm down, turn off grief, and cooperatively return to their normal routine as we disengage and demobilize. Even in the best of times, students are not always in control of their emotions. Feelings may be expressed unexpectedly and at inconvenient times. While the expression of laughter or playfulness may seem incongruous, both are part of an array of acceptable emotions. Teachable moments abound, as students learn that people are affected and react in different ways. As responders, we use unfolding events as opportunities to empathize, teach, and encourage understanding.

We want to leave the school community with the resources to feel hopeful and empowered. We foster dependency rather than empowerment when the response continues longer than needed. It is helpful to keep in focus that recovery from a traumatic event is the norm (Johnson, 2006; Sandoval & Brock, 2009; Vernberg et al., 1996).

Stay the Course, But Avoid Staying Too Long

As I interviewed colleague Doug DiRaddo, a district team coordinator, the discussion moved to issues of disengagement. Doug believes that when the team extends a response for more than a few days, it goes beyond psychological first aid in most cases. Sometimes we stay longer than necessary. With practice, over the years, the team becomes adept at getting in and getting out—engaging, doing what the team is supposed to do, and then leaving in an efficient manner.

Doug observed that in nearly every crisis, an administrator or teacher raises the question, "How do you know they are not trying to get out of class?" This seems less an issue and easier to detect on the elementary level but more difficult in middle and high school.

Doug recalled a high school response when ten or fifteen students in the large counseling area engaged in normal conversation with laughter. Three team members observed several other students, who were very quiet. While all kinds of emotions, including laughter, may occur during grieving and recovery, the conversation and humor of these students did not appear related to the deceased student, or to their grief. After awhile, Doug decided to test the situation by directing the group to return to regular class schedules. After giving them passes to rejoin their classes, he said they could return for additional help. Then he waited for students to filter back. They did not.

Strategies to Support Return to Routine

Students who have a difficult time returning to their routines may benefit from strategies beyond simply encouraging them to return to their pre-crisis schedule. Doug outlined several strategies framed as questions. Real problem solving may help the troubled student design a plan to address the question, "How can we get you through today?"

For the more severely affected student, the problem may be framed, "How can we get you through this afternoon?" or "How can we get you back to class?" or "How can we get you through the next two hours?" A re-integration technique includes guided questions or statements to develop coping strategies.

Questions to Facilitate Return to Routine

1. Compared to yesterday, how do you feel today?
2. Do you have a support system of friends, family, faith, or a trusted person at school?
3. What is your action plan to get through today and tomorrow?

These questions can lead to brainstorming, problem-solving, and an action plan.

Statements to Facilitate a Return to Routine

- If I feel _____, I will take a break, see a counselor if necessary, and return to class as soon as I am able.
- If I feel _____, I will look at the blackboard or close my eyes and visualize a favorite place, or
  - ✓ Use deep breathing, or
  - ✓ Think of pleasant memories, or
  - ✓ Read the "power card" I carry, describing my struggle, strategies, goals, or I will look at a photo or note from home that is reassuring.

231

✓ If I feel ____, I know I can check in with a counselor at lunch.

✓ If I feel____, I can make it to 11:45 or 2:10 when I can talk with a helping person.

Reestablishing routine is reinforced when the response concludes and disengagement occurs with minimal disruption.

Teachers are informed, supportive, and on the lookout for students who need attention. Systems of support are in place for those who are still distressed.

A "case manager" (usually a school counselor) is assigned to monitor students identified as at risk for stress reactions.

Everything is documented in a resource file for referrals.

Examining Outcomes for Effectiveness

The PREPaRE Model addresses crisis teams examining the response with several types of assessment methods, including 1) *needs assessment* "to identify areas to be addressed, so that plans and strategies may be developed," 2) *process analysis* "to understand what was done and by whom, and to assess whether these activities were consistent with established plans," and 3) *outcome evaluation* "to assess the effectiveness of stated objectives and/or crisis prevention, preparedness, response and recovery activities" (Brock et al., 2009). During examination, the team can discuss general questions such as: "What was effective about the response?" and "How could the response have been more effective?" and "What lessons learned can be applied to future responses?"

PREPaRE also describes criteria that generate data indicating the effectiveness of outcomes and readiness for disengagement. "The school crisis response can be concluded when all individuals have obtained the knowledge and/or support they need to cope with crisis generated problems" (Brock et al., 2009). Therefore, response conclusion does not require that crisis-generated problems are *solved,* only that individuals can *cope effectively.*

PREP<u>a</u>RE:
"Outcomes That Reflect Effectiveness"

Data-Driven Criteria to Evaluate
Readiness for Disengagement

- Responders have provided crisis intervention indicated by psychological triage;
- Individuals with psychopathology have been provided appropriate treatment and referral;
- Individuals with maladaptive coping behaviors have been referred to appropriate professionals and potential lethality has been reduced;
- Aggressive, delinquent, and criminal behavior occur in school at or below pre-crisis levels;
- Students attend school at or above pre-crisis attendance rates;
- Student academic functioning is at or above pre-crisis levels.

Importance of District Team Debriefing for Demobilization and Closure

PREP<u>a</u>RE recommends debriefing with crisis responders to examine response effectiveness and to care for the caregiver. This is particularly important for the district team since demobilization for most responders means leaving the team support network and returning to schools and families not familiar with their experience.

Demobilization of crisis teams after a severely traumatic event should include plans for a timely closure debriefing session. While each team member may be affected differently and to varying degrees, every member benefits from peer support and a recovery plan to fit individual needs. After disengaging, it remains important to continue supporting teachers and other staff who need it (Brock et al., 2009).

Main Aspects of Debriefing for Closure

It is useful to ask a writer to document debriefing themes. Here's how a closure debriefing works.

- Caregivers tell stories and express their feelings.
- Caregivers discuss the most difficult aspects of the response and what went well.
- Caregivers document effective interventions along with data that demonstrates return to pre-crisis capacity.
- Caregivers discuss "what could we have done better?" And, they consider whether policy and procedures should be modified.
- Caregivers ask and answer, "What did we learn about our team or crisis response that will be helpful in the future? Can we identify challenges unique to this response?"
- How are we taking care of ourselves? Are we equipped with individualized recovery plans?

Closure

Reaching *closure* following a traumatic incident may be more complicated and elusive than the specific acts comprising disengagement and demobilization. Closure is more a state of mind, like finding meaning or acceptance or purpose as one looks to the future. The way disengagement is conducted can help the responder and others reach closure, but there is no timetable. For many who have experienced tragic events, closure may not even be an operative term. We continue to carry some events with us, perhaps taking comfort that others share our experience and knowing that we have something of value to share with others.

22

Compound Stress
of Dual Tragedies

Abstract

Two middle school students are accidentally killed within one month. The first is accidentally shot to death by a friend. The second is struck and killed by a car. This case study describes crisis counseling and interventions after each incident, including equity of remembrance and the impact of successive traumatic events on the staff and student body. Sample letters to parents are included. *Themes are: 1) effects of repeated trauma; 2) issue regarding equity of memorials; 3) system-wide triage; 4) addressing intense anger.*

INTRODUCTION

The accidental death of a middle school student at the beginning of the school year was devastating. Imagine the impact of a second sudden, accidental death of a student exactly one month after the first. Not only are the emotions of the first death re-visited by the impact of the second, but impressionable middle school students begin to imagine being "cursed" and dreading what that date next month might bring.

Joel Meyers and Norman Pitt (1976) wrote about traumatic events strikingly similar to what occurred at this school. Two students died suddenly in accidents one month apart. Some children began engaging in disruptive classroom behavior; some experienced symptoms of anxiety disorders; bomb threats were called in; superstitious rumors circulated that a third student would die. Meyers and Pitt used a consultative approach to develop a teacher workshop providing psychoeducation to address 1) student feelings, 2) the bereavement process, 3) teacher feelings, and 4) recommendations. Students were encouraged but not pressured to express their feelings and concerns, which were addressed to support effective coping. Stabilizing and educating adult caregivers prepared them to recognize student needs. This had a positive impact on the recovery process. After the intervention, teachers reported a significant reduction in students' disruptive behavior.

The present case study provides an example of how a previous case study can inform the response to a similar situation (Meyers & Pitt, 1976).

Here's what happened. Two ninth grade boys skipped school in early September and burgled a house where they found two handguns in a shoebox. While engaging in horseplay with one of the guns, one boy fatally shot his fourteen-year-old friend in the head. He called 9-1-1, then panicked and fled. The survivor pleaded guilty to manslaughter and was treated, while incarcerated, for post-traumatic stress disorder for killing his best friend. As part of the adjudication, the court required him to speak to young people about the danger of guns.

PREVENTION/MITIGATION

Jimerson et al. (2012b) point out that prevention may not always be possible, but a flexible, comprehensive crisis plan can include preparation for specific incidents such as sudden, accidental death, including the suicide or homicide of a student or a staff member. Planning for unusual, severely traumatic events can mitigate trauma, support grief and coping, and educate caregivers when a crisis occurs. Having two sudden student deaths, one the accidental shooting and the other, a girl struck by a car, in close temporal proximity is extremely rare. The effect of the two tragic events compounded the trauma and challenged the capacity to respond (Jellinek & Okoli, 2012).

236

PREPAREDNESS

Preparing comprehensive, yet flexible response plans can promote psychological first aid and long term follow-up for the unexpected death of students or staff (Jimerson et al., 2012b). These types of severely traumatic events do not lend themselves to school-wide drills and practice involving students, but can be considered and practiced using discussion-based exercises such as tabletop drills and workshops (Reeves et al., 2010).

Jellinek and Okoli (2012) and Jimerson et al. (2012b) recognized that students who experience the sudden, violent death of a relative or close friend are at high risk for psychological trauma. Brymer et al. (2012a) observe that a school's history of previous adverse events is among the key factors influencing how it responds to a traumatic incident. Worden (2009) cautions that reactions to sudden death are often intense and expressed by a variety of emotions, including sadness, shock, anger, fear, guilt, numbness, and confusion. It is reasonable to expect that unexpected traumatic incidents repeated in close proximity could place students at higher risk for stress reactions, increase perceptions of potential threat, and generate more intense feelings of shock, fear and anger. During a second crisis, it makes sense for the responder to anticipate the higher level of risk and intense feelings. Meyers and Pitt (1976) demonstrated the benefits of informing and emotionally stabilizing a school staff and encouraging, but not pressuring students to express their feelings and concerns.

RESPONSE

While both boys had attended the middle school the previous year, they were registered to attend a district high school in the current year. The victim had even practiced during the summer with the high school football team. His personality was outgoing and he was popular. He was described as being "loved" by seventh and eighth grade students at the middle school. The tragedy touched students and staff throughout the district. While conducting *primary triage*—identifying students and staff who potentially needed direct support—responders determined that the crisis team should be deployed to both the high school and the middle school (PREPaRE Model: Primary Triage: Evaluating Psychological Trauma). Responders were also sent to a second high school and an elementary school where students knew the victim. As it turned out, the need was most extensive at the middle school.

An e-mail sent to the administration and staff of the affected middle and high schools directed all media questions to the superintendent's office. The superintendent assumed this task because of the sensitive nature of the incident, the need for consistent responses to questions, and the desire to reduce the burden on building administrators. Consultation between principals and superintendent was ongoing.

Triage and Crisis Counseling: Dealing with Grief and Intense Anger

Responders provided intensive crisis intervention for individuals and for groups at the middle school for several days (PREPaRE Model: Provide Interventions and Respond to Psychological Needs). To inform the broad scope of triage assessment, students completed a form responding to the following statement, "When I heard the news about the death of _____, a former middle school student, my reaction was _____." The form also invited students to check one of the following choices: "I would like to speak with a counselor today" or "I do not need to speak with a counselor at this time." The forms were maintained by a school counselor who was also a member of the district team. As an immediate screening device, the forms were reviewed by the counselor and members of the crisis team during debriefing sessions, serving one aspect of ongoing triage.

About thirty students received crisis intervention services in small groups and individually. During these interventions, responders began the process of *secondary triage*—monitoring reactions during interventions to determine if students and staff had adequate support, or needed more intensive treatment (PREPaRE Model: Secondary Triage: Evaluating Psychological Trauma). In addition to anticipated grief for the victim, many expressed strong feelings of anger toward the shooter. Some made statements like, "It was a plot to kill him" or "He did it on purpose." Responders listened and feelings were accepted, but conclusions about the shooter's intentions were challenged.

It was frustrating for the responders to address the many comments and questions about the shooter's motivation since these details were unknown. Emphasis was placed on known facts, the shooter's claim that it was a horrible accident, and how both boys made a series of tragic mistakes that day. Crisis counselors had teachable moments, but little legal information. Court proceedings were ongoing. Students were educated about the negative impact of rumors. Circumstances and statements ultimately led to placing responsibility with the teen who pulled the trigger, but also established that it was done accidentally, with no intention to harm.

Anger is often one of the emotions observed during grief reactions, especially when there is a sudden, violent death. However, "off target" anger directed toward peers because they were smiling or not expressing sorrow in an "appropriate" manner was also observed (Jellinek & Okoli, 2012). This generally led to teachable moments about different perspectives toward the deceased and the variety of ways people express grief. Educating students about various reactions and tolerance for differences was an important focus of intervention (PREPaRE Model: Psychoeducation). While angry *feelings* expressed during crisis counseling were accepted, if a student threatened the shooter or another with physical harm, a contract was required stating the student would not retaliate against the shooter or someone not grieving the "right" way. There was discussion about peaceful alternatives and ways were explored to support the constructive expression of feelings. The student was advised that an administrator would be informed of the contract and would follow-up as a non-punitive, supportive resource.

RECOVERY

The circumstances of this traumatic incident were laden with strong emotions. Perhaps due to factors such as the confusing circumstances of the sudden death and the deceased student's non-status on the middle school roster, the opportunity for a school-wide memorial or recognition was not provided. A teenager had fatally shot his friend, and more information, understanding, and time would be needed to wade through the nightmare and try to make sense of it. For a few students, *tertiary triage* identified the need for ongoing monitoring and referral for further treatment (PREPaRE Model: Tertiary Triage: Evaluating Psychological Trauma). Unfortunately, the student body of this middle school would not have much time to again experience normal routine.

RESPONSE

Second Tragedy Compounds Trauma

Exactly one month after the shooting, a seventh grade girl was struck and killed by an automobile early one evening while crossing a four-lane roadway. While she was not as well known in the school as the shooting victim, there was a large outpouring of sadness. The school community was severely impacted by the cumulative effect of a second tragedy. Many students who had been affected by the first death needed to be seen again by crisis counselors, whether or not they knew the more recent victim. We learned the important lesson that students or staff may exhibit delayed stress reactions and that such reactions may not surface until triggered by a subsequent event (PREPaRE Model: Evaluating Psychological Trauma: Idiosyncratic Consequences of Crisis Exposure). Responders were prepared to treat reactions associated with both events.

The contrast in circumstances and personalities of the two deceased young people illustrates that these factors mediate the intensity of reactions and response needs. The boy was generally well known and died a violent, shooting death. The girl's death was more clearly accidental. She was quiet, with some interesting, apparently contradictory qualities. She was artistic and often wore black in the "gothic" style, but was also active and admired in a local Girl Scout troop. Some who were counseled had not understood or accepted her, resulting in the need to work through guilt feelings. The circumstances of the boy's death left more anger to be addressed.

The school administrators, counselors, nurse, and secretaries were extremely sensitive in accommodating the district team during a time when they were personally reeling. In turn, specific members of the crisis team were assigned to support the principal and other administrators, overwhelmed by the weight of the second fatality. Secretaries were provided a script to help them respond to phone inquiries. The school and district crisis teams met for an early morning briefing where they planned together support for students, staff, and community. Primary triage was a priority, accomplished by brainstorming to identify students in close emotional proximity to the recently deceased student (friends, Girl Scout members, homeroom and subject classmates) and those vulnerable to re-traumatization. The school's phone tree was activated to inform staff of a 7 a.m. meeting in the library.

The principal took the lead, while school psychologists and counselors helped facilitate the early morning staff meeting. The focus was on supporting staff members and providing them with information to monitor and support students (PREPaRE Model: Caregiver Training: Psychoeducation). Teachers and support staff were provided information about the unique challenges and potentially intense level of reactions that could be associated with a second sudden, traumatic incident in close proximity to the first. Key points reviewed were student reactions to trauma, how to listen and be supportive, the need to monitor student reactions, and if necessary, how to refer a student to the crisis team for supportive intervention. Teachers and support staff had been e-mailed practical information about understanding reactions and helping students cope. Staff was also reminded about caring for themselves and each other, and the availability of floating substitute teachers and supportive resources if needed.

Triage and Crisis Intervention: Planning, Supporting, Informing

In the wake of the death of the second student, the middle school library was set up for triage of students needing support

241

when they entered the building. Six groups of paired counselors visited every classroom to support students and teachers, and to gather information to evaluate needs. The purpose of these brief classroom meetings was to provide students with knowledge of crisis facts, address their questions and concerns, and with their teachers, to begin to identify students needing further intervention (PREPaRE Model: Classroom Meetings). A psychoeducational process was conducted in the home room and classes of the deceased student due to the emotional proximity of these students to her. This more direct level of intervention shared crisis facts while dispelling rumors, informed students about and normalized common crisis reactions, provided information about maladaptive reactions and how to cope, helped caregivers identify students needing further intervention, and helped students develop a plan that included strategies for managing stress (PREPaRE Model: Student Psychoeducational Group).

Approximately 30-40 students were seen individually or in small groups throughout the day. The library was spacious for both large and small groups. It had adjoining rooms where counselors could meet with students individually, or in small groups when needed. Bottled water, tissues, writing and art materials were made available. Students were given the opportunity to express sympathy in a "memory book" and on a paper mural to be sent to the family (PREPaRE Model: Ensure Perceptions of Safety and Security: Providing Opportunities to Take Action). The nature of the comments in the memory book and on the mural were monitored for depressive or "at risk" statements as part of *secondary triage,* and to make certain they were appropriate for the family. Students were informed that the principal would present the book and mural to the family prior to the funeral.

Primary triage began at the initial team briefing. Those identified as vulnerable were seen either individually or in small, homogeneous groups having similar reactions. Some referred students entered the library together, forming small groups. Others wandered in alone, and either joined an appropriate group or talked with a responder individually. Those providing interventions constantly conducted *secondary triage* to identify those who were at risk and in need of follow-up and possible referral.

A letter from the principal was sent home to the family of every student, informing them of the second tragic death. The crisis team debriefed several times throughout the day to share themes expressed during crisis interventions, generate names of students needing follow-up, arrange for parent contacts, and plan the next interventions. These debriefings were planned by crisis team leaders in consultation with the principal with care to make certain that significant stakeholders could attend. Debriefings were generally planned during lunch and after school, with team leaders informing team members of the time and location.

The crisis team determined which students were successfully adjusting and satisfying emotional needs through natural support systems, and which students and staff appeared to need additional intervention or referral for treatment (PREPaRE Model: Secondary Triage: Evaluating Psychological Trauma). At random times throughout the day there were spontaneous, informal meetings involving the principal and team leaders or counselors making necessary decisions or discussing pressing issues.

District provision of substitute teachers was helpful, but their contribution to triage was limited since they did not know the students. The substitutes provided relief for teachers who needed to talk with a colleague or responder, or who wanted to attend the funeral. District support also included helpful consultation by the superintendent and other administrators. The graphics department quickly provided copies of the letters sent home with students at the end of the day.

The sudden, accidental death of a young girl is the kind of traumatic event that touches many district schools. To generate the names of other vulnerable students, contacts were made with principals and counselors at two elementary schools, two other middle schools, and the high school where two of the victim's siblings were students. As a crisis team leader in conversation with the Girl Scout troop leader, I suggested strategies for support (PREPaRE Model: Reestablish Social Support Systems) including referral of troop members to a community agency that supports grief if needed.

243

RECOVERY

A friend of the male shooting victim expressed the legitimate complaint that the opportunity to express memories through a book and murals had not been available after he died (PREPaRE Model: Special Considerations When Memorializing an Incident). He was helped to write a "memory" letter to the shooting victim's mourning family. In hindsight, the school crisis team realized the need to be equitable in planning the extent of appropriate memorial activities (PREPaRE Model: Examine Effectiveness of Crisis Prevention and Intervention). A notable exception is memorialization after a death by suicide, which requires a separate set of cautions regarding how to remember the student while distancing from the self-destructive act (Erbacher et al., 2015; Hart, 2012; Jellinek & Okoli, 2012; Ruof & Harris, 1988; Zenere, 2009a).

The process of emotional healing was underway, and students and staff appeared cared for and supported. *Tertiary triage* was ongoing for students considered vulnerable and needing to be monitored or referred for more intensive support (PREPaRE Model: Tertiary Triage: Evaluating Psychological Trauma). By the morning of the third day of the response, relatively normal routine was reestablished. It does not always happen this quickly when so many are affected, but having a structured and organized response did help facilitate the recovery process.

Some staff from the middle school attended the funeral on the morning of the fourth day. They included the principal and other administrators, the school psychologist, a school counselor, and several teachers. According to family wishes, students were welcome to attend, but families were advised through letters, that children must be accompanied by a parent or guardian. School staff dispersed themselves throughout the chapel, so they could be in proximity to most of the grieving students. A limited number of crisis responders and school counselors remained available at the school on the day of and the day after the funeral to process students' thoughts and feelings as needed.

District and school administrators expressed gratitude for the response effort by schools throughout the district who contributed key personnel, including school psychologists, counselors, nurses, and social workers. Appreciation was also extended to the blended school and district crisis team for working to meet the significant needs of a school population in turmoil (PREPaRE Model: Caring for the Caregiver). When ongoing anxiety was detected, school staff reassured students that the school was not "cursed" and that another student death the next month was highly unlikely. That date passed uneventfully.

Lessons Learned: Reflection and Discussion

1. Young students often display a keen sense of fairness, and should have options for memorializing a classmate whether the number of students who choose to be involved is three or three hundred. Plan memorial options that respect the deceased student regardless of popularity. *What steps would you take to ensure equity and appropriate remembrance options?*

2. When there is a death in the school community, take steps to ensure that triage (identifying students and staff who need direct support) occurs at every school where it is needed. *How can these steps be incorporated into triage?*

3. When there is a sudden or violent death in the school community, there may be instances of "off target" blame, anger, or threats toward innocent students. Often such threats are made by students predisposed to anger or bullying. *What are some ways a crisis intervenor can defuse a potentially volatile situation, and turn it into a teachable moment?*

4. Students must have the option to acknowledge a fellow student's death, regardless of circumstances. Care must be taken not to celebrate, permanently memorialize, or glorify deaths resulting from suicide, criminal, or high-risk behavior.

∼

Letters sent to parents/guardians, edited for confidentiality, follow.

District / School Letterhead

Dear Parents,

Our community and school experienced a tragic event that saddens us deeply. Two former students from last year's eighth grade class were involved in a shooting incident resulting in the death of one of them. We extend our deepest sympathy to the victim's parents, family, and schoolmates.

[School Name] Middle School staff wishes to be supportive and sensitive to all students and their families in helping them cope with this tragedy. This morning, counselors, psychologists, and social workers visited each class to provide students with facts and to dispel rumors. We offered assistance to students having difficulty coping with this news.

We encourage you to listen carefully to your child, answering questions openly and honestly, and letting the children know that we don't have all of the answers about death. Our school staff and district personnel are available to students who need special attention and support.

On behalf of the [School Name] Middle School staff, thank you for your understanding and concern during this difficult time.

Sincerely,
Principal

District / School Letterhead

Dear Parent/Guardians:

The funeral service for _[Student Name]_ will be held on [Date] at [Church and location]. Visitation begins at 10 a.m. followed by a Mass at noon.

If your child plans to attend the service, please do not send your child to school that day. Please escort your child to the service. This will not only show support for the _____ family during their time of grief, but will allow you, the primary caregiver, to be with your child to provide emotional support. It is advisable that no student attend the service without a parent.

At the conclusion of the service, please do not bring your child to school. Children will probably need time to reflect on the events of the past week. Therefore, it is strongly recommended that students _not_ return to school after the funeral.
Sincerely,
Principal

School Letterhead

Dear Parents

Our school and our community has again experienced a great tragedy. We are deeply saddened by the untimely death of [Student Name], a seventh grader, [Day] evening after a pedestrian accident. Our heartfelt sympathy is extended to her parents, family, and schoolmates.

The [School Name] Middle School staff wishes to be supportive and sensitive to all students and their families as we cope. This morning, counselors, psychologists, and social workers visited each class to provide facts as well as assistance to grieving students.

We encourage you to listen carefully to your child, answering questions openly and honestly. Let them know we don't have all of the answers about death. Our school staff and district personnel will be available to students who need special attention and support.

The funeral service for _[Student Name]_ will be on [Date] at the [Name] Funeral Home at [location]. Visiting hours begin at 10 a.m. followed by the service at noon. We advise that no student attend the service without a parent.

If your child plans to attend, please plan to escort your child to the service for emotional support. Do not bring your child to school after the service on that day. Your presence will show support for the _____family during their time of grief. For your child to be excused, please provide a note explaining the absence.

We strongly recommend being with your children after the service as they will probably need time to reflect on the week's events.

On behalf of the [School Name] Middle School staff, thank you for your understanding and concern during this difficult time.

Sincerely,
Principal

23

Leadership and Teamwork

Reflections

From the time the team is established, its leadership style influences its effectiveness during crisis response. Key to maintaining effectiveness is keeping the team vital, energetic, coordinated, and interested in developing skills and seeking knowledge.

Adapting Leadership Styles to Crisis Response

Crisis response is a complex mission requiring multifaceted approaches to leadership. These approaches establish norms that can either enable or obstruct group functioning and effective teamwork. Crisis response often requires a range of services and interventions. Traumatic events quickly consume the time and energy of a single individual, especially if the caregiver is on staff at the affected school. For those shrouded in their school's grief, the ability to evaluate situations and make decisions may be compromised. In these circumstances, the leadership of an outside team can help members of a school team become functional again and able to resume leadership roles. A team approach that coordinates tasks and shares leadership reduces caregiver stress while increasing the effectiveness of interventions.

The complex nature of crisis response is well suited for flexible, shared leadership models such as situational and functional approaches. When a team communicates well, many responders may be observing, sensing, and sharing what needs to be done. It is an immense relief when the weight does not fall on one harried administrator or team leader. While decisive leadership and quick decisions are necessary in some contexts, there remain many opportunities for discussion, consultation, consensus and shared leadership. At times, team members can perform a variety of leadership functions. A well-functioning team becomes more responsive, more competent, and more efficient than any one member.

Leadership Models: Situational and Functional

Situational Leadership Model

In situational models, the facts and circumstances dictate the most appropriate leadership style. Within a particular context, style must be relevant to the task and to the group's skills, developing competence, commitment, and motivation (Blanchard et al., 1985; Fiedler, 1967; Fiedler, 1994; Fiedler et al., 1976; Hersey, 1985; Hersey & Blanchard, 1977).

Chaotic or dangerous emergencies generally require authoritative, directive leadership and quick decision-making. This leadership style can originate from a recognized command center or team leader in the field, often the school principal, or designee. In the event of fire or school bus accident, the Fire Marshal assumes absolute control of the scene. During a crime-related crisis such as a school shooting, command generally comes from law enforcement. After the storm that occurs at the onset of a sudden, chaotic crisis, and after the team has had the opportunity to deliberate and plan interventions, the leadership and decision-making can be both shared and consensus-driven. Given the changing demands of each situation, a trained and experienced team can readily adjust to the most effective leadership style for each crisis.

Three case studies illustrate leadership styles that meet crisis needs.

1. During the terminal illness of a kindergarten teacher, the school principal and counselor had time to consult with the district team and plan with staff. They shared leadership functions and developed resources to support students, teachers, and com-

munity. Support for teachers was especially needed. Their preparations mitigated emotional trauma after the teacher died.

2. Classmates witnessed the sudden death of a middle school student, triggering an emergency that initially required directive, authoritative control by administrators, teachers, and emergency medical services. After the initial shock, the blended school and district teams shared leadership during consensus-driven briefings, ongoing triage, and planned interventions for severely traumatized students. Unanticipated problems arose, including insufficient student input in planning a memorial and insufficient emotional support for staff. Collaboration led the team to a better understanding of how best to resolve those issues.

3. The crossroads encountered after a teacher raped a sixth grader called for clear, directive leadership. Students and teachers were traumatized, the entire school community devastated. A system-wide approach included strong support for response team members, who needed ongoing reassurance and security to work effectively with students. The team leader sensed system-level needs, such as conflict resolution among teaching teams. As the response evolved, shared leadership emerged. The team collaborated on plans for interventions that included conflict resolution.

Fiedler's Contingency Model (1967) includes a discussion of leadership in stressful situations such as crisis response. He recommends a match between the strength of the leader's style and the situational challenge. The leader's ability to handle stress is a key variable in determining control of a situation. Fiedler indicates that leaders having the appropriate style, characteristics, and experience will be most effective during school crises.

Functional Leadership Model

In a functional model, any team member can assume leadership roles so long as that member furthers team goals and addresses *task* or *maintenance* functions (Adair, 1996, 2006; Hackman & Walton, 1986; Hackman & Wageman, 2005a, 2005b). The group's *task* is to pursue their work objectives (what group members want to accomplish). Tasks that advance group goals can include keeping discussions on task, giving and seeking information, clarifying, summarizing, consensus testing, task setting, directing, and time keeping. Group *maintenance* consists of its social and emotional morale—how satisfied group members are with their interactions and relationships. Maintenance functions that facilitate positive feelings leading toward interpersonal satisfaction can include encouraging ideas, solving interpersonal problems, expressing group or individual feelings, gate-keeping to encourage participation, compromise, and team building.

When a group emphasizes task functions but no maintenance, initial productivity can be high. But, even when the group loves its task, it risks eventual conflict, dissatisfaction, and burnout. The flip side is that all maintenance but no task can be fun and it can initially produce group harmony, but it will likely lead to stagnation, disillusionment, and failure to accomplish goals. While optimal levels of task and maintenance can vary with each group's purpose, it makes sense to balance relatively high levels of both task and maintenance. Crisis team leaders and members can monitor the group for necessary task and maintenance functions.

Applying the principles of functional leadership to school crisis planning, selected team members can organize counseling interventions while others can consult with the teaching staff, conduct triage, manage parental concerns, or work with the media. The school principal has ultimate responsibility for the response. There is generally consultation among the school and district teams, with the principal central to major decision-making. The principal may choose to exercise broad-based leadership, designate a colleague, or delegate leadership roles to responding team leaders, while focusing on administrative functions such as constructing letters to families, contacting a grieving family, and leading staff and community meetings.

Distributed leadership models combine elements of situational and functional leadership (Harris, 2008; Ritchie & Woods, 2007; Spillane, 2006; Spillane et al., 2004). Depending upon situational needs, various school and crisis functions can be a collective responsibility shared by administration with individuals and teams designated to assume leadership in their areas of expertise.

Yukl's Multiple Linkage Model (2012) combines aspects of

situational and functional leadership approaches. Leaders can influence work situation variables by developing and improving individual and group performance. His emphasis on teamwork, intervening situational variables, and organization of the task structure aligns with PREP<u>a</u>RE's application of the Incident Command System (ICS) to the structure of complementary roles and functions on school crisis teams (PREP<u>a</u>RE Model: School Crisis Teams: ICS Activities of the School Crisis Team).

PREP<u>a</u>RE's Incident Command System

The PREP<u>a</u>RE Model describes an Incident Command System with a team structure of complementary roles and functions. Under a hierarchical command framework are collaborating sections, including Planning (Thinkers), Operations (Doers), Logistics (Getters), and Finance (Payers). During a response, the operations section provides the most direct interventions to students and staff, supported by other sections and led by the Incident Commander (IC) and crisis management team (Brock et al., 2009). This structure helps teams organize and view responders as part of an interdependent, multidisciplinary system of functional leadership. A Unified Command Structure (UCS) provides leadership in more complex responses, which involve multiple agencies. (National Incident Management System, 2004)

Concepts central to the Incident Command System are *division of labor* and *span of control,* both of which support shared leadership. Division of labor means that according to their knowledge and training, team members are assigned to tasks within one or more of the sections of the command system. This creates an atmosphere of shared influence and many opportunities to exert leadership functions. Span of control means that in most cases a person cannot be in charge of more than seven, and optimally no more than five team members. This also contributes to the opportunity for many responders to coordinate and lead various functions. (Brock et al., 2009)

The reality of our district responses prior to PREP<u>a</u>RE was less hierarchical than the ICS model. There has tended to be less leadership from a district or school level person such as an Emer-

253

gency Operations Director or Incident Commander as prescribed by the model. The superintendent is generally visible and supportive at the affected school early in a crisis. After the initial team briefing and faculty meeting, the superintendent often withdraws from the scene while remaining available for consultation, serving as media liaison, and approving support systems such as the provision of substitute teachers or extra funding when needed. The school principal can assume or delegate the role of Incident Commander to the extent that she or he is comfortable.

Leadership of day to day activities such as debriefing, planning, and decision-making is generally shared among district and building team leaders—usually the school psychologists and counselors. Open communication is facilitated through processes such as sharing information, providing feedback about effectiveness and needs, and brainstorming on how to proceed. The counselors and school psychologist assigned to the affected school are encouraged to gradually take leadership roles in planning and implementing interventions, to the extent they are able. They often overcome their own grief to do remarkable work with their students and staff.

School Principal and Crisis Response Team
A System of Reciprocal Support

While blended school and district teams benefit immeasurably from the support of the building administrator, there must be reciprocal support for the administrator. Throughout the crisis, it is crucial to support the principal's efforts. The response team should seek ways to help the principal accomplish administrative and maintenance tasks. Beyond administrative duties, the principal takes on a tremendous emotional load, feeling the weight of responsibility for what is happening in the school community.

Since the leadership and support of building administration is integral to the response, there is a concerted effort to plan team debriefings at times when the principal and assistant principals can participate and be involved in decision-making. Involving the administrators is, at times, difficult given the demands placed on building administrators during crises (Poland & Poland, 2004). While bearing the burden of their personal trauma, principals must direct routine school business with the added demands of the crisis or threat, heightened student and staff needs, communication with families, media scrutiny, possible liability, and often interaction with police, community agencies, and other service providers (Mears, 2012).

DiRaddo and Brock (2012) observe that nearly all principals face multiple crises throughout their careers. The principal's leadership is essential in deciding the type and extent of a crisis and the appropriate level of response. Trained administrators, crisis teams, and teachers help to facilitate an efficient, organized response that reaffirms a sense of security for students and the school community (DiRaddo & Brock, 2012).

Sharing the Leadership Load: Partnerships and Collaboration

No crisis responder—counselor, school psychologist, or administrator—should have to be a Lone Ranger. No caregiver should be forced to go it alone, without operational or emotional support. A small, rural school district should plan in advance, either to partner with other nearby "buddy" districts and community agencies, or with the nearest large district (PREPaRE Model. School Crisis Teams: Collaboration with Crisis Response Partners). The task, during a severe or catastrophic incident is simply too complex and multifaceted to be confronted by one, two, or even a few able people—especially if their school has been affected and their students and staff are experiencing trauma. A trained team, collaboration, and shared leadership are necessary.

Even the Lone Ranger, the fictional masked hero who "led the fight for law and order in the early west" was not alone. He rode with his Native American friend Tonto from place to place on the plains fighting a lonely but determined battle against lawbreakers preying on citizens. Tonto had the Lone Ranger's back, often putting himself at risk to gather information during a crisis. He was a trusted confidant, sounding board, and problem solver. He understood that his masked friend needed lots of help.

255

The Lone Ranger's mask was a symbol that his mission was more important than his personal identity. His goal was to empower people and leave them better off than when he arrived. He and Tonto had an uncanny knack for leaving at just the right moment. As they left in a "cloud of dust," someone would invariably ask, "Who was that masked man?" They were gone; the people regained control and believed they could care for themselves.

In *The Wisdom of Teams,* Katzenbach and Smith (1993) discuss what makes effective teams and leaders. From their viewpoint, successful team leaders believe they need not make all key decisions, nor assign all key jobs. Consistent with functional leadership, the authors recognize that any member who genuinely believes in the team's purpose can help lead it toward higher performance. Their description of collaborative leadership applies to crisis teams:

> Successful team leaders instinctively know that the goal is team performance instead of individual achievement, including their own...Team leaders act to clarify purpose and goals, build commitment and self confidence, strengthen the team's collective skills and approach, remove externally imposed obstacles, and create opportunities for others. Most important, like all members of the team, team leaders do real work themselves. (p. 131)

Team leaders also learn when their "action can hinder the team, and how their patience can energize it." Knowing they do not have all the answers, team leaders believe success depends on the combined contributions of all members working toward a common purpose. They avoid actions that may constrain the free flow of ideas or intimidate team members. They recognize that the leader's belief in what the team is doing can be "incredibly powerful" (Katzenbach & Smith, 1993).

Essential Qualities:
Crisis Leadership and Teamwork

Given the goals and challenges of school crisis response, essential qualities associated with effective leaders are magnified.
1. Comfort with taking and sharing leadership;
2. Supporting the mission before, during and after crises; and
3. Supporting resilience among affected persons and team members.

Comfort with Taking and Sharing Leadership

- Team leaders develop comfort with the responsibility of dealing with trauma.
- Team leaders defer leadership when appropriate, to the fire marshal, law enforcement, incident commander, school principal, or team members, but never defer the consultative role.
- Team leaders understand that the principal is the school leader, in consultation with the superintendent, incident command and team leaders, although the principal may delegate leadership to those with expertise in crisis intervention.
- Team leaders are ready to take control and make quick decisions when necessary, but are also ready to enlist their colleagues rather than to resolve situations alone.
- Team leaders are flexible, able to use a directive or consensus-driven approach depending on the crisis and they consistently encourage open communication of ideas, feelings, and constructive feedback.
- Team leaders share leadership functions and initiative with team members, while coordinating interventions through briefings and communication in the field.
- Team leaders defer leadership in areas where they lack expertise, and they gain knowledge through consultation and study.

Supporting the Mission:
Before, During and After Crises

- Team leaders build the skills of team members through opportunities for training and professional development in crisis intervention, and also leadership, communication, problem solving, decision-making and teamwork.
- Team leaders continuously encourage performance improvement and empowerment through *personal mastery* (Senge, 2006).
- Team leaders are familiar with community resources and proactively plan with police and fire departments, mental health agencies, hospitals, and crisis management resources.
- Team leaders understand that under duress, the use of checklists, protocols, and forms can be helpful in supplementing knowledge and memory.
- Team leaders schedule team briefings and debriefings and set agendas with input from team members and school staff.
- Team leaders are familiar with triage during response and are content with partial resolution and stabilization of individuals in preparation for referral when needed.
- Team leaders ensure that affected students are escorted to appropriate settings for classroom, group, and individual interventions where trained responders are present.
- Team leaders are present at faculty, staff, and school community meetings.
- With school administrators, team leaders ensure ongoing communication and sharing of appropriate information with students, school staff, parents/guardians, and grieving families.
- To meet student and staff needs, team leaders advocate provision of educational information as needed to administrators, teachers, and support staff (secretaries, cafeteria workers, custodians, and bus drivers).
- Team leaders consult with school administrators prepar-

258

ing letters and memoranda with updates to the school community.

- Aware that teams sometimes get stuck, team leaders review strategies, problem-solve, or seek consultation to resolve issues.

Supporting Resilience
Among Affected Persons and Team Members

- As part of systemic support, team leaders give priority care not only to students, staff, and families, but also to response team members. They recognize the imperative of emotionally stabilizing school staff so they can care for their students.
- Team leaders seek opportunities to educate stakeholders *before* crises and to share psychoeducation *during* and *after* crises.
- During a crisis, team leaders seek opportunities to foster resilience among responders and those who are directly affected. They do this by modeling resilient leadership, optimism, decisiveness, integrity, and effective communication (Everly, 2011).
- To emphasize administrator and staff contributions and foster their self-respect under circumstances that could promote confusion and helplessness, team leaders adopt a side-by-side, consultative approach (Caplan, 1964, 1970; Meyers et al., 1979; Meyers & Pitt, 1976).
- Team leaders can inspire responder resiliency by adopting a *self-efficacy model* (Bandura, 1982; 1997) which recognizes prior success and encourages an optimistic and confident attitude. It can mean offering interpersonal support, coaching team members, and teaching stress management (Everly, 2011).
- While intervening to meet the needs of those affected, leaders encourage empathy but guard against vicarious trauma, which could immobilize responders.
- Team leaders guard against vicarious trauma by monitoring their own emotions and need for relief. They take seri-

ously the concept of "care for the caregiver."

- Team leaders emphasize the importance of closure debriefings to examine response effectiveness and lessons learned; they plan coping strategies to mitigate responder stress reactions.

Conducting effective crisis response requires understanding the varied roles of players, and the harmony of their interdependent parts in the concerted effort. The leader is a team player and the team is part of the leadership. The leader and the team follow each other in service to the task. The task is best served when an interactive process between team and leaders maintains and validates team efforts.

Those who assume leadership roles should be conscious of their personal leadership style and their comfort levels relative to the situational need. For example, one leader may find it challenging to assert an authoritative style. The challenge for another may be to welcome shared functional leadership when needed. Self-knowledge and understanding situational need allows the thoughtful leader to assume appropriate, constructive control while encouraging fellow responders. The words of the Chinese philosopher Lao-Tzu illuminate. Paraphrasing, "The worst leaders, people fear and hate. The good leaders, people honor and praise. As for the best leaders, people do not notice their existence. When the best leaders' work is done, the people say, 'We did it ourselves.' "

Leadership Makes a Difference

On a deep level, a leader can be a catalyst for cohesion, energy, a sense of shared purpose, self-care, and enthusiasm for both mundane and significant tasks. Leadership can create extraordinary teamwork or it can stifle interaction and initiative.

Kouzes and Posner (2012) describe five practices of exemplary leadership relevant to school crisis response that "make extraordinary things happen in organizations." When they *Model the Way,* leaders affirm shared values by their actions. During crises, team leaders model practice that aligns values with active engagement. When they *Inspire a Shared Vision,* leaders enlist others in supporting an exciting vision. Team leaders inspire the commitment of crisis responders by sharing a passionate belief in the process of recovery. When they *Challenge the Process,* leaders search for innovative opportunities to improve. During crises, team leaders confront unique situations and creatively adapt interventions to achieve positive outcomes. To *Enable Others to Act,* leaders build collaborative relationships that strengthen team members' determination to serve. Crisis team leaders seek to empower others, solve problems collaboratively, and share leadership. When team leaders *Encourage the Heart,* they show appreciation for contributions to the mission, which creates a culture of celebration and a spirit of community. During and after crisis response, team leaders communicate appreciation for people's struggle to be resilient, for their acts of kindness, and for the best aspects of human nature under the worst circumstances.

A leader can help a team understand its mission and strive to accomplish that mission with determination and excellence. A leader can help individual team members define their roles, realize their strengths, exert leadership, and recognize each other as part of an interdependent system of support. Good leaders can help develop effective and sometimes amazing team performance.

In the film *Hoosiers,* a high school basketball coach appears single minded and autocratic, emphasizing fundamentals and insisting on best practices. Play the game the right way, develop your skills, be a complete player, depend on teamwork rather than individual talent. At the same time that he challenges his players, he supports their efforts to improve as a team, encouraging the community to respect them, and instilling confidence in all players, including the least talented. When a star-caliber player joins the team, he fits in with their ethic and practice, enhancing his outstanding play and the play of his teammates. Eventually the team begins to believe it can accomplish its goals, deriving strength from each other and from their faith. Ultimately, they assume shared leadership and influence decision-making when it counts the most. When teams work together effectively, they can achieve dramatic results.

My Journey Toward Leadership

My journey toward leadership was not easy. In the formative stages, peers sometimes saw me as a leader although I did not. During graduate school, I discovered styles of leadership that felt comfortable and fit my personality. I took more initiative and some risks. In the process, I discovered and nurtured more assertive and animated aspects of my personality.

Significant growth occurred for me in graduate school at Temple University and while volunteering as a teacher at Project Learn. The graduate program provided a social support network and laboratory for personal growth. My experiences at Project Learn complemented graduate studies, making everything more real.

At first, I felt culture shock at Project Learn. It was not Hogwarts, the fictional school for magic, though it captured the magic of learning. There I realized the power of education motivated by curiosity and joy rather than coercion and fear.

When students at Project Learn called me "teacher," I reflected on what that meant. When a respected teacher observed me tutoring a student and said I had "power," I was puzzled. Eventually, I realized that exerting power does not need to dominate others. Rather, it is the ability to empower others by building trust and helping them accomplish their own learning goals. I enjoyed this leadership role.

Many years later, in my professional work as a school psychologist, I assumed situational leadership upon realizing that my assigned middle school and the entire district had no crisis prevention, preparation, or response plan. I wrote a manual for the middle school and conducted training. I presented on the topic at our state conference and with colleagues, advocated for a district-wide team. We established and trained a team characterized by shared leadership. While I chose to be a school psychologist, it feels like leading a crisis response team chose me.

We developed a model in which several coordinators took leadership of various aspects of the district team response. Early in its existence, the team deployed to an elementary school in response to a horrific incident. After a briefing and faculty meeting, district administrator Dr. Ben Ellis said to me as he prepared to return to the district building, "You are in charge."

At that point, I had knowledge and skills consistent with team leadership, but defined myself as one of the coordinators rather than as a team leader. This crisis needed a leader to work closely with the principal to coordinate interventions. While there was still plenty of shared leadership, the expression of confidence in me by that administrator made an impression on my self-perception as a leader. In the turmoil of crisis, my reluctant journey toward leadership felt validated. Encouragement from an esteemed colleague helped me reach a place of broader self-acceptance and service.

24

Homicide
of a High School Student

Abstract

When a popular high school student is shot to death, the tragedy
is the most recent in a series that traumatizes the community
and its school. One challenge for responders is to legitimize grief
while distancing from the student's destructive involvement in
the drug scene. Our attention turns to cultural competence. An
African American school counselor shares insight into unique
aspects of triage; an administrator discusses the inclusion of
grieving students across racial boundaries. Facing barriers, the
mostly white responders build bridges with African American
students. A sample letter to the community is included. *Themes
are: 1) the effects of repeated trauma on students and staff; 2)
boundaries, barriers, and bridges to cultural competence; 3) issues of
relative need and inclusion in triage; 4) the drug counterculture.*

INTRODUCTION

Effects of Repeated Trauma

The district's crisis team responded three times in one
year to a high school where students were at risk in
neighborhoods where gun violence led, too often, to
serious injury or death. Sometimes a teenager made bad choices
and engaged in high-risk behavior. Other times, an innocent

265

was caught in crossfire. If the crisis team felt the burden of three mobilizations to the school within one year, imagine how threatened the students felt in the midst of frequent violence. A school's history of previous adverse events and its experiences with crisis intervention influence how a school copes with a traumatic incident (Brymer et al. 2012a).

The cycle of violence takes a toll on young people. A brief literature review follows.

PREVENTION/MITIGATION

Children are generally more vulnerable to traumatic events than adults are; childhood psychological trauma can have long-term impact on personality development, and on cognitive and coping abilities (Barenbaum et al., 2004). Some high school students experience severe emotional trauma throughout their childhood and adolescence. While addressing the effects of violent loss on urban youth, Pynoos and Nader (1990) challenge the myth that young people living in environments with cumulative grief experiences become immune to the psychological effects. This mistaken belief can lead to offering little or no intervention services to support students' grief and recovery. The cycle of minimal treatment for violent trauma "increases the possibility of long-term enduring grief." Crisis teams must have both the knowledge of the effects of cumulative exposure to violent trauma and the skills to intervene. Jellinek and Okoli (2012) and Jimerson et al. (2012b) recognized that students who experience the sudden, violent death of a relative or close friend are at high risk for psychological trauma (PREPaRE Model: Evaluating Psychological Trauma).

Violence uniquely affects the grief of urban children (Zenere, 2009b). "Although theirs is a journey that may be foreign to those not raised in environments scarred by such events, it … can be contextually understood. Thus, it is critical that the school mental health practitioner be aware of the factors that influence a child's pathway through bereavement." The effect can be devastating.

The ongoing violence and death in some neighborhoods are compared with the traumatic experience of children living in a war zone (Bell & Jenkins, 1991).

The repetition of traumatic violence can result in debilitating social, emotional, physical, and cognitive symptoms. Parson (1994) describes "urban violence traumatic stress response syndrome" resulting from children's chronic exposure to violence. While a child may initially react with shock and disbelief, "with each subsequent loss exposure, affective responses may become increasingly blunted," according to Zenere (2009b), who catalogs research on some of the developmental outcomes, including social withdrawal, aggressiveness, and/or the consumption of harmful substances (Lubit et al., 2003). Other outcomes may include dissociation, intrusive thoughts, recurrent dreams, flat affect (a severe reduction in emotional expressiveness), or a need to be in constant motion (Ehrenreich, 2001; ICISF, 2006; Parson, 1994). When repeatedly exposed to traumatic incidents, children begin burying their emotions, a process that can lead to unhealthy, sometimes violent outcomes (Zenere, 2009b).

The research speaks to the despair and depression of inner city African American students, who year after year see friends, relatives, older and younger community members die violently on the streets where they live. Some of these deaths are traceable to involvement in the drug trade, or to gangs, or to conflicts resolved with weapons, but many involve simply being in the wrong place at the wrong time (Wong et al., 2007). While some schools and communities unite to discourage involvement with drugs and violence, these problems continue to affect young people.

PREPAREDNESS

Athey and Moody-Williams (2003) emphasize the seriousness of training the crisis teams to be aware of the cultural values, traditions, and needs of each diverse school community (PRE-PaRE Model: Cultural Considerations). They suggest maintaining information about race and ethnicity, languages spoken, local history of race relations, history of trauma, and other pertinent local data. They explain the benefits of becoming familiar with com-

267

munity resources, respected leaders, and language interpreters. They suggest being prepared to implement solutions to cultural problems arising from a crisis. Response teams must understand how various ethnic groups seek help and they must learn cross-cultural outreach strategies. Crisis teams must strictly avoid using prejudicial stereotypes or labels. Young (1997) suggests learning the community's cultural norms on the way emotional pain and grief are expressed, and the reactions and rituals associated with death.

Horowitz et al. (2005) found that African American children and parents prefer to seek emotional support from family members rather than professionals they do not trust. In a study of African American children exposed to chronic violence, Jones (2007) identifies kinship support, an Afro-centric perspective, and spirituality as protective factors. Other researchers connect the church, the religious community, and collaborative religious coping (God and self, working together to solve problems) as additional sources of social support and resilience among African Americans (Kim & McKenry, 1998; Molock et al., 2006).

Summarizing the research, Brock et al. (2009) suggest "school-based mental health professionals seeking to help African American students cope with crises should be particularly aware of the formal kinship support, which may embody values of harmony, interconnectedness, authenticity, and balance, and (they should be) aware of the importance of the Black church."

As crisis responders at the high school, we recognized the significance of kinship, expressed in support provided by trusted educators and peers. The effect was powerful (PREPaRE Model: Reestablish Social Support Systems).

While schools are hard-pressed to prevent neighborhood violence, preparation for response to sudden, violent death as part of a comprehensive school safety, prevention, preparedness, and response plan is vital (Jimerson et al., 2012b). An effective program can provide the kind of care and interventions that might prevent future tragedy (PREPaRE Model: Developing Resilience and School Connectedness: Cultivate Internal/External Resilience).

268

RESPONSE

At the high school where the crisis response team returned three times in one year, a senior had been killed the previous spring. A shooting in the fall left a tenth grade girl seriously injured. The following spring arrived with the shooting death of a popular senior. School counselor Iman Turner learned of the latest tragedy from a student weeping outside his office. School administration confirmed the incident she described to him. The injured young man was taken by ambulance to the hospital. His mother returned to Delaware from work in another state only to see her son taken off life support and die, the latest casualty in the drug war that plagued his community. The district crisis team mobilized the next morning at the invitation of the school administration.

Prior to the faculty meeting before the start of the school day, the school and district response teams met for a briefing. An assistant principal and the counselors led the school team. The acting principal reminded the team that, in these difficult times, as educators and helping professionals, we needed to take care of each other as well as students and staff. The administrator's reminder contained wisdom that comes from enduring a cycle of senseless and sad experiences. He tempered his sensitive leadership with the knowledge that his staff was beleaguered by repeated trauma. When a team's need for self-maintenance is not recognized and met, the team might soon find it exceedingly difficult to accomplish its task (PREPaRE Model: Caring for the Caregiver). Commenting on the impact of increased urban violence, Johnson (1998) writes, "Nowhere has this been worse than the inner city, and no one experiences it more closely than the staff of an inner-city school."

Initial Briefing

Some of the main points of discussion and planning at the early morning briefing included (PREPaRE Model: Crisis Communication Guidelines):

- Sharing facts, as we knew them.
- Discussing what information and supports to provide

teachers and staff at the faculty meeting. Information included a prepared statement to be shared in class with students, anticipated emotional reactions, and monitoring for students needing referral for crisis counseling.

- Discussing what to say—and not say—to students.
- Preparing for triage and support of students in the library and adjacent rooms, including specific areas for large and small groups, and individual counseling. Bottled water, tissues, and fresh fruit would be in the library.
- Brainstorming resulted in generating the names of students expected to need support. These included possibly affected students who were:
    1. In school on the day of the initial briefing
    2. Out of school on the day of the initial briefing
    3. Attending other schools that needed to be contacted.
- Planning to document the names of students receiving interventions. These students might also generate names of peers needing support.
- Planning to observe recurrent expressed themes and identify the needs of students and staff during the interventions.
- Planning to bring the names of counseled students and expressed themes to a debriefing tentatively scheduled around lunchtime. Periodic debriefings would be ongoing throughout the response, and would include these topics:
    1. Sharing salient information about the response;
    2. Sensing needs of students and staff, and planning interventions to meet ongoing needs;
    3. Planning crisis counseling based on triage, and assigning responsibility to contact parents and guardians of students most affected;
    4. Funeral arrangements and wishes of the family, when available.
- Planning support for the administration, including preparation of letters to the school community by the acting principal; contact with the family of the deceased;

270

addressing the media; and arranging to have letters copied at district office.

During the briefing, there was discussion of expected strong feelings, especially sadness, anger, and confusion. The team needed to guide expressions of anger in constructive directions and to anticipate anger and confusion related to the choices and activities that put the victim at risk. An intervention goal was to support grief for the young man while encouraging distance from his self-destructive involvement in the drug trade. We anticipated that the variety of emotional reactions would present teachable moments. Beyond the obvious dangers of the drug scene, we know that people's grief reactions vary to the same situation.

We talked about the response to the similar tragedy a year earlier and tried to apply lessons from that experience to the present case. The results were mixed. We anticipated opportunities to form groups in which students could network and support each other (PREPaRE Model: Reestablish Social Support Systems). We expected opportunities for affected students to seek crisis counseling and support from people they knew and trusted. We needed a plan to monitor student needs throughout the school's physical plant, including areas difficult to monitor. We considered having at least one trusted interventionist, who lived in the community, available in the large group counseling area of the library. We found that no matter what steps are contemplated, it is very difficult, and perhaps impossible to reaffirm perceptions of safety in the face of repeated violence. We knew too that crisis responders must not assure safety that cannot be assured (PREPaRE Model: Reaffirm Physical Health and Safety: Providing Accurate Assurances).

Cultural Boundaries, Barriers and Bridges

As the response unfolded, we realized that while planning is helpful, events do not always go according to plan. The agony, the anger, the tension among dozens of neighborhood students was palpable. They were black and most of the district responders were white. Initially they seemed inaccessible to our support. In previous high school responses, it was typical for students to seek comfort from small peer groups that crisis counselors could work with. The present groups seemed different — their boundaries more guarded, less permeable. Many formed their own tight, private, support system in which grief was evident but at the same time hidden behind closed mouths and faces devoid of expression. Some of the silence was probably shock, but there were also tears. One student, who spoke incoherently, was either under the influence of drugs, facing emotional collapse, or both. Sometimes in crisis response, the incredible becomes the norm. Several responders noticed a trickle of blood flowing from a crude bandage around a student's lower leg. He was sent to the school nurse for treatment of a gunshot wound.

The library, where students were to receive *psychological triage,* was nearly empty. Sporadically students trickled in, and there were instances of individual or small group psychological first aid. In these instances, compassion and empathy from responders knew no racial boundaries or division. However, in this circumstance, large groups of grieving black students were faced with many counselors whom they did not know. We were strangers to them, mostly white strangers. I imagine their expectation was that we had little understanding of their sorrow, their despair, or their world. We could genuinely care, try to connect, maybe even provide a measure of help by our presence, or a word or some brief intervention (PREPaRE Model: Identifying and Responding to Emotionally Overwhelmed Students).

During this difficult time at the high school, it often seemed that skills, caring, and cultural competence were not enough. I'm not knocking cultural sensitivity. Cultural understanding was definitely helpful, but I'm especially thankful for our African American colleagues, who were sensitive, skilled, and familiar with the students, their culture and community. These colleagues included the acting principal, two assistant principals, the counselor, and two interventionists. Each of them understood what the students were experiencing and they remained to support the students long after the district response team had left campus. These colleagues understood their students on a deeper level than I imagined. I learned later that each of these educators had experienced the violent death of meaningful people in their own lives. They felt kinship with the suffering students, a kinship that was forged in mutual pain and, for that reason, was invaluable (PRE-PaRE Model: Developing Resilience and School Connectedness: Cultivate Internal/External Resilience).

During the first day of response, we learned that a group of twelve to fifteen young men and women were huddled close and secure in the small basement office of a staff member who lived in their community and who provided comfort and support for students in their time of need. His work in the school supported academic and behavioral success, especially for students with challenging behaviors. They chose to be together in his office, protected like a tiny fortress supporting each other, but not accessible to our counseling. We allowed them their safe space and privacy (PREPaRE Model: Reaffirm Physical Health and Safety/ Reestablish Social Support Systems). We tentatively offered group counseling, but it was difficult in that crowded, rectangular office, nearly overflowing as a human barrier to the intrusion of more adults. What helped most was the presence of adults who had been in these students' lives, whom they knew and trusted— the African American counselor, assistant principal, and social worker from our district response team. They took the lead. Other responders wove a system of support for them.

One assistant principal, who had seen too much of this kind of misery, freely expressed her grief. She shed tears for the latest victim of street crime and for the students and staff who grieved his loss. She met with grieving students in her office and spent time with students in the staff member's basement office. Two social workers from the district response team supported her efforts. The assistant principal showed me a video she had taken on her cell phone of a pep rally where the deceased student was smiling, handsome, and happy in his role as master of ceremonies. He was obviously talented. It was heartbreaking to know his potential was snuffed out by gunshot.

Eventually, all of the students needing support were encouraged to use the library and adjoining rooms where they could be together or get crisis counseling from those they knew, as well as from some of the counselors on the crisis team. The team gained better access to the most affected students and we monitored their emotional status (PREPaRE Model: Secondary Triage: Evaluating Psychological Trauma). The change presented an opportunity to engage in a structured PREPaRE intervention, "Student Psycho-educational Group"(Brock et al., 2009) where student questions were answered and rumors dispelled. We discussed and helped to normalize reactions while using *secondary triage* to identify maladaptive reactions of students possibly needing referral. We taught stress management strategies. We identified and reinforced positive support systems and adaptive coping, including the development of stress management plans. The students used art materials that were provided, and seemed consoled in doing so. Many contributed to a memory book for the grieving family (PREPaRE Model: Providing Opportunities to Take Action).

Those who were grieving included students in their senior year, some of them college bound. All were connected to the neighborhood where they live. Many of them knew who bought drugs, who sold them, and who had guns in the criminal subculture. Some felt responsible for not saving their fellow student who had died. School counselor Iman Turner described crisis counseling as being willing to sit in silence, to listen, to hear their stories, to understand, and to ask questions for clarification. His goal was to help students reflect on their own questions and figure out what they needed to do.

Iman outlined the work that was ahead. Short-term tasks were to grieve, to support the family of the deceased student, and to maintain academic goals. Long-term tasks included persuading students that they could reject the path to drugs and violence and encourage others to do the same. They could connect with faith-based support networks; and they could make commitments to themselves, their health, and to their families. They could tell family and friends of their love for them and they could give all that they have to give to become better people. These themes helped students mourn this loss, and to distance them from destructive choices by challenging them to strive for fulfilling lives (PREPaRE Model: Providing Opportunities to Take Action).

One student who sought counseling stood out because he was different. A tall, lanky, white youth, known to be involved in the drug scene, appeared shaken. Maybe he was scared, and identifying with the deceased student, whom he probably knew through an unfortunate sharing of bad choices. Haunted by fearful insights, he knew the mourning that was in progress could have been for him. Several times, he came looking for school counselor, Iman Turner. Feeling traumatic stress, he sought consolation in the counselor he trusted, one with whom he had a relationship that transcended race and ethnicity.

Triage: Unique Issues and Relative Need

In this response, as in others, there were nuances of pain and opportunities for learning. When I visited the school counselor, Iman Turner, to hear his views on the response, he discussed a challenging aspect of *psychological triage* associated with violent death in the drug counterculture. Some young people in the community glorified the combat, elevated the violence, and viewed the dead teenager as a fallen warrior, a hero. While an element of reverence was present, it was not necessarily grief or mourning. While stunned, and perhaps confused by the killing, they felt connected by street life, using and selling drugs, and being part of the gun counterculture. They were shocked and perhaps saddened, but not necessarily in the throes of sorrow like the students and community members who grieved for the young man. Iman leveled with them. They were not the priority in triage. He respected their feelings, but his priority was to be available to those grieving the loss of a friend, a neighbor, a classmate (PREPaRE Model: Secondary Triage: Evaluating Psychological Trauma).

The counterculture young people appeared almost in awe of the circumstances of the death. They were generally respectful, but did not display the kind of grief demonstrated by other students who knew the victim as a vibrant, complicated human being who had made bad choices. Some who grieved had grown up with him. Others had been with him through four years of high school, getting to know and appreciate his hopes, dreams, and aspirations. Now they grieved dreams not deferred, but snuffed out.

The school counselor elaborated on the need to explore the feelings of the counterculture youth whose interest ranged from curiosity to worship—and possibly grief. He respectfully explored their feelings with them, sorting out those who truly needed grief counseling. He talked with them honestly about differences in various reactions to the death. For those caught up in the counter-culture mystique of drugs and violence, he exercised a profound teachable moment. The drug culture, with its money, materialism, and temporary highs, seduces poor urban youth who are without hope or dreams. They soon learn how fickle the drug culture is when a temporary high turns into long-term addiction, and fast money becomes a target on the back of those who have suc-cumbed to its abridged charms. Drug culture truth is concealed, its promise of affluence is a lie. Drugs kill hope for the future and drugs kill young men and women.

Iman took the opportunity to plant the seed, hoping it would grow. He left the students with challenges: Reflect on this death. Reflect on your lifestyle. Contemplate change. Think about mak-ing choices that are life affirming, rather than self-destructive. "You can come back and talk with me. You don't need to die," he said. Through all of this, Iman grieved for the young man who died. The counselor was frustrated. He wanted to prevent sense-less deaths.

RECOVERY

At the funeral, the deceased student was remembered with affection, but the eulogies did not glorify the actions that led to his death (PREPaRE Model: Special Considerations When Memo-rializing an Incident). The aftermath of the funeral signaled a reasonable return to normal routine at the high school.

After the response, an assistant principal shared insights from her perspective. We discussed the frustration of embracing grieving students under circumstances in which bad choices lead to homicide. We responded to a situation devastating to a com-munity. She said, however, we ought not restrict the response to those we think are affected—that we could have and should have included all students in the response. While letters were sent home to the entire school community, we had clearly focused interventions on the genuine, obvious need of black students, most from the neighborhood of the deceased student.

The assistant principal spoke of being approached by white students who felt the loss of their classmate. They said they felt "out of it." They did not feel as though they had the opportunity to take part in the grieving. For some of them, the young man's death evoked feelings associated with the loss of a family member or a friend. While it is understandable that the focus of attention was African American students, the response should have been more inclusive in reaching out to all students troubled by this tragedy (PREPaRE Model: Examine Effectiveness of Crisis Prevention and Intervention).

Valarie Molaison (2003) dispels the myth that when a student dies, we should inform only those most closely affected.

> When someone dies in the school community, it affects the entire community. True, some will be affected more than others, but tragic or untimely deaths are often met with strong emotional reactions, even in those who did not know the person. Further, it is not possible to discern who will or will not be closely affected by the death. Sometimes people have links with one another outside of school that are not known by school officials.

Saltzman et al. (2001) emphasize the need to collect information about students from multiple sources, using multiple methods. They provide a school-based screening and group treatment protocol for adolescents exposed to community violence.

The assistant principal said that, in a crisis, racial barriers between responders and students are not of uppermost importance. Students experiencing grief are generally receptive to the provision of care, comfort, and support, but cultural competence is necessary. She asked, "How would I, as a black crisis responder, feel intervening with all Asian American students and families grieving the death of an Asian American student? Could I be more helpful if I was sensitive to and had a deeper understanding of the Asian experience and culture?"

In retrospect, I believe there are many ways to demonstrate cultural competence. It is helpful when the larger culture embraces and values other cultures while accommodating their norms. There can be expressions of respect for individuals and their culture. It helps to be interested and willing to ask, to learn about, and to understand cultural differences and similarities. I never underestimate the power of empathy, respectfully shared across cultural traditions and values. Whenever possible, we must strive to include school and community leaders, crisis responders, and language interpreters who are trusted sources of comfort (PRE-PaRE Model: Specific School Crisis Planning Issues: Cultural Considerations).

∽

Some years later, I returned to the high school to interview an administrator. In the hallway at the door to the counseling suite, one counselor, who I knew, pressed a cell phone to her ear. Walking by, I heard her say the word "killed." After all these years, my ears were attuned to tragic discourse. Though she said it softly, the word seemed to reverberate through the corridor. School staff congregated in the library. I gazed through the double doors and saw members of the district crisis response team—my colleagues, my friends. As she entered the library, the counselor with the cell phone told me a male student had been shot and killed during a robbery.

I declined her invitation to enter the library as I had retired and was no longer a team member. Although my feelings were mixed, it would have been inappropriate to join a cohesive team that had strong leadership. I wanted to be involved yet felt relief that I did not have to be. Feeling a need, a pull to be with the team, I knew my heart was with them. I felt for them. A part of me will always be with the team.

Lessons Learned: Reflection and Discussion

1. Repeated, violent traumatic incidents in neighborhoods near schools have a cumulative, debilitating effect on students and staff. *What steps would help a crisis team to guide students and staff in coping with the terrible effect of repeated violence and death?*

2. It is beneficial for the crisis team to understand cultural norms such as the expression of emotional pain, reactions to trauma, and sources for social support among African American youth. Most beneficial is having trusted school and district responders who are African American. *How can a crisis team develop an understanding of cultural norms and the value of diverse team membership? What are the benefits?*

3. A violent or deadly outcome of criminal or high-risk behavior generates confused and contradictory feelings such as sadness and anger in grieving students. *How do crisis counselors legitimize the expression of grief for a young man killed in drug-related violence while encouraging distance from, and constructive anger toward his destructive choices?*

4. Students initially ignored the library set-up for triage and intervention in favor of the small office of a trusted African American staff member, where the security of peer support was available. *How can responders respect students' need for peer support and security? How can responders encourage students to reduce the defensive boundaries that they feel in favor of benefiting from access to all available resources?*

5. Triage after urban violence presents unique challenges, such as having to distinguish the different needs of those who grieve the death from those in awe of a "fallen warrior." *How are priorities set? And how are different needs addressed in triage and crisis counseling?*

6. In this case study, crisis responders held a false, unstated assumption that only African American students needed to grieve and receive support. *Without minimizing the anguish and needs of African American students, how can the team support all students in their grief and desire to recognize the death of a fellow student?*

The following is an edited letter to parents and guardians after a homicide.

District / School Letterhead

Parents and Guardians of [School Name] High School Students:

On Friday, [Date], our high school lost a member of its family to an act of senseless violence in the city of _____. [Name of Student] was scheduled to graduate with his class on June 1. Instead he will be mourned by many and buried in the coming days.

Our students, faculty, and staff observed a moment of silence today, and grew a little closer in memory of a classmate, friend and student. Faculty and staff, the district crisis team, Wellness Center staff, counselors, school psychologist, and nurse met this morning in advance of our students' arrival. Throughout the day all students and staff were offered the opportunity to speak directly with a counselor to express their sadness and grief.

I speak from the unfortunate experience of losing a loved one when I say that death is extremely difficult to discuss with a child. If you recognize that your child is experiencing grief as a result of this tragic event, I urge you to seek counseling either through referral by your private physician or by contacting one of our guidance counselors at [phone number]. Our counselors have done an outstanding job in listening to the children and providing guidance and support. The mental health and physical well-being of our students is paramount always. We will continue to offer support throughout the week.

Please contact me directly, or any member of the administrative staff with your concerns or questions. Thank you for your continued support for our students, faculty, and staff.

Sincerely,
Acting Principal

25

Systems Thinking

Reflections

Maintaining the energy and vitality of even the best programs and teams is a challenge. As a crisis responder, one of the most exciting aspects of team maintenance is expanding the group's learning and awareness. Each new response evokes lessons learned from past responses, but also provides an opportunity to apply the knowledge gained from models such as PREPaRE and the awareness that comes from systems thinking (Brock, 2011; Brock et al., 2009; Reeves et al., 2011).

In *The Fifth Discipline* (2006), Peter Senge states that systems thinking requires us to "give up the illusion that the world is created in separate, unrelated forces…" He describes a rainstorm:

> A cloud masses, the sky darkens, leaves twist upward, and we know that it will rain. We also know that after the storm, the runoff will feed into groundwater miles away, and the sky will grow clear by tomorrow. All these events are distant in time and space, and yet they are all connected within the same pattern. Each has an influence on the rest, an influence that is usually hidden from view. You can only understand the system of a rainstorm by contemplating the whole, not any individual part of the pattern. (pp. 6-7)

Senge views human endeavors as systems "bound by invisible fabrics of interrelated actions." He observes that being "part of that lacework" makes it more difficult to see the "whole pattern of change… We tend to focus on snapshots of isolated parts of the system, and wonder why our deepest problems never seem to get solved. Systems thinking is a conceptual framework, a body of knowledge and tools that [have] been developed… to make the full patterns clearer, and to help us see how to change them effectively."

Many theorists, researchers, and practitioners have contributed to our understanding of human systems. They developed concepts and techniques to help navigate systems and interacting subgroups. They have been courageous explorers of human relations, charting maps that help identify how the dynamic interaction of variables impacts the system as a whole. This knowledge has enabled us to intervene on many levels to address problems. We are able to become process observers and to diagnose group and system needs. We can then intervene to facilitate change, moving people and organizations toward conflict resolution and solutions that promote recovery.

The Systems Work of Kurt Lewin and Salvador Minuchin

Theorists Kurt Lewin and Salvador Minuchin have made immense contributions through their work on systems theory. Both Lewin and Minuchin developed theoretical frameworks and applications that have expanded our understanding of systems and ways of modifying them to produce positive outcomes. They have helped us see and comprehend more of the world by recognizing its complexity and connectedness. We can appreciate the nuances of social interaction and apply constructs that simplify complexity. That, in turn, enables us to fashion and adapt techniques with people and systems in distress. We are able to see human interaction more clearly, and to design interventions that rally the processes of constructive change.

Kurt Lewin

In his empirical research, Kurt Lewin collected scientific data to explain factors that influence motivation, leadership, and problem solving. He developed and applied techniques to improve group processes. An influential study by Lewin, Lippitt, and White (1939) examined the effects of *autocratic, democratic,* and *laissez-faire* leadership styles on groups and their members. That research demonstrated that significant social issues could be studied experimentally. Lewin sought to develop a problem-solving process that takes into account forces acting upon problem situations.

Lewin's ideas, including *Field Theory* (1951) revolutionized the study of group dynamics, organizational development, and systems change. Lewin's *force field analysis* uses vectors to illustrate forces that move toward or away from desired goals. These *helping and restraining* forces are in opposition, but constitute a balance, or "quasi-stationary equilibrium" that represents the current state of affairs. Systemic movement toward the ideal state of affairs (or desired goals) is achieved by designing interventions that change the opposing forces. *Helping forces,* which move in the direction of the ideal state can be strengthened or developed; *restraining forces,* which move away from the ideal state can be weakened or removed. The change agent may choose to intervene on one or more of the helping or restraining forces, thus changing the equilibrium and consequently, the system as a whole.

Four Basic Questions of Force-Field Analysis

- What are the factors likely to restrain movement toward the desired state?
- What are the factors likely to help movement toward the desired state?
- What actions might weaken or remove factors that restrain movement toward the desired state?
- What actions might strengthen or develop factors that support movement toward the desired state?

283

In school crisis response, movement toward the desired state is facilitated by interventions that begin the process of recovery and the return to pre-crisis capacity.

Salvador Minuchin

In his book, *Families and Family Therapy* (1974), Salvador Minuchin applied systems thinking to enhance our understanding of dynamic family structures and interaction. His "structural family therapy" provides "a body of theory and techniques that views the individual as part of a larger social context." Within the family social system, the individual must adapt and change, but in so doing, also influences other family members. The individual is a part of the system in which relationships are influenced by interacting structures that are part of the whole.

The family system must be able to adapt to changing circumstances. There must be a sufficient range of "alternative transactional patterns" and flexibility to use them when the system is stressed or needs restructuring. "The boundaries of the family subsystems must be firm, yet flexible enough to allow realignment when circumstances change... If a family responds to stress with rigidity, dysfunctional patterns occur..." Dysfunctional systems usually include unresolved conflict within and between subsystems of the family; these patterns can be rigidly maintained. Therapeutic work often involves recognizing, exploring, and developing alternatives to the patterns of conflict that block improvement in the family's relationships. Through knowledge of family structures, conflict resolution, and a variety of techniques, the family system can be unbalanced, creating a disequilibrium that promotes change and guides movement toward more effective, satisfying, growth-oriented and functioning relationships.

Minuchin's approach was a courageous departure from the *medical model,* with its focus on the patient as the site of pathology and source of the problem. In traditional psychiatric diagnosis, data is gathered about the patient, who is given a label and targeted for treatment. In structural family therapy, the *identified patient* is viewed as a family member who is the "symptom carrier," expressing a problem whose etiology is not within the indi-

284

vidual but within the family system. While the identified patient will need special attention, "the whole family must be the target of therapeutic interventions."

The process of diagnosis involves broadening the conceptualization of the problem, including the family context and interactions. Constructive change in the individual follows the resolution of conflicts and changes in the "transactional patterns" of the family as a whole and within its subsystems. Similarly, during triage in crisis response, the most traumatized individuals are identified as needing special attention and follow-up. However, systems thinking prescribes that the entire interacting community be evaluated to determine whether various levels of intervention are needed. Similar to structural family therapy, school crisis response may uncover a need to resolve conflicts within and between subsystems such as teachers, students, administrators, parents, responders and others, that can block collaboration and progress toward recovery.

Minuchin developed creative ways to diagnose the functional (or adaptive) and the dysfunctional (or maladaptive) aspects of family systems. In his approach, the therapist temporarily *joins* the family system, experiencing and understanding firsthand the interpersonal dynamics, transactions, conflicts, and roles that maintain the system. From this perspective, the therapist observes how family members relate to their "newest member" (the therapist) and to each other, analyzes functional and dysfunctional relationships, and makes a *structural diagnosis*. Similarly, the crisis responder joins a system—not as therapist, but as the newest part of a community in distress to assess crisis impact, observe relationships and reactions, empathize with those affected, learn about their context, experience conflicts that block recovery, and determine system-wide and individual needs and interventions.

Out of a family crisis can come insights that will ultimately build relationships and strengthen the family system. Similarly, response to a school crisis can be an intervention that builds relationships and strengthens individuals and schools coping with traumatic events. While it is important not to intervene when normal processes of coping make intervention unnecessary, not intervening when action is clearly needed can compound a trag-edy. Knowledge of dynamic human systems supports the effective diagnosis of group and individual needs, facilitates targeted inter-ventions, and can be a critical asset in purposeful crisis response.

School Crisis Response and Systems Thinking

The work of Lewin and Minuchin contribute to the appre-ciation and application of group dynamics and systems theory to understanding schools in crisis. A *system* can be described as a collection of interdependent parts, people, or groups having a reciprocal influence on one another and a common purpose or task. Each part of the system can perform different roles, but each contributes to accomplishing the system's overall goal. Schools constitute a complex and interconnected system of various sub-groups including students, teachers, administrators, parents, grade levels, teaching teams, classrooms, the PTA, teacher's union, cafeteria and custodial staff, and more. The system as a whole, and its interacting subgroups, must be evaluated in the context of a school crisis.

Triage: Evaluating and Understanding Needs

The PREPaRE Model takes a systems perspective during multi-phased triage, using multiple variables to evaluate incident severity and to determine the level of response needed. The model takes into account personal risk factors and warning signs that indicate the degree of psychological trauma (PREPaRE Model: Evaluating Psychological Trauma). Triage reveals the varying degree to which a crisis affects many individuals and groups across multiple locations throughout the system. Triage also uncovers the variability of the nature and circumstances of crises, creating constellations of symptoms and needs.

Considering system-wide need is also prescriptive, since vari-ous types of interventions or no intervention may be appropriate for different individuals and groups. The responder best serves those affected by differentially addressing their needs with an awareness that needs can change. The type of intervention and degree of emotional support differs significantly for those severely traumatized and for those only mildly affected (PREPaRE Model: Levels of Crisis Interventions). A traumatic incident may also generate intense feelings of anger, frustration, guilt or blame, as well as misunderstood feelings that require conflict resolution with individuals or subgroups.

During triage, we generally think of meeting student needs first, but systems thinking reminds responders they must often attend to affected groups of teachers, administrators, support staff, families, other affected schools, and the community at large. System-wide intervention is critical since response disengagement must leave students with stabilized adults who are able to effectively cope, solve problems, and care for them. Systems thinking reminds responders that they are part of the system, and must be included in plans for self-care, support and recovery.

Applying Systems Thinking to Crisis Recovery

The work of Lewin and Minuchin demonstrates that we can move systems damaged by traumatic incidents toward recovery by a variety of interventions that address problems. Applying Lewin's force-field analysis to crisis response, it is possible to develop variables that promote healing and to weaken (or remove) variables that block movement toward recovery. School administration and staff—in key positions to promote student recovery—can benefit from a consultative approach that strengthens them through education about effective response, and the reactions, and needs of students and staff. A consultative approach can suggest ways to implement helpful interventions, and it can flag signals that warrant a student referral (PREPaRE Model: Caregiver Training).

Examples of variables that promote movement toward recovery include reuniting students with support systems (PREPaRE Model: Reestablish Social Support Systems); educating the community about grief reactions; empowering students and staff by forming committees to plan memorials and performing constructive actions, such as creating a memory book for a grieving family; or establishing a chapter of Students Against Drunk Driving (S.A.D.D.) (PREPaRE Model: Ensure Perceptions of Safety and Security: Providing Opportunities to Take Action). Other inter-

287

ventions that promote recovery are structured discussion groups (PREPaRE Model: Psychoeducation: Classroom Meetings), reading young students a book with a relevant theme (bibliotherapy), or providing an opportunity for creative expression such as writing, drawing, or storytelling.

Application of Lewin's model leads to interventions that weaken or remove obstacles to recovery. Examples include controlling traffic and crowds, calming and preparing parents prior to reunification, and managing the media to minimize trauma for affected students. Providing *psychological first aid* to those in need can mitigate stress reactions. Constuctive, culturally competent preparation for difficult events such as funerals and anniversary dates can turn potential obstacles to recovery into events that promote resilience and healing.

Systems thinking enables responders to view crisis response as a dynamic, multidimensional event. In looking at the whole, the responder can perceive many ways to intervene in support of those affected, and to influence crisis variables in the direction of healing. Crisis response is more comprehensive when the team considers the entire interacting, interdependent system as it develops needed interventions. Instead of intervening in only one part of the system, intervention can be multifaceted, addressing more than one variable at the same time. Variables blocking recovery can be removed at the same time that variables supporting recovery are enabled.

Basic Emotional and Existential Issues

Sometimes crisis response must consider themes generated by a traumatic incident that go beyond the usual measures of providing psychological first aid and facilitating recovery. Short- and long-term response can address basic, yet profound issues such as safety and security, trust in others and in 'the system,' or faith in self or spiritual forces greater than ourselves. While initial response focuses on psychological first aid and immediate needs, sensitivity to the deeper issues can alleviate, or it can exacerbate emotional pain. Crisis response that recognizes emotional and existential issues can constructively accept them through cre-

288

ative expression and discussion, honest reassurance of safety and trust, and respect for faith-based and spiritual beliefs. Response that ignores emotional and existential issues presents a potential obstacle to resolution. Systems thinking helps us perceive what the eye cannot see—the deeper, meaningful issues and relationships that go beyond a formidable traumatic incident. Sometimes these issues are subtle. Other times they are as glaring as the elephant in the room that nobody talks about. Speaking of elephants, let's talk about one.

∽

A folktale helps illustrate some implications of systems thinking or its absence. The tale involves several blind men trying to describe an elephant. One feels the elephant's trunk and reports that the animal is straight and hollow like a pipe. The second man feels a leg and declares the elephant solid and mighty like a column. The third man feels the elephant's ear and remarks with assurance that the animal is flat and broad, like a rug. Each man insists that his is the true description, but of course, each man is only partially correct because he correctly describes only part of the whole.

The elephant is composed of its parts. While saying an elephant is the combination of its parts is simplistic, we can identify an elephant by describing its individual parts. Still, an elephant is more than the sum of its trunk, legs, ears, tusks or characteristic trumpeting voice. Systems theory and Gestalt psychology remind us that the whole is greater than the sum of the parts. While an elephant certainly consists of tangible parts that can be seen and felt, the word "elephant" connotes a concept even larger than its substantial self—a colossus. The elephant can be described as mighty, even majestic, and sacred to some, having an amazing memory (if you believe it), symbol of the jungle for some, or symbol of the circus for others. The dog not only wags its tail and barks, it is 'man's best friend.' The duck not only waddles and quacks, it represents a humorous caricature named 'Donald,' or a bird sought by hunters.

289

The blind men in the folktale inform our understanding of systems. Being able to identify the parts helps us recognize and appreciate the whole. But fixating on one or another part gives us a partial and possibly harmfully narrow view of what is at stake. We don't want the trees to obscure the forest, nor do we want the forest to hide the trees. Consider aesthetic and practical value in perceiving both the trees and the forest. And, when a tree does fall in the forest, it affects the entire eco-system. Trees are varied and beautiful, each making a unique contribution to the viability and wealth of the forest. The forest as a whole has magnitude and meaning beyond a combination of trees. Systems thinking enables easy movement between specific details and the big picture to make sense of all aspects of a scene.

It is understandable that crisis responders tend to react at first to individual, observable parts of the system. Like the men in the folktale, they use their senses to grasp immediate needs and, only later, to the unfolding themes that speak to the challenges emerging from a traumatic event. These challenges touch individuals and the community. Crisis response becomes a dynamic process of striving to understand the variety of needs and themes of both the individual parts and the distressed system as a whole—carefully intervening to support resilience and healing. Crisis response strives to initiate a meaningful, sometimes spiritual process of grief and renewal that appreciates the dynamic and varied aspects of the trees and the forest, the parts and the whole, to promote hope and recovery.

Appendices

A Powerful Lesson

Jay Spilecki was a scholar—athlete, talented, respected, and well liked by his high school peers. One tragic night changed everything.

When Jay died in an automobile accident, it was not confirmed during crisis response that his death was related to alcohol consumption. Later, when the medical examiner released his blood/alcohol level, his death became a cautionary tale for young people, largely through the efforts of his parents.

Jay's parents reached out through their grief to cooperate with the school's crisis response team to comfort the students. Jay's mother, Sue Spilecki, penned a poignant article, reprinted here with her permission.

A Short Walk

By Sue Spilecki

(Used by permission)

It's a short walk from the Charter School of Wilmington, where I teach, across Lancaster Pike to the Silverbrook Cemetery. I make that walk every year with about 250 Charter School students—freshmen who are in my Health and Wellness classes. When we leave school, they think they're going on some sort of physical fitness field trip. By the time we return, they've learned a powerful lesson about the dangers of underage drinking and drunk driving—a lesson that I hope stays with them for the rest of their lives.

In 1996, my son, Jay, was a senior in high school. He was a happy, fun-loving kid—not at all different from the kids I see in high school now. That December, he attended a dance with some friends and later ended up at a party where they were drinking alcohol.

I learned that at about 1:45 a.m., he tricked the designated driver into giving him the car keys. He and two friends jumped into a car to check out another party. On Whitby Road in Sharpley, he lost control of the car and hit a tree. He died instantly.

My ninth grade health and wellness students don't know any of this when we set out on our walk across Lancaster Pike. Happy and talkative when we leave the school, they grow quiet when we step on to the grass of the cemetery. By the time I have them gather around my son's grave, they are silent and nervous.

I tell them the lesson is about under-age drinking and driving under the influence of alcohol. I ask if any of them know a family affected by a drunk driver. A few raise their hands. Then I say, "Now, you all know someone because you all know me."

I then tell them Jay's story. I stress to them that he was an awesome high school student with a bright future and loads of friends and a family that loved him, just like them. And, like them, he knew lots of kids who drank and made poor decisions, but nothing bad ever happened, so what was the big deal?

But bad things do happen. I learned that fact in 1996.

Since then, I've learned that two-thirds of Delaware's 11th graders drink alcohol and one in four binge drink. I know that 11th graders who drink are 16 times more likely to get in a car with a driver who is a minor and has been drinking than those who don't drink. I know that they're three times more likely to be forced to have unwanted sexual intercourse, four times more likely to be arrested, and six times more likely to use other drugs.

I share these and other statistics with my students. It would be great if they remember these facts, but what I really want them to remember is that they're not indestructible. Bad things can and do happen to kids just like them. They must not drink and drive.

Parents must remember to be parents to their kids and not buddies. Especially as we move into the "party" season—graduations, beach, "senior week"—all this can translate into tragedy if parents do not step up and actively prevent underage drinking.

Don't serve alcohol to your kids and their friends under the mistaken notion that by keeping them at your house you're keeping them safe. Join me in the effort to enact a "social host" law in Delaware, to hold people responsible for underage drinking on their property.

Parents—and all adults—must play a more active role in preventing underage drinking. You can learn more about teens and drinking by visiting parentsstepup.org, a website established by Delaware's Department of Services for Children, Youth and Their Families.

Or, like my ninth graders, you can learn more by joining me on a short walk across Lancaster Pike.

Sample Survey of School Crisis Responders

While I was discussing the educational purposes of this book with Michael Roth, a graduate of the counseling psychology program at Temple University, he suggested developing a survey to gather information about the experiences of new and experienced school crisis responders. This information could be useful in developing training and support for responders. Readers are invited to adapt these survey questions, which were devised by Michael Roth and Jeff Roth.

---

1. Indicate your experience working as a school professional.

Circle one:

Internship only   1-5 years   6-10 years   11-20 years
over 20 years

2. Indicate your current school job title, or internship program.

Circle one:

Psychologist   Counselor   Social Worker   Nurse
Other: _____

3. Have you responded to a school crisis as a member of a school response team, a district team, both school and district teams, or neither team?

Circle one:

School   District   Both   Neither

4. How many school crises have you responded to as a member of a school or district response team?

Circle one:

None   One   Two   Three to Five   Six to Nine   Ten or More

5. What were the most difficult aspects of your response experience?

6. What specific knowledge or skills were most helpful during the response?

7. What personal qualities are most helpful to your effectiveness as a responder?

8. What personal qualities are obstacles to your effectiveness as a responder?

9. What are the most significant lessons learned during the response?

10. What knowledge or skills would be most helpful for meeting the challenges of school crisis response in the future?

Adamson & Peacock (2007) surveyed school psychologists regarding their experiences and perceptions of crisis response. High percentages of participants indicated their schools had crisis intervention plans, teams, and training, but many suggested that additional training would improve their response capability. The idea of conducting more research on school crisis response training and practice deserves consideration.

Bibliotherapy
Talking About Death, Coping and Recovery

Lifetimes: A Beautiful Way to Explain Death to Children by B. Mellonie and R. Ingpen. Bantam Books, 1983.

    Suggested Age Range: 4–9 years

    Theme: A poetic description of the cycle of life.

I Miss You: A First Look at Death by P. Thomas. Illust. by L. Harker. Barron's Educational Series, 2001.

    Suggested Age Range: 4–9 years

    Theme: Helps children understand that death is a natural part of the cycle of life, and that feelings are important and can be expressed.

When Dinosaurs Die: A Guide to Understanding Death by L.K. Brown. Illust. by M. Brown. Little, Brown Books for Young Readers, 1998.

    Suggested Age Range: 4–12 years

    Theme: Explaining death using compassionate dinosaurs. Some sections very intense.

The Fall of Freddie the Leaf: A Story of Life for All Ages by L. Buscaglia. Slack Inc., 1982.

    Suggested Age Range: 4 years–adult

    Theme: A warm, simple story describing how leaves change with the passing seasons as an allegory for the balance of life and death.

Children Also Grieve: Talking about Death and Healing by L. Goldman. Photos by L. Goldman. Jessica Kingsley Publishers, 2005.

    Suggested Age Range: 4 years–adult

    Theme: Dialogue helps caregivers support children coping with the death of a close friend or relative. Interactive sections encourage children to share reactions.

Gentle Willow: A Story for Children About Dying by J.C. Mills. Illust. by C. Pillo. APA: Magination Press, 2010.

Suggested Age Range: 4 years–adult

Theme: A book written for children who may be terminally ill and for children who know them. Encourages expression of feelings.

Help Me Say Goodbye: Activities for Helping Kids Cope When a Special Person Dies by J. Silverman. Fairview Press, 1999.

Suggested Age Range: 5–8 years

Theme: Creative activities to help children cope with the death of a loved one.

Helping Children Think About Bereavement: A Differentiated Story and Activities to Help Children Age 5–11 Deal With Loss by H. Butler. Routledge, 2013.

Suggested Age Range: 5–11 years

Theme: Helps children develop the emotional vocabulary to talk about death.

How It Feels When a Parent Dies by J. Krementz. Alfred A. Knopf, 1993.

Suggested Age Range: 6–16 years

Theme: Children talk about the death of a parent.

My Life By Me: A Kid's Forever Book by B. Barber. APA: Magination Press, 2011.

Suggested Age Range: 7–11 years

Theme: A personal memory book for children who are terminally ill.

Healing Your Grieving Heart: 100 Practical Ideas for Kids by A. Wolfelt. Companion, 2001.

Suggested Age Range: 8–12 years

Theme: A book of helpful ideas for healing and recovery.

Talking with Children and Young People About Death and Dying by M. Turner. Illust. by B. Thomas. Jessica Kingsley Publishers, 2006.

Suggested Age Range: 8 years–adult

Theme: A book that acknowledges the grief process, including children's common fears.

Don't Despair On Thursdays!: The Children's Grief-Management Book by A. Moser. Illustrated by D. Melton. Landmark Editions, 1996.
> Suggested Age Range: 9 years–adult
> Theme: This book informs children about the grieving process, helps them deal with feelings of grief when people or pets die, gives them tools to cope, and offers them hope.

Tear Soup: A Recipe for Healing After Loss by P. Schwiebert and C. DeKlyen. Illust. by T. Bills. Portland, OR: Grief Watch, 2008.
> Suggested Age Range: 9 years–adult
> Theme: Facing the pain of grieving and gaining support needed for healing.

Part of Me Died Too: Stories of Creative Survival Among Bereaved Children and Teenagers by V. Fry. Dutton, 1995.
> Suggested Age Range: 10 years–adult
> Theme: Stories of coping by children dealing with death of family members or friends.

You Are Not Alone: Teens Talk About Life After the Loss of a Parent by L. Hughes. Scholastic Press, 2005.
> Suggested Age Range: 12–18 years
> Theme: The process of grieving and dealing with life after the death of a parent, interspersed with testimonials by teenagers about grief and coping.

Through My Eyes: A Journal for Teens by L. Kranz. Cooper Square, 1998.
> Suggested Age Range: 12–18 years
> Theme: A book of journaling about grief for teenagers.

When Will It Stop Hurting?: Teens, Loss, and Grief by E. Myers. Illust. by K. Adams. Scarecrow Press, 2006.
> Suggested Age Range: 12–18 years
> Theme: A self-help guide for teenagers dealing with grief.

I Will Remember You: What To Do When Someone You Love Dies: A Guidebook Through Grief for Teens by L. Dower. Scholastic Books, 2001.

Suggested Age Range: 12 years–adult

Theme: Advice, anecdotes, poems and songs to help grieving teens.

The Grieving Teen: A Guide for Teenagers & Their Friends by H. Fitzgerald. Simon & Schuster/Touchstone Press, 2000.

Suggested Age Range: 12 years–adult

Theme: Helps teenagers understand grief reactions, feelings, support groups, recovery.

Helping Teens Cope With Death by The Dougy Center. Dougy Center, 1999.

Suggested Age Range: 13–18 years

Theme: This very helpful book explains adolescent grief reactions and provides tips for parents on supporting teens, including dealing with anniversaries.

The Healing Your Grieving Heart Journal for Teens by A.D. Wolfelt. Companion Press, 2002.

Suggested Age Range: 13–18 years

Theme: A journal that supports the teenager's grief process, including open-ended questions that facilitate understanding and the exploration of feelings.

Chicken Soup for the Soul: Grieving and Recovery: 101 Inspirational and Comforting Stories about Surviving the Loss of a Loved One by J. Canfield, M.V. Hansen, and A. Newmark. Chicken Soup for the Soul Publishing, 2011.

Suggested Age Range: 16 years–adult

Theme: A collection of comforting stories about grieving and recovery.

Talking About Death: A Dialogue Between Parent and Child by E.A. Grollman. Drawings by S. Avishai. Beacon Press, 2011.

Suggested Age Range: 18 years–adult

Theme: A guide for parents to help children through the death of a loved one.

Helping the Grieving Student: A Guide for Teachers by The Dougy Center. Dougy Center, 1998.

Suggested Age Range: 18 years–adult

Theme: A valuable resource for teacher training, support staff, and administrators.

Death and Dying of a Mother

After Charlotte's Mom Died by C. Spelman. Illust. by J. Friedman. Albert Whitman, 1996.

Suggested Age Range: 5–9 years

Theme: A six year old girl feels sad and angry after her mom dies in a car accident.

The Brightest Star! by K.M. Hemery. Illust. by R. Boldt. Centering Corporation, 1998.

Suggested Age Range: 5–11 years

Theme: A young girl grieving the death of her mother, is comforted and reminded of her mother's love by looking at the brightest star in the sky.

Mama's Window by L. Rubright. Illust. by D. Smith. Lee & Low Publishing, 2005.

Suggested Age Range: 8–11 years

Theme: A young boy must live with his uncle after the death of his mother.

The Leanin' Dog by K.A. Nuzum. HarperCollins, 2010.

Suggested Age Range: 8–12 years

Theme: The sudden appearance of a dog helps an 11-year-old girl cope with grief and stress reactions associated with the accidental freezing death of her mother in a storm.

The Linden Tree by E. Matthews. Milkweed Editions, 2007.

Suggested Age Range: 8–13 years

Theme: When an 11 year old girl's mother dies of meningitis, she must cope with grief, find her role on the family's rural farm, and understand her father's remarriage.

Walk Two Moons by S. Creech. HarperCollins, 1994.

Suggested Age Range: 9 years–adult

Theme: A story about re-defining the self with the help of

grandparents and a friend, after a mother dies. Native American theme

The Tiger Rising by K. Di Camillo. Candlewick Press, 2002.
　Suggested Age Range: 10–15 years
　Theme: A 12 year old boy's new friendship with a girl and his discovery of a caged tiger in the woods, help him understand his father and grieve the death of his mother.

Home Before Dark by S.E. Bridges. Banks Channel Books, 2000.
　Suggested Age Range: 12 years–adult
　Theme: A teenage girl who had been living in a station wagon, tries to settle on a tobacco farm. She copes with her mother's death and later, her father's wish to remarry.

Motherless Daughters: The Legacy of Loss by H. Edelman. Da Capo Press, 2006.
　Suggested Age Range: 12 years–adult
　Theme: This book deals with the death of the mothers of girls and women.

The Friends by R. Guy. Laurel Leaf Books, 1995.
　Suggested Age Range: 12 years–adult
　Theme: A mother's death and father's autocratic control creates a gulf between best friends. African American and Indian cultural themes

Death and Dying of a Father

　Samantha Jane's Missing Smile: A Story About Coping With the Loss of a Parent by J. Kaplow and D. Pincus. Illust. by B. Spiegel. APA: Magination Press, 2010.
　Suggested Age Range: 4–8 years
　Theme: A child experiences her father's death and finds tools to re-discover happiness.

Daddy's Chair by S. Lanton. Illust. by S.O. Haas. Lantern Press, 2013.
　Suggested Age Range: 4–8 years
　Theme: A book about memories of a father who died of cancer. Jewish mourning rituals.

Mama Does the Mambo by K. Leiner. Illust. by E. Rodriguez. Hyperion, 2001.

 Suggested Age range: 5–8 years

 Theme: A young girl tells the sad story of her father's death. Latina theme

Flamingo Dream by D.J. Napoli. Illust. by C. Felstead. Greenwillow, 2002.

 Suggested Age Range: 5–8 years

 Theme: After her father's death from cancer, a young girl creates a book celebrating their last year together.

Everett Anderson's Goodbye by L. Clifton. Illust. by A. Grifalconi. Holt, 1983.

 Suggested Age Range: 5–9 years

 Theme: A story of coping with the death of a father. African American theme

Saying Goodbye to Daddy by J. Vigna. Illust. by J. Vigna. Albert Whitman, 1991.

 Suggested Age Range: 5–10 years

 Theme: After her father is killed in a car accident; a little girl is helped through fear, loneliness and anger by her mother and grandmother.

A Father Like That by C. Zolotow. Illust. by LeUyen Pham. HarperCollins, 2007.

 Suggested Age Range: 5–11 years

 Theme: A young boy imagines life with a father he never knew.

Upside-Down Cake by C. Carrick. Illust. by P. Bouma. Clarion, 1999.

 Suggested Age Range: 7–12 years

 Theme: A young boy and his father, who is dying of cancer, celebrate the father's last birthday together.

Sunflowers and Rainbows for Tia: Saying Goodbye to Daddy by A.K. Greene. Illlust. by C. Love. Centering Corporation, 1999.

 Suggested Age Range: 8–12 years

Theme: A young girl and her family cope with the death of her father.

Black Jack Jetty: A Boy's Journey Through Grief by M.A. Carestio. APA: Magination Press, 2010.
Suggested Age Range: 8–13 years
Theme: A boy learns to cope with the death of his father, a soldier in Afghanistan.

Praying to A.L. by J. Caseley. Greenwillow Books, 2000.
Suggested Age Range: 10–16 years
Theme: A teenager, grieving for her father who recently died, remembers special moments, including their mutual interest in the life of Abraham Lincoln.

Listen to the Fig Tree by S.B. Mathis. Puffin, 1990.
Suggested Age Range: 12 years–adult
Theme: A young black woman, who is blind, copes with her mother's alcoholism and the approaching anniversary of her father's murder. African American theme.

A Death in the Family by J. Agee. Bantam, 1969; Penguin Classics, 2009.
Suggested Age Range: 15 years–adult
Theme: The sudden, accidental death of a father impacts a family.

Tiger Eyes by J. Blume. Bantam Doubleday Dell, 1981; Delacorte, 2013.
Suggested Age Range: 15 years–adult
Theme: A girl finds meaning after the sudden, tragic murder of her father.

Death and Dying of a Grandmother

One More Wednesday by M. Doray. Illust. by M. Doray. Greenwillow Books, 2001.
Suggested Age Range: 4–8 years
Theme: When a little bunny's grandmother dies, he remembers good times and asks his mother about death.

Grandma's Gone to Live in the Stars by M. Haynes. Illust. by M. Haynes. Albert Whitman, 2000.

    Suggested Age Range: 4–8 years

    Theme: The death of a beloved grandmother, told by a young child as she says goodbye.

Grandma's Purple Flowers by A.J. Burrowes. Lee & Low Publishers, 2000.

    Suggested Age Range: 5–8 years

    Theme: A girl narrates the story of her grandmother's death. African American theme

Bubby, Me, and Memories by B. Pomerantz. Union of American Hebrew Congregations, 1993.

    Suggested Age Range: 5–8 years

    Theme: A story about coping with the death of a grandmother. Jewish theme

A Season for Mangoes by R. Hanson. Clarion, 2005.

    Suggested Age Range: 5–9 years

    Theme: A girl describes her feelings, while saying goodbye to her grandmother in her own, personal way. Jamaican theme

Nana Upstairs and Nana Downstairs by T. dePaola. Illust. by T. dePaola. Putnam, 1973.

    Suggested Age Range: 5–13 years

    Theme: A story of recovery after the death of a grandmother and great grandmother.

Bluebird Summer by D. Hopkinson. Illust. by B. Anderson. Greenwillow Books, 2001.

    Suggested Age Range: 6–11 years

    Theme: After their grandmother's death, two children on her farm work to recreate her spirit by finding some of the things she loved.

Annie and the Old One by M. Miles. Illust. by P. Parnall. Little, Brown & Co., 1985.

    Suggested Age Range: 6–12 years

    Theme: A dying grandmother explains the cycle of life.

Native American, Navajo theme.

Felita by N. Mohr. Illust. by R. Cruz. Penguin Putnam, 1979; Puffin, 1999.
    Suggested Age Range: 7–11 years
    Theme: Coping with prejudice and the death of a grandmother. Puerto Rican theme.

Grandma's Scrapbook by J. Nobisso. Illust. by M. Hyde. Gingerbread House, 2000.
    Suggested Age Range: 7–12 years
    Theme: An older girl recalls tender memories of summers spent with her grandmother, with a scrapbook as the vehicle for story telling.

Death and Dying of a Grandfather

Where Is Grandpa? by T.A. Barron. Illust. by C.K. Soentpiet. Puffin, 2001.
    Suggested Age Range: 4–8 years
    Theme: A child's first person description of the death of Grandpa.

The Two of Them by Aliki. Illust. by Aliki. HarperCollins, 1987.
    Suggested Age Range: 4–8 years
    Theme: A child's love for her grandfather continues after his death.

The Happy Funeral by E. Bunting. Illust. by Dinh Mai Vo. HarperCollins, 1982.
    Suggested Age Range: 5–7 years
    Theme: A little girl honors her grandfather by helping make preparations for his funeral. Chinese-American theme

Blue Roses by L. Boyden. Illust. by A. Cordova. Lee & Low Publishers, 2002.
    Suggested Age Range: 5–8 years
    Theme: A girl grieving her grandfather's death has a dream. Native American theme

Poppy's Chair by K. Hesse. Illust. by K. Life. Scholastic, 2000.

Suggested Age Range: 5–10 years
Theme: A girl experiences stages of grief, before accepting her grandfather's death.

Gran-Gran's Best Trick by D. Holden. APA: Magination Press, 1989.
Suggested Age Range: 5–11 years
Theme: A girl talks about a special relationship with her grandfather and difficulty coping with his death from cancer.

Blackberries in the Dark by M. Jukes. Alfred A. Knopf, 1985; Yearling, 1994.
Suggested Age Range: 7–12 years
Theme: A boy and his grandmother share feelings about the death of his grandfather.

Grandpa Loved by J. Nobisso. Illust. by M. Hyde. Gingerbread House, 2000.
Suggested Age Range: 7–12 years
Theme: Memories of what his grandpa loved transports a boy to fond places they shared.

When Grandfather Journeys Into Winter by C.K. Strete. Greenwillow, 1979.
Suggested Age Range: 7–12 years
Theme: A young boy struggles to accept his grandfather's rapidly approaching death. Native American theme

My Grandson Lew by C. Zolotow. Harper & Row, 1974; Trophy, 1985.
Suggested Age Range: 7–12 years
Theme: A boy deals with loneliness by sharing memories after his grandfather's death.

A Ring of Endless Light by M. L'Engle. Dell, 1980; Square Fish, 2008.
Suggested Age Range: 10 years–adult
Theme: A teenage girl experiences emotional highs and devastating lows while coming to terms with death as an affirmation of the wholeness of life.

Death and Dying of a Sibling/Relative/Teacher

You Hold Me and I'll Hold You by J. Carson. Illust. by A. Cannon. Scholastic, 1992.

    Suggested Age Range: 4–7 years

    Theme: At her great aunt's memorial service, a young girl's father helps her deal with all the people by wisely whispering, "You hold me and I'll hold you."

Ben's Flying Flowers by I. Maier. Illust. by M. Bogade. APA: Magination Press, 2012.

    Suggested Age Range: 4–8 years

    Theme: A young girl remembers her brother, finding comfort in understanding that although he died, her happy memories of him live on.

I Remember Miss Perry by P. Brisson. Illust. by S. Jorisch. Dial Press, 2006.

    Suggested Age Range: 4–10 years

    Theme: A boy is helped to cope with the accidental death of his kind teacher.

I Don't Have an Uncle Phil Anymore by M. Pelligrino. Illust. by C. Kempf. APA: Magination Press, 1998.

    Suggested Age Range: 4–10 years

    Theme: A young boy copes with the death of an adored uncle.

A Little Bit of Rob by B.J. Turner. Illust. by M. Backer. Albert Whitman, 1996.

    Suggested Age Range: 4–10 years

    Theme: A young girl and her parents cope with her brother's death.

Nadia The Willful by S. Alexander. Illust. by L. Bloom. Pantheon Books, 1983.

    Suggested Age Range: 6–12 years

    Theme: Nadia reacts when her favorite brother dies and her father decrees that no one can talk about him.

What is Goodbye? by N. Grimes. Illust. by R. Colon. Hyperion, 2004.
Suggested Age Range: 8–12 years
Theme: A brother and sister use poetry to describe feelings, grieving for their brother.

Mick Harte Was Here by B. Park. Yearling Press, 1996.
Suggested Age Range: 8–12 years
Theme: A young girl affectionately tells about her eccentric, lively brother, who died in a bicycle accident while not wearing a helmet.

Can You Hear Me Smiling? A Child Grieves a Sister by A.R. Jackson. Illust. by L. Lawhon. Child & Family Press, 2004.
Suggested Age Range: 8–12 years
Theme: A sister tenderly describes her older sister's illness and death.

Stolen Words by A.G. Koss. American Girl, 2001.
Suggested Age Range: 8–12 years
Theme: A girl copes with the death of her aunt by re-writing her aunt's stolen diary, whch contains references to the Holocaust. Jewish theme

Beat the Turtle Drum by C. Greene. Viking Press, 1976; Yearling, 1979.
Suggested Age Range: 8–12 years
Theme: A story about the death of a sister and emotions of the surviving sister.

Kira-Kira by C. Kadohata. Atheneum Press, 2004.
Suggested Age Range: 8 years–adult
Theme: A young girl idolizes her older sister, who dies of lymphoma. The family attempts to cope with their loss. Japanese American theme

Missing May by C. Rylant. Scholastic, 2004.
Suggested Age Range: 9–18 years
Theme: A girl and her uncle cope with the death of her beloved aunt, with a new friendship playing a significant role.

Birdland by T. Mack. Scholastic, 2003.
> Suggested Age Range: 12–16 years
> Theme: A 14 year old boy copes with the death of his older brother, who loved jazz great Charlie Parker, by exploring his journal and poetry.

Recovering From the Loss of a Sibling: When a Brother or Sister Dies by K.F. Donnelly. iUniverse, 2000.
> Suggested Age range: 12 years–adult
> Theme: This book explores the issues, questions and feelings of surviving siblings.

A Summer to Die by L. Lowry. Houghton Mifflin, 1977; Ember, 2007.
> Suggested Age Range: 12 years–adult
> Theme: A teenage girl mourns the death of her sister from leukemia over the summer.

Death and Dying of a Friend

A Story For Hippo by S. Puttock. Illust. by A. Bartlett. Scholastic, 2001.
> Suggested Age Range: 4–8 years
> Theme: When Monkey's best friend Hippo dies, questions are answered in a way that very young children can understand.

Chester Raccoon and the Acorn Full of Memories by A. Penn Illust. by B. Gibson Tanglewood, 2009.
> Suggested Age Range: 4–8 years
> Theme: Mother raccoon helps her son cope with his friend's death with fond memories.

I Had A Friend Named Peter: Talking to Children About the Death of a Friend. by J. Cohn. Illust. by G. Owens. Wm. Morrow, 1987.
> Suggested Age Range: 4–13 years
> Theme: When a young boy dies after being hit by a car, children talk about the death of their friend. Introduction provides helpful guidelines

A Taste of Blackberries by D. Smith. Illust. by M. Wimmer. HarperCollins, 1973, 2004.

    Suggested Age Range: 7 years–adult

    Theme: After the funeral of a friend who dies of an allergic reaction to bee stings, a boy picks blackberries for the grieving mother.

Rain Is Not My Indian Name by C. L. Smith. Illust. by L. Earley HarperCollins, 2001.

    Suggested Age Range: 8–12 years

    Theme: After the death of her best friend, a girl stays in seclusion, but finally takes a job as a newspaper photographer covering a summer youth camp. Native American theme

Bridge to Terabithia by K. Paterson. Illust. by D. Diamond. HarperCollins, 1977, 2004.

    Suggested Age Range: 9–14 years

    Theme: A surviving friend struggles with guilt, but builds new, supportive relationships.

When a Friend Dies: A Book for Teens About Grieving and Healing by M.E. Gootman. Free Spirit Press, 1994.

    Suggested Age Range: 13–18 years

    Theme: A book about coping and healing after the death of a teenage friend.

Running Loose by C. Crutcher. Greenwillow Books, 2003.

    Suggested Age Range: 13 years–adult

    Theme: A teenager learns about sportsmanship, love and death, when his girlfriend dies.

Me and Earl and the Dying Girl by J. Andrews. Amulet Books, 2012.

    Suggested Age Range: 14–adult

    Theme: Creative, somewhat alienated teenage boys become friends with a girl dying of leukemia, and make a film for her when she stops treatment.

The Fault in Our Stars by J. Green. Dutton Books, 2012.

    Suggested Age Range: 14–adult

Theme: Profound questions about death, life and love emerge from the relationship between two teenagers who meet at a cancer support group for young people.

The Big Hang-Up by W.E. Huntsberry. Lothrop, 1970.
Suggested Age Range: 15 years–adult
Theme: Young teenage survivors experience grief and guilt, after a friend is killed in an auto accident involving drinking and driving.

Death and Dying of a Pet/Animal

My Pig Amarillo by S. Ichikawa. Philomel, 2003.
Suggested Age Range: 4–7 years
Theme: When a young boy's pet pig dies, his grandfather comforts him. Latino theme

Goodbye Mousie by R.H. Harris. Illust. by J. Ormerod. Aladdin, 2004.
Suggested Age Range: 4–8 years
Theme: After the death of his pet mouse, a little boy learns that sadness and memories are part of saying goodbye.

Helen the Fish by V. Kroll. Illust. by T. L. Weidner. Albert Whitman, 1992.
Suggested Age Range: 4–8 years
Theme: A story about the death of a pet goldfish.

Goodbye, Brecken by D. Lupton. Illust. by D. Lupton. APA: Magination Press, 2013.
Suggested Age Range: 4–8 years
Theme: The death of a young girl's dog is her first experience with grief.

When a Pet Dies by F. Rogers. Putnam, 1988; Puffin, 1998.
Suggested Age Range: 4–10 years
Theme: This book explores various feelings that a child may have when a pet dies.

Badger's Parting Gifts by S. Varley. HarperCollins, 1992.
Suggested Age Range: 4–11 years

Theme: This book deals with the death of a beloved badger.

The Tenth Good Thing About Barney by J. Viorst. Illust. by E. Blegvad. Atheneum, 1971, 1987.
Suggested Age Range: 4–12 years
Theme: Fond memories of a pet cat help with understanding, meaning and recovery.

For Every Dog An Angel by C. Davis. Lighthearted Press, 2004.
Suggested Age Range: 4 years–adult
Theme: A story about dealing with the death of a pet dog.

For Every Cat An Angel by C. Davis. Lighthearted Press, 2004.
Suggested Age Range: 4 years–adult
Theme: A story about dealing with the death of a pet cat.

Saying Goodbye to Lulu by C. Demas. Illust. by A. Hoyt. Little, Brown, 2004, 2009.
Suggested Age Range: 5–7 years
Theme: A girl expresses feelings about caring for an old dog until its death, and then meeting a new puppy.

The Dead Bird by M.W. Brown. Illust. by R. Charlip. Harper & Row, 1985.
Suggested Age Range: 5–8 years
Theme: Children find a dead bird, give it a burial and remember it.

Jasper's Day by M.B. Parker. Illust. by J. Wilson. Kids Can Press, 2002.
Suggested Age Range: 5–8 years
Theme: A young narrator tells the story of a pet dog with cancer, who is about to be euthanized. The family honors their pet's life.

It Must Hurt A Lot: A Book About Death and Learning and Growing by D. Sanford. Illust. by G. Evans. Multnomah Press, 1985.
Suggested Age Range: 5–8 years
Theme: Describes a boy's anger, grief and eventual acceptance of his pet dog's death.

Hachiko: The True Story of a Loyal Dog by P. Turner. Houghton Mifflin, 2004, 2009.

Suggested Age Range: 5–10 years

Theme: A dog returns to a train station every day for ten years to wait for his person, who had died. When the dog dies, he is honored with a bronze statue. Japanese theme

Sammy in the Sky by B. Walsh. Illust. by J. Wyeth. Candlewick Press, 2011.

Suggested Age Range: 5–13 years

Theme: After the death of a hound dog, a girl keeps his spirit alive with fond memories.

The Christmas Day Kitten by J. Herriott. Illust. by R. Brown. St. Martin's Press, 1986.

Suggested Age Range: 6–12 years

Theme: The relationship between a dying cat and its owner is beautifully described.

When Violet Died by M. Kantrowitz. Parents Magazine, 1973.

Suggested Age Range: 6–12 years

Theme: When a bird dies, the importance of a ceremony in accepting death is shown.

My Friend Fish by M. Hegwood. Holt, 1975.

Suggested Age Range: 7–12 years

Theme: A child has a friendship with a fish that dies. African American theme

Kate, The Ghost Dog: Coping With the Death of a Pet by W.L. Wilson. Illust. by Soud. APA: Magination Press, 2010.

Suggested Age Range: 8–13 years

Theme: A story about coping with the death of a pet dog.

Sounder by W.H. Armstrong. Illust. by J. Barkley. HarperCollins, 1969.

Suggested Age Range: 10 years - adult

Theme: The story of struggling sharecroppers and Sounder, their loyal hunting dog. African American theme

Old Yeller by F. Gipson. HarperCollins, 1956; Perennial Classics, 2009.
>Suggested Age Range: 10 years–adult
>Theme: Heartwarming story about a boy and his dog in the Texas hills.

Suicide/Prevention

Bart Speaks Out: Breaking the Silence on Suicide by J.P. Goldman. Western Psychological Services, 1998.
>Suggested Age Range: 6–12 years
>Theme: A family dog speaks out about his confusion and grief after his owner's suicide.

A Hole in the World by S. Hite. Scholastic, 2001.
>Suggested Age Range: 11 years–adult
>Theme: A teenager sent to live on a relative's farm after the suicide of an appreciated farmhand, finds himself dealing with profound questions about life and death.

Face at the Edge of the World by E. Bunting. Clarion, 1988.
>Suggested Age Range: 11 years–adult
>Theme: A boy tries to understand his best friend's suicide.

But I Didn't Say Goodbye: Helping Children and Families After a Suicide by B. Rubel. Griefwork Center, 2009.
>Suggested Age Range: 11 years–adult
>Theme: Describes the life changing experience of a boy, whose father died by suicide.

Passing Through by C. Gerson. Dell, 1980.
>Suggested Age Range: 13 years–adult
>Theme: A high school girl copes with her older brother's suicide with help from a friend.

When Living Hurts by S. Gordon. Urj Press, 1985, 2004.
>Suggested Age Range: 13 years–adult
>Theme: This book helps troubled teenagers, adults, and their friends by teaching them to cope with feelings that might lead to more severe depression or suicide.

The Owl's Song by J.C. Hale. Doubleday, 1974; Starfire, 1990.
Suggested Age Range: 13 years–adult
Theme: A story about a young boy's struggle for self worth, dealing with alcoholism and suicide. Native American theme

Camilla by M. L'Engle. Square Fish, 2009.
Suggested Age Range: 13 years–adult
Theme: After her mother's suicide attempt, a daughter realizes that parents are fallible, and discovers affirmation for the value of life.

Remembering the Good Times by R. Peck. Dell, 1985.
Suggested Age Range: 13 years–adult
Theme: A boy and girl are aware that a friend is overwhelmed by the pressures in his life, but never suspect he was considering suicide.

Ordinary People by J. Guest. Penguin, 1982.
Suggested Age Range: 15 years–adult
Theme: A teen attempts suicide after his brother drowns in an accident. He experiences emotional pain and fragile family relationships, while being helped to recover.

My Son, My Son by I. Bolton. Bolton Press, 1983.
Suggested Age Range: 16 years–adult
Theme: A mother's story of surviving the suicide of her son—offers hope, reassurance, practical emotional support.

No Time to Say Goodbye: Surviving the Suicide of a Loved One by C. Fine.
Harmony Press, 1999.
Suggested Age Range: 16 years–adult
Theme: Written by the survivor of her husband's suicide, the author captures insights and makes practical, honest suggestions to help other survivors.

After a Parent's Suicide: Helping Children Heal by M. Requarth. Healing Hearts Press, 2008.
Suggested Age Range: 18 years - adult
Theme: A book that provides understanding, comfort and

suggestions to help children and teens heal after the suicide of a parent.

Bullying/Prevention

The Last Laugh by J. Aruego and A. Dewey. Dial, 2006.
Suggested Age Range: 4–7 years
Theme: A picture book in which a clever duck outwits a bullying snake.

Ellen, the Elegant Elephant by C. D'Amico and S. D'Amico. Arthur A. Levine, 2004.
Suggested Age Range: 4–7 years
Theme: A young elephant is nervous about her first day of school, but feels better wearing her grandmother's hat for good luck. Then, the teasing starts.

Jungle Bullies by S. Kroll. Illust. by V. Nguyen. Cavendish, 2006; Two Lions, 2013.
Suggested Age Range: 4–7 years
Theme: Larger jungle animals bully the smaller ones to get what they want, until a mother monkey teaches them that everyone benefits from sharing.

The Bully Blockers Club by T. Bateman. Illust. by J. Urbanovic. Whitman, 2004.
Suggested Age Range: 4–8 years
Theme: Friends and bystanders stick up for each other, taking a stand against bullying.

Bully B.E.A.N.S. by J. Cook. National Center for Youth Issues, 2009.
Suggested Age Range: 4–8 years
Theme: Bystanders realize that they can stop bullying.

Yoon and the Jade Bracelet by H. Cecorvits. Farrar, Straus & Giroux, 2008.
Suggested Age Range: 4–8 years
Theme: When standing up to a bully does not resolve the problem, friends tell adults.

Hooway for Wodney Wat by H. Lester. Illust. by L. Munsinger. Sandpiper, 2011.

> Suggested Age Range: 4–8 years
> Theme: Rodney is teased because of speech difficulties, but stands up to the class bully.

Nobody Knew What to Do: A Story About Bullying by B.R. McCain. Whitman, 2001.

> Suggested Age Range: 4–8 years
> Theme: Encourages children to tell adults about bullying so that they may intervene.

Myrtle by T.C. Pearson. Illust. T.C. Pearson. Farrar, Straus, & Giroux, 2004.

> Suggested Age Range: 4–8 years
> Theme: A kind aunt helps Myrtle learn how to cope with a mean, bullying neighbor.

The Brand New Kid by K. Couric. Illust. by M. Priceman. Doubleday, 2000.

> Suggested Age Range: 4–9 years
> Theme: A boy from Hungary is teased in school because he looks different.

Amazing Grace by M. Hoffman. Illust. by C. Binch. Dial, 1991.

> Suggested Age Range: 4 years–adult
> Theme: When Grace plays a special role in the school play, she endures sexist and racist reactions, but gets support from her mother and grandmother. African American theme

Swimmy by Leo Lionni. Illust. by L. Lionni. Dragonfly Books, 1973.

> Suggested Age Range: 4 years–adult
> Theme: A bully fish is scared off when a school of little fish band together.

Stop Bullying Bobby!: Helping Children Cope with Teasing and Bullying by D. Smith-Mansell. Illust. by S. Riggio. New Horizon Press, 2004.

> Suggested Age Range: 4 years–adult

Theme: A girl helps a new kid being bullied, by involving her parents and teacher.

Ruby and Bubbles by R. Winstead. Dial, 2006.
Suggested Age Range: 5–7 years
Theme: A pet bird helps Ruby deal with two bullying girls who target her.

Stars in the Darkness by B. Joosse. Chronicle, 2001.
Suggested Age Range: 5–7 years
Theme: A young boy and his mother seek creative ways to save his older brother from gang violence. African American theme

The Berenstain Bears and the Bully by S. Berenstain and J. Berenstain.
Random House, 1996.
Suggested Age Range: 5–8 years
Theme: When little sister is beaten up by a bully at school, she learns a lot more than either ignoring, or standing up to her.

Shrinking Violet by C. Best. Farrar, Straus & Giroux, 2001.
Suggested Age Range: 5–8 years
Theme: A shy little girl has the courage to stand up to a bully's teasing and saves her school from disaster.

The Name Jar by Y. Choi. Dell Dragonfly Books, 2003.
Suggested Age Range: 5–8 years
Theme: A young child is teased on the school bus because of her Korean name.

How to Make Friends with a Giant by G. Choldenko. Illust. by A. Walrod. Putnam, 2006.
Suggested Age Range: 5–8 years
Theme: A new boy is teased because he is tall, but a friendship helps others accept him.

The Sissy Duckling by H. Fierstein. Illust. by H. Cole. Simon & Schuster, 2005.
Suggested Age range: 5–8 years
Theme: A happy duckling is teased, but continues to bake

and do the things he likes best.

Goggles! By E.J. Keats. Puffin, 1998.
Suggested Age Range: 5–8 years
Theme: Boys outwit neighborhood bullies who try to take their motorcycle goggles. African American theme

Candy Shop by J. Wahl. Illust. by N. Wong. Charlesbridge, 2004.
Suggested Age Range: 5–9 years
Theme: A boy and his aunt comfort a candy shop owner from Taiwan, when bigots write hurtful words on the sidewalk.

The Juice Box Bully: Empowering Kids to Stand Up for Others by B. Sornson and M. Dismondy. Illust. by K. Shaw. Ferne Press, 2010.
Suggested Age Range: 5–12 years
Theme: This book empowers "bystanders" to actively discourage bullying.

Oliver Button Is a Sissy by T. dePaola. Illust. by T. dePaola. Voyager Books, 1979.
Suggested Age Range: 5 years–adult
Theme: A boy is teased because of his "sissy" interests, but follows his strengths.

Eddie Longpants by M. Levert. Groundwood, 2005, 2011.
Suggested Age Range: 6–8 years
Theme: A very tall boy becomes the target of a bully.

A Play's the Thing by Aliki. HarperCollins, 2005.
Suggested Age range: 6–9 years
Theme: When a class puts on a play that deals with a bully, the real class bully learns a lesson about getting along with others.

Pinky and Rex and the Bully by J. Howe. Illust. by M. Sweet. Spotlight, 2006.
Suggested Age Range: 6–9 years
Theme: Pinky learns about himself while defending his favorite color pink, and his friendship with a girl, from the neightborhood bully.

Benjamin and the Word/Benjamin y la palabra by D.A. Olivas. Pinata, 2005, 2011.

Suggested Age Range: 6–9 years

Theme: After Benjamin beats his friend in a game of handball, there is name calling, and his father gets involved in conflict resolution. Latino theme

I Get So Hungry by B. Moore Campball. Illust. by A. Bates. Putnam, 2008.

Suggested Age Range: 6–10

Theme: A little girl is teased about her weight until a teacher joins with her to live a healthier lifestyle.

Say Something by P. Moss. Illust. by L. Lyon. Tilbury House, 2008.

Suggested Age Range: 6–10 years

Theme: This story makes the point that one witness can help stop bullying.

Blue Cheese Breath and Stinky Feet: How to deal with Bullies by C. De Pino. APA: Magination Press, 2004.

Suggested Age Range: 6–13 years

Theme: A boy devises a plan with the help of parents and teacher to deal with a bully.

Stop Picking on Me: A First Look at Bullying by P. Thomas. Barron's Educational Series, 2000.

Suggested Age Range: 6–12 years

Theme: An informative, interactive book about understanding and dealing with bullies.

The Sneetches and Other Stories by Dr. Suess. Random House, 1961.

Suggested Age Range: 6 years–adult

Theme: Dr. Suess offers four short stories with social meaning. *Sneetches* is a story that indirectly comments on injustice based upon race, religion or gender bias.

Shredder-Man: Secret Identity by W. Van Draanen. Illust. by B. Biggs. Yearling, 2006.

Suggested Age Range: 7–10 years

Theme: A young boy characterized as a "nerd", is the target of the school bully until the boy creates a cyber super hero called Shredder-Man.

They Call Me Chicken: A Story of Courage by J. Caporale. Illust. by W. Summers. Xlibris Corporation, 2005.

Suggested Age Range: 7–13 years

Theme: A boy called "chicken" by bullies learns to cope and feel good about himself.

Bully by P. Polacco. Putnam Juvenile, 2012

Suggested Age Range: 7–16 years

Theme: A girl courageously stands up for her friend, who is a target of cyberbullying.

Bullies Are a Pain in the Brain by T. Romain. Illust. by T. Romain. Free Spirit, 1997.

Suggested Age Range: 8–13 years

Theme: This book addresses understanding and dealing with bullies.

Is It Because? by T. Ross. Illust. by T. Ross. Barron's Educational Series, 2005.

Suggested Age Range: 8–14 years

Theme: A boy being bullied by a classmate wonders why, and reaches some profound answers that help him to cope.

Blubber by J. Blume. Atheneum, 2002.

Suggested Age Range: 8 years–adult

Theme: A girl who is overweight is bullied by classmates, a leader and followers.

Loser by J. Spinelli. HarperCollins, 2003.

Suggested Age Range: 9–12 years

Theme: A young boy is considered a strange "loser" by class-mates, but he remains optimistic with family support that enables positive feelings about himself.

My Secret Bully by T. Ludwig. Illust. by A. Marble. Tricycle Press, 2005.

Suggested Age Range: 9–13 years

Theme: A girl's perspective on bullying, explores feelings and helpful strategies.

Physical/Sexual Abuse and Prevention

Let's Talk About Saying No by J. Berry. Scholastic, 1996.

Suggested Age Range: 3–7 years

Theme: This book explores the assertive expression of feelings, and how to say "No".

Uncle Willy's Tickles: A Child's Right to Say No by M. Aboff. Illust. by K. Gartner. APA: Magination Press, 2003.

Suggested Age Range: 3–8 years

Theme: Introduction to understanding body boundaries and a child's right to say no.

It's My Body: A Book to Teach Young Children How to Resist Uncomfortable Touch by L. Freeman (Britain). Illust. by C. Deach. Parenting Press, 1982.

Suggested Age Range: 3–8 years

Theme: Sensitively teaches young children to distinguish "good touch" and "bad touch".

Your Body Belongs to You by C. Spelman. Illust. by T. Weidner. Whitman, 1997.

Suggested Age Range: 3–9 years

Theme: Preventing child sexual abuse in an assertive manner, without being frightening.

Some Parts are Not for Sharing by J.K. Federico. Tate Publishing, 2009.

Suggested Age Range: 4 years–adult

Theme: A pair of friendly fish teach young children about parts of the body, appropriate boundaries, and that some parts are private.

Kids Helping Kids Break the Silence of Sexual Abuse by L.L. Foltz. Lighthouse Point Press, 2003.

Suggested Age Range: 4 years–adult

Theme: Survivors of sexual abuse share lessons about healing and staying safe.

Some Secrets Hurt by L.K. Garner. Illust. by B. Speth. Shadow Mountain, 2009.

Suggested Age Range: 4 years–adult

Theme: A young victim of sexual abuse finds the courage to tell.

I Said No! A Kid to Kid Guide to Keeping Private Parts Private by Z. King and K. King. Illust. by S. Rama. Boulden Publishing, 2008.

Suggested Age Range: 4 years–adult

Theme: This book helps children set healthy boundaries from a kid's perspective and helps caregivers discuss sexual abuse and problematic situations.

The Right Touch: A Read-Aloud Story to Help Prevent Child Sexual Abuse by S. Kleven. Illust. by J. Bergsma. Illumination Arts Publishing, 1998.

Suggested Age Range: 4 years–adult

Theme: A trusted caregiver can read this gentle story to teach young children about sexual abuse and how to prevent it. This book affirms that abuse is not the child's fault.

Mia's Secret by P. Ledwon. Illust. by M. Mets. Tundra Books, 2006.

Suggested Age Range: 4 years–adult

Theme: Little Mia is feeling powerless and frightened, having promised to keep a secret about being sexually abused.

Please Tell!: A Child's Story About Sexual Abuse by J. Ottenweller. Illust. by J. Ottenweller. Hazelden Publishing, 1991.

Suggested Age Range: 4 years–adult

Theme: A young girl who was sexually abused by a family member encourages others who have been abused to speak out.

My Body Is Private by L. Girard. Illust. by R.S. Pate. Whitman, 1984.

Suggested Age Range: 5–12 years

324

Theme: The conversation of a mother and daughter is a lesson about privacy and saying "No" to touching that makes the girl feel uncomfortable.

Hear My Roar: A Story of Family Violence by G. Watts. Illust. by B. Hodson. Annick Press, 2009.
Suggested Age Range: 6–9 years
Theme: A family of bears provide an allegory about family violence and taking action to break the cycle of abuse.

The Berenstain Bears Learn About Strangers by S. Berenstain and J. Berenstain.
Random House, 1985.
Suggested Age Range: 6–10 years
Theme: Bear cubs learn about safety and rules for dealing with strangers.

Healing Days: A Guide For Kids Who Have Experienced Trauma by S. Farber Straus.
Illust. by M. Bogade. APA: Magination Press. 2013.
Suggested Age Range: 6–11 years
Theme: Resource to empower children who have been physically or sexually abused.

Not in Room 204: Breaking the Silence of Abuse by S. Riggs. Illust. by J. Zollars. Whitman, 2007.
Suggested Age Range: 6 years–adult
Theme: A teacher conducts a lesson on stranger danger and supports a young girl who confides to her about being abused by her father.

No More Secrets for Me: Sexual Abuse is a Secret No Child Should Have to Keep by O. Wachter. Illust. by J. Aaron. Little, Brown & Co., 2002.
Suggested Age Range: 7 years–adult
Theme: This book helps parents and caregivers teach children warning signs of sexual abuse and the importance of talking about abuse if it happens.

The Magic Half by A. Barrows. Bloomsbury USA Childrens, 2009.

Suggested Age Range: 8–12 years
Theme: Time travel is the vehicle to tell a story of child abuse. A suspenseful, engaging tale that may be quite scary for young children.

Finding Safety: Boundaries for Teenagers: How to Recognize and Protect Yourself from Abuse by C. Marlowe. First Book Library, 1999.
Suggested Age Range: 13 years–adult
Theme: This book empowers teens and adults dealing with or surviving sexual abuse.

When Something Feels Wrong: A Survival Guide about Abuse for Young People
by D. Pledge. Free Spirit, 2002.
Suggested Age Range: 13 years–adult
Theme: This is a valuable resource for teenagers seeking positive ways to deal with sexual abuse and begin the healing process.

Hope in Patience by B. Fehlbaum. Westside Books, 2010.
Suggested Age Range: 14 years–adult
Theme: A story about a sexually abused teenager, who experiences traumatic reactions and with help, begins the difficult process of healing.

Teaching Children with Down Syndrome about Their Bodies, Boundaries, and Sexuality by T. Couwenhoven. Woodbine House, 2007.
Suggested Age Range: 16 years–adult
Theme: A book of stories, examples and suggestions for parents and caregivers of children with special needs, about affection, sexual relationships, and abuse prevention.

Sibling Abuse: Hidden Physical, Emotional and Sexual Trauma by V.R. Wiehe.
Sage Publications, 1997.
Suggested Age Range: 18 years–adult
Theme: This book sensitively tells the hidden story of sibling sexual abuse, including personal accounts of survivors, insights, and suggestions for prevention and treatment.

Serious Illness/Hospital Experience

When Mommy Is Sick by F. Sherkin-Langer. Illust. by K. Life. Whitman, 1995.

    Suggested Age Range: 3–8 years

    Theme: A child deals with mother's illness, hospitalization and separation.

Franklin Goes To The Hospital by P. Bourgeois. Illust. by B. Clark. Scholastic, 2011.

    Suggested Age Range: 3–8 years

    Theme: A turtle is scared to go to the hospital for an operation, but learns that you can be both scared and brave.

Going to the Hospital by A. Civardi and M. Bates. Usborne, 2005.

    Suggested Age Range: 3–10 years

    Theme: Reassurance when a boy spends a night in a hospital after an ear operation.

My Grandpa Had a Stroke by D. Butler. Illust. by N. Wong. APA: Magination Press, 2007.

    Suggested Age Range: 4–8 years

    Theme: Offers age-appropriate information to help young children and families cope with feelings and adjust when a loved one has a stroke.

Sometimes My Mommy Gets Angry by B. Campbell. Illust. by E.B. Lewis. Puffin, 2005.

    Suggested Age range: 4–8 years

    Theme: A girl learns to cope with a mother having severe, disturbing mood swings.

Striped Shirts and Flowered Pants: A Story About Alzheimer's Disease for Young Children by B. Schnurbush. Illust. by C. Pillo. APA: Magination Press, 2007.

    Suggested Age Range: 4–8 years

    Theme: A young girl learns with reassurance from her family how Alzheimer's Disease will affect her grandmother, and discovers how to cope with her feelings.

Do I Have to Go to the Hospital?: A First Look at Going to the Hospital by P. Thomas
> Illust. by L.Harker. Barron's Educational Series, 2006.
> Suggested Age Range: 4–8 years
> Theme: Helps children undertand the need to go to the hospital and what to expect.

What About Me? When Brothers and Sisters Get Sick by A. Peterkin.
> Illust. by F. Middendorf. APA: Magination Press, 1992.
> Suggested Age Range: 4–8 years
> Theme: Helps young children and families deal with the complicated feelings of having a sibling with a serious illness.

Madeline by L. Bemelmans. Viking Press, 1939, 2000.
> Suggested Age Range: 4–9 years
> Theme: A young girl has a hospital experience and emergency surgery.

Whistle for Willie by E.J. Keats. Illust. by E.J. Keats. Viking Press, 1964, 1998.
> Suggested Age Range: 4–9 years
> Theme: A story about a boy's hospital experience and support. African American theme

Curious George Goes to the Hospital by M. Rey and H.A. Rey. Houghton Mifflin, 1966.
> Suggested Age Range: 4–9 years
> Theme: A little primate has a hospital experience and emergency surgery.

Our Mom Has Cancer by A. Ackermann and A. Ackermann.
> American Cancer Society, 2000.
> Suggested Age Range: 4–10 years
> Theme: Daughters write about having a mother fighting cancer.
> *Sad Days, Glad Days: A Story About Depression* by D. Hamilton. Illust. by G. Owens. Whitman, 1995.
> Suggested Age Range: 4–10 years

328

Theme: A young girl experiences sad and glad days, because of her mother's depression.

Why is Mommy Sad? A Child's Guide to Parental Depression by P. Chan. Illust. by L. Faust. Current Clinical Strategies Publishing, 2006.

Suggested Age Range: 4–11 years

Theme: A book designed to be read together by children and parents about depression.

The Rainbow Feelings of Cancer: A Book for Children Who Have a Loved One with Cancer by C. Martin and C. Martin. Illust. by C. Martin. Hohm Press, 2001.

Suggested Age Range: 4–11 years

Theme: A daughter's illustrations and thoughts about her mother's illness, cancer.

When Mommy Had Cancer by T. Rawlins. Illust. by Jean Sanchez. WestBow, 2013.

Suggested Age Range: 4–11 years

Theme: A boy tells about his mother having cancer, receiving treatments, and helping.

The Surgery Book: For Kids by S. Bhatia. AuthorHouse, 2010.

Suggested Age Range: 4–11 years

Theme: Reassuringly prepares children for tonsil removal, but helps with any surgery.

Grandma's Soup by N. Karkowsky. Illust. by S.O. Haas. Kar-Ben Publishing, 1989.

Suggested Age Range: 5–9 years

Theme: A young girl deals with her grandmother's confusion and disorientation due to Alzheimer's disease. Jewish theme

Promises by E.M. Winthrop. Illust. by B. Lewin. Clarion, 2000.

Suggested Age Range: 5–9 years

Theme: The story of a girl dealing with her mother's cancer chemotherapy treatments.

Now One Foot, Now the Other by T. dePaola. Illust. by T. dePaola. Penguin, 1981.

Suggested Age Range: 5 years–adult

Theme: When a young boy's grandfather has a stroke, the boy teaches his grandfather to walk just as his grandfather had done for him.

Always My Grandpa: A Story for Children About Alzheimer's Disease by L. Scacco. Illust. by N. Wong. APA: Magination Press, 2005.

Suggested Age Range: 6–10 years

Theme: A young boy gently learns about the course of Alzheimer's Disease.

Wishing Wellness: A Workbook for Children of Parents With Mental Illness by L.A. Clarke. Illust. by B. Matthews. APA: Magination Press, 2006.

Suggested Age Range: 6–12 years

Theme: Workbook sensitively designed to help children process feelings and fears about having a parent with severe mental illness.

The Year My Mother Was Bald by A. Speltz. Illust. by K. Sternberg. APA: Magination Press, 2003.

Suggested Age Range: 8–13 years

Theme: A girl's journal about the year her mother was diagnosed and treated for cancer.

Friends Till the End by T. Strasser. Laurel Leaf Books, 1982.

Suggested Age Range: 12 years–adult

Theme: A student in high school is diagnosed with leukemia, affecting fellow students.

I Never Promised You a Rose Garden by J. Greenberg. Holt, 1964; St. Martin's, 2008.

Suggested Age Range: 15 years–adult

Theme: An intelligent young girl who has schizophrenia struggles through self-destructiveness, while demonstrating wit and courage.

Tragic Human Events/Violence

Changes, Changes by P. Hutchins. Aladdin, 1987.
Suggested Age Range: 2–6 years
Theme: A picture book without words that illustrates an experience with fire, encouraging young children to verbalize their thoughts and feelings.

Fire Fighters by N. Simon. Illust. by P. Paparone. Aladdin, 1998.
Suggested Age Range: 2–6 years
Theme: A book that teaches fire safety by following a team of firefighting dalmatian dogs from their firehouse home to the scene of a fire.

A Chair for My Mother by V. Williams. Illust. by V. Williams. Greenwillow, 1984.
Suggested Age Range: 3 years–adult
Theme: A child, her mother and her grandmother save their pennies to purchase a comfortable armchair, after their furniture is lost in a fire. African American theme

A Terrible Thing Happened by M.M. Holmes. Illust. by C. Pillo. APA: Magination Press, 2000.
Suggested Age Range: 4–8 years
Theme: A story of children who have witnessed violence or trauma. Includes suggestions for parents or caregivers

Jenny Is Scared! When Sad Things Happen in the World by C. Shuman. Illust. by C. Pillo. APA: Magination Press, 2003.
Suggested Age Range: 4–8 years
Theme: A story to comfort and help young children cope with being aware of threats of violence and terrorism in the world.

Why Are You So Scared?: A Child's Book About PTSD by B. Andrews. Illust. by K. Kirkland. APA: Magination Press, 2011.
Suggested Age Range: 4–8 years
Theme: Recognizes children's feelings and reassures them they are not responsible for a parent's sadness, anger, or despair– feelings that do not negate parental love.

From Far Away by R.N. Munsch and S. Askar. Illust. by M. Martchenko. Annick Press, 1995.
    Suggested Age Range: 4–8 years
    Theme: A young girl moves to Canada from a country at war and adjusts to a new language and customs.

The Cello of Mr. O by J. Cutler. Illust. by G. Couch. Penguin, 1999.
    Suggested Age Range: 5–9 years
    Theme: Frightened residents of a bombed city find hope in the courage of a musician.

Sadako and the Thousand Paper Cranes by E. Coerr. Illust. by E. Young. Penguin, 1997.
    Suggested Age Range: 5–12 years
    Theme: After the bombing of Hiroshima, a young girl dying of leukemia demonstrates amazing spirit, focusing her energy on folding 1,000 paper cranes. Japanese theme

It's Still a Dog's New York: A Book of Healing by S. Roth. National Geographic, 2001.
    Suggested Age Range: 5–12 years
    Theme: After the tragedy of September 11, 2001, two dogs deal with fear, sadness and anger, and discover they can find healing by helping others.

Shelter Folks by V. Kroll. Illust. by J. Naimo Jones. Eerdman's Publishing, 1995.
    Suggested Age Range: 5–15 years
    Theme: A nine year old girl is at first ashamed, but adjusts to living in a shelter.

The Butterfly by P. Polacco. Puffin Press, 2009.
    Suggested Age Range: 6–9 years
    Theme: A little girl discovers her family is hiding a Jewish family in Nazi occupied France. Monique and Sevrine meet secretly and become friends. Jewish theme

Your Move by E. Bunting. Illust. by J. E. Ransome. Harcourt, 1998.

Suggested Age Range: 6–12 years

Theme: When a ten year old boy's gang initiation endangers his six year old brother, they find the courage to reject violence.

Why Did It Happen? Helping Children Cope in a Violent World by J. Cohn. Morrow Junior Books, 1994.

Suggested Age Range: 6–12 years

Theme: A young boy is helped to cope with a violent act in his neighborhood and is reassured by caring adults. Coping with secondary trauma.

When Something Terrible Happens: Children Can Learn to Cope with Grief by M. Heegaard. Illust. by children. Woodland Press, 1996.

Suggested Age Range: 6–12 years

Theme: A book for children exposed to violent or traumatic events.

It Doesn't Have to Be This Way: A Barrio Story/No Tiene Que Ser Asi by L.J. Rodriguez.

Children's Book Press, 1999.

Suggested Age Range: 6–12 years

Theme: A young boy becomes reluctantly involved with a local gang, until a violent event involving his cousin, forces him to make a critical choice. Latino theme

Fly Away Home by E. Bunting. Illust. by R. Himler. Clarion, 1991.

Suggested Age Range: 6–14 years

Theme: A homeless boy and his father live in an airport.

Terrible Things: An Allegory of the Holocaust by E. Bunting. Illust. by S. Gammel. The Jewish Publication Society, 1996.

Suggested Age Range: 6 years–adult

Theme: An allegorical introduction to the Holocaust, using forest animals to encourage children to recognize and stand against injustice. Jewish and Universal theme

Benno and the Night of Broken Glass by M. Wiviott. Illust. by J. Bisaillon. Kar-Ben Publishing, 2010.

Suggested Age Range: 7–11 years

Theme: The story of a violent night of Nazi terror told through the eyes of a cat. Jewish and Universal theme

The Harmonica by T. Johnston. Illust. by R. Mazellan. Charlesbridge Publishing, 2008.

Suggested Age Range: 8–12 years

Theme: Inspired by a true story, a young Polish boy survives a concentration camp and the Holocaust with a harmonica given to him by his father. Jewish and Universal theme

Sami and the Time of the Troubles by F.P. Heide and J.H. Gilliland. Illust. by T. Lewin. Clarion, 1992.

Suggested Age Range: 8 years–adult

Theme: A young brother and sister live and strive to have a future in war-torn Lebanon.

One April Morning: Children Remember the Oklahoma City Bombing by N. Lamb. Illust. by F. Cooper. Lothrop, Lee & Shepard, 1996.

Suggested Age Range: 10 years–adult

Theme: Promotes understanding of how a child reacts to violent tragedy.

Lost in the War by N. Antle. Dial, 1998.

Suggested Age Range: 12–16 years

Theme: The story of a young girl's struggle to cope with a mother who is still haunted by traumatic experiences as a nurse during the war in Vietnam. Illustrates PTSD

Young People From Bosnia Talk About War by H. Fireside and B.J. Fireside.

Enslow Publishers, 1996.

Suggested Age Range: 12 years–adult

Theme: Youths who experienced war talk about fears, doubts and hope for the future.

The Disappearance by R. Guy. Laurel Leaf, 1991.

Suggested Age Range: 12 years–adult

Theme: A young teenager is acquitted of murder charges,

but becomes a suspect when a girl disappears. African American theme

Thanks to My Mother by S. Rabinovici. Translated by J. Skofield. Puffin Books, 2000.

> Suggested Age Range: 12 years–adult
> Theme: The moving story of how a young Jewish girl and her mother survive the Holocaust. Jewish theme

Behind the Eyes by F.X. Stork. Dutton Juvenile, 2006.

> Suggested Age Range: 13–19 years
> Theme: A teenage boy tries to cope and survive after the violent death of his older brother, and threats from the gang culture. Latino theme

Grief Girl: My True Story by E. Vincent. Delacorte, 2007.

> Suggested Age Range: 13–19 years
> Theme: Story of a teenage girl, her older sister and younger brother, whose parents are killed in a terrible car crash that leaves them dealing with grief and survival.

A Grief Like No Other: Surviving the Violent Death of Someone You Love by K. O'Hara. Marlowe, 2006.

> Suggested Age Range: 18–adult
> Theme: Insights and suggestions to help survivors of the violent death of a loved one.

Wheels Down: Adjusting to Life After Deployment by B. Moore and C. Kennedy. APA: Magination Press, 2011.

> Suggested Age Range: 18–adult
> Theme: Ideas and strategies to aid adjustment of returning service persons and families.

Natural and Accidental Disasters

Changes, Changes by P. Hutchins. Aladdin, 1987.

> Suggested Age Range: 2—6 years
> Theme: A picture book without words that illustrates an experience with fire, encouraging young children to verbalize their thoughts and feelings.

Rhinos Who Rescue by J. Mammano. Chronicle Books, 2007.
 Suggested Age Range: 2—6 years
 Theme: Firefighters are represented as rhinos making exciting rescues.

Fire Fighters by N. Simon. Illust. by P. Paparone. Aladdin, 1998.
 Suggested Age Range: 2—6 years
 Theme: A book that teaches fire safety by following a team of firefighting dalmatian dogs from their firehouse home to the scene of a fire.

Symphony # 6, The Pastoral. Op. 68 by L.V. Beethoven.
 Suggested Age Range: 2 years–adult
 Theme: A beautiful symphony evokes the coming of a storm, the turbulence of thunder and lightening, and finally the tranquility that invites animals out into the forest. Danced or narrated with children, it helps them find comfort during a storm.

Clifford and the Big Storm by N. Bridwell. Scholastic, 1995.
 Suggested Age Range: 3—6 years
 Theme: Clifford the dog helps a little girl find shelter during a hurricane.

A Coloring Book: After the Tornado by B.F. Corder and T. Haizlip. North Carolina Division of Mental Health. Available through the American Red Cross.
 Suggested Age Range: 3–7 years
 Theme: A coloring book for dealing with tornados and other natural disasters.

It's Mine! by L. Lionni. Dragonfly Books, 1996.
 Suggested Age Range: 3—7 years
 Theme: Frogs argue until they begin helping each other during a scary storm and flood.

Franklin and the Thunderstorm by P. Bourgeois. Illust. by B. Clark. Scholastic, 1998.
 Suggested Age Range: 3–8 years
 Theme: A story that helps overcome the fear of thunder and lightening.

Katy and the Big Snow by V.L. Burton. Illust. by V.L. Burton. HMH, 1943, 1971, 2009.

Suggested Age Range: 3–8 years

Theme: A red tractor courageously serves as a snowplow during a huge blizzard.

A House of Leaves by K. Soya. Illust. by A. Hayashi. Philomel, 1987.

Suggested Age Range: 3—8 years

Theme: During a rain shower, a girl shares shelter with insects under a leafy canopy.

A Chair for My Mother by V. Williams. Illust. by V. Williams. Greenwillow, 1984.

Suggested Age Range: 3 years—adult

Theme: A child, her mother and her grandmother save their pennies to purchase a comfortable armchair, after their furniture is lost in a fire. African American theme

Flash, Crash, Rumble, and Roll by F. Branley. Illust. by E. Emberley. Crowell, 1964.

Suggested Age Range: 4–8 years

Theme: A book that provides explanations for the various sounds of a storm.

Dot the Fire Dog by L. Desimini. The Blue Sky Press, 2001.

Suggested Age Range: 4—8 years

Theme: Dot the dalmatian lives at the firehouse and sees how the firefighters work.

River Friendly, River Wild by J. Kurtz. Illust. by N. Brennan. Aladdin, 2007.

Suggested Age Range: 4—8 years

Theme: A young girl describes the Red River flood and the evacuation of her family.

That Sky, That Rain by C. Otto. Illust. by M. Lloyd. HarperCollins, 1992.

Suggested Age Range: 4—8 years

Theme: A girl and her grandfather move farm animals into

the barn before a storm.

Earthquack! by M. Palatini. Illust. by B. Moser. Simon & Schuster, 2005.
> Suggested Age Range: 4—8 years
> Theme: Barnyard animals are afraid of what they believe is an earthquake.

The Snowy Day by E. J. Keats. Puffin, 1976 (Reprint).
> Suggested Age Range: 4—10 years
> Theme: A little boy explores his urban neighborhood after a snowstorm.

Thunder Cake by P. Polacco. Penguin, 1997.
> Suggested Age Range: 4 years–adult
> Theme: A grandmother reassures her frightened granddaughter by telling her that the ominous dark clouds of a coming storm are just the ingredients of a thunder cake.

City in the Winter by E. Schick. Macmillan, 1970.
> Suggested Age Range: 5–9 years
> Theme: A small boy and his grandfather are housebound by a blizzard.

Mary Jo's Grandmother by J.M. Udry. Illust. by E. Mill. Whitman, 1972.
> Suggested Age Range: 5–9 years
> Theme: During a snowstorm, Mary Jo gets help from her grandmother.

The Storm Book by C. Zolotow. Illust. by M. Graham. HarperCollins, 1952, 1989.
> Suggested Age Range: 5–9 years
> Theme: A summer storm slashes across the land, culminating with a reassuring rainbow.

Tornado by B. Byars. Illust. by D. Ben-Ami. HarperCollins, 2004 (Reprint).
> Suggested Age Range: 6—10 years
> Theme: In a storm cellar during a tornado, a family listens to stories about a dog.

The Day the Hurricane Happened by L. Anderson. Illust. by A. Grifalconi.

    Scribner's, 1974.

    Suggested Age Range: 6–13 years

    Theme: Grandpa tells frightened children what to expect about an imminent hurricane.

Umbrella by T. Yashima. Viking Press, 1958, 1977.

    Suggested Age Range: 7–11 years

    Theme: A story about the reassurance of a new umbrella on a rainy day.

The Big Rain by Françoise Seignobosc. Omnibus, 2003.

    Suggested Age Range: 7–13 years

    Theme: During a flood, a story about being saved from a farm house by a boat.

Little Toot on the Mississippi by H. Gramatky. G.P. Putnam's Sons, 1973.

    Suggested Age Range: 7–13 years

    Theme: Tugboat survives a flood, evoking feelings about floods and scary experiences.

Tornadoes! By G. Gibbons. Holiday House, 2010 (Reprint).

    Suggested Age Range: 8—12 years

    Theme: Text and illustrations describe tornadoes and what to do if one approaches.

I'll Know What to Do: A Kid's Guide to Natural Disasters by B. Mark and A. Layton. Illust. by M. Chesworth. APA: Magination Press, 1997.

    Suggested Age Range: 8–13 years

    Theme: Aids recovery from trauma caused by natural disasters.

Stormy Night by M. Lemieux. Illust. by M. Lemieux. Scholastic, 1999.

    Suggested Age Range: 8–14 years

    Theme: A young girl lies awake on a stormy night thinking about life and death.

Tornado! by J. Fradin and D. Fradin. National Geographic Children's Books, 2011.

    Suggested Age Range: 10 years—adult

    Theme: Descriptions of real tornadoes with awesome photographs that contribute to understanding their power and affect on people.

Green Angel by A. Hoffman. Scholastic, 2010.

    Suggested Age Range: 13 years–adult

    Theme: Green, age 15, struggles to survive, after her family dies in a disaster.

REFERENCES

Adair, J. (1996). *Not bosses but leaders: How to lead the way to success.* Kogan Page Ltd.

Adair, J. (2006). *How to grow leaders: The seven key principles of effective leadership development.* Kogan Page Ltd.

Adamson, A.D., & Peacock, G.G. (2007). Crisis response in the schools: A survey of school psychologists' experiences and perceptions. *Psychology in the Schools, 44* (8), 749-764.

Aiello, A. (2010). In the presence of heartbreak: An intern's personal reflections on crisis response. *NASP Communiqué, 39* (1).

American Psychiatric Association (2000). *Diagnostic and statistical manual of mental disorders (DSM-IV-TR) (4th ed).* Washington, DC: APA.

Arvay, M. and Uhlemann, M. (1996). Counsellor stress in the field of trauma: A preliminary study. *Canadian Journal of Counselling/Reveu Canadienne de Counseling (2).*

Athey, J. & Moody-Williams, J. (2003). Developing cultural competence in disaster mental health programs: Guiding principles and recommendations. Washington, DC: US Department of Health and Human Services.

Bandura, A. (1982). Self-efficacy mechanism in human agency. *American Psychologist, 37,* 122–47.

Bandura, A. (1997). *Self-efficacy: The exercise of control.* New York: W.H. Freeman.

Barenbaum, J., Ruchkin, F., & Schwab-Stone, M. (2004). The psychosocial aspects of children exposed to war: Practice and policy initiatives. *Journal of Child Psychology and Psychiatry, 45,* 41–62.

Barkin, L. (2011). *The Comfort Garden: Tales from the Trauma Unit.* San Francisco: Fresh Pond Press.

Bates, M. & Spears, B. (2010, July). *Emergency management considerations for students and staff with disabilities.* Paper presented at the U.S. Department of Education, Office of Safe and Drug-Free Schools Readiness and Emergency Management for Schools Final Grantee Meeting. Boston, MA.

Bear, G.G. (2010). *School discipline and self-discipline: A practical guide to promoting prosocial student behavior.* New York: Guilford Press.

Bell, C., & Jenkins, E. (1991). Traumatic stress and children. *Journal of Health Care for The Poor and Underserved, 2,* 175–88.

Blanchard, K.H., Zigarmi, P. & Zigarmi, D. (1985). *Leadership and the one minute manager: Increasing effectiveness through situational leadership.* New York: Morrow.

Blaustein, M. (2013). Childhood trauma and a framework for intervention. In E. Rossen and R. Hull (Eds.). *Supporting and educating traumatized students: A guide for school-based professionals (pp. 3–21).* New York, NY: Oxford University Press.

Bolnik, L., & Brock, S.E. (2005). The self-reported effects of crisis intervention work on school psychologists. *The California School Psychologist, 10,* 117–124.

Bonanno, G.A. (2004). Loss, trauma, and human resilience: Have we underestimated the human capacity to thrive after extremely aversive events? *American Psychologist, 59,* 20–8.

Bradshaw, C.P., Mitchell, M.M., & Leaf, P.J. (2010). Examining the effects of schoolwide positive behavioral interventions and supports on student outcomes. *Journal of Positive Behavior Interventions, 12,* 133–148.

Brent, D.A., McMakin, D.L., Kennard, B.D., Goldstein, T.R., Mayes, T.L., & Douaihy, A.B. (2013). Protecting adolescents from self-harm: A critical review of intervention studies. *Journal of the American Academy of Child and Adolescent Psychiatry, 52,* 1260-1271.

Brickman, H.K., Jones, S.E., & Groom, S.E. (2004, May). Evolving school crisis management since 9/11. *Education Digest,* 69(9), 29–35.

Bride, B.E. (2007). Secondary traumatic stress among social workers. *Social Work, 52,* 63–70.

Brock, S.E. (2002a). Crisis Theory: A foundation for the comprehensive school crisis response team. In S.E. Brock, P.J. Lazarus, & S.R. Jimerson (Eds.), *Best practices in school crisis prevention and intervention* (pp. 5–17). Bethesda, MD: National Association of School Psychologists.

Brock, S.E. (2002b). Estimating the appropriate crisis response. In S.E. Brock, P.J.Lazarus, & S.R. Jimerson (Eds.), *Best practices in school crisis prevention and intervention* (pp. 355–66). Bethesda, MD: National Association of School Psychologists.

Brock, S.E. (2002c). "Identifying psychological trauma victims." In S.E. Brock, P.J. Lazarus, & S.R. Jimerson (Eds.), *Best practices in school crisis prevention and intervention* (pp. 367-83). Bethesda, MD: National Association of School Psychologists.

Brock, S.E. (2011). *PREPaRE Workshop #2: Crisis intervention and recovery: The roles of school-based mental health professionals.* (2nd ed.). Bethesda, MD: National Association of School Psychologists.

Brock, S. E. (2012). Preparing for school crisis intervention. In S.E. Brock & S. R. Jimerson (Eds.) *Best practices in school crisis prevention and intervention* (pp. 265–83; 2nd ed.). Bethesda, MD: National Association of School Psychologists.

Brock, S. E. & Davis, J. (2008). Best practices in school crisis intervention. In A. Thomas & J. Grimes (Eds.), *Best practices in school psychology* V. Bethesda, MD: National Association of School Psychologists.

Brock, S.E., & Jimerson, S.R. (2004). Characteristics and consequences of crisis events: A primer for the school psychologist. In E.R. Gerler, Jr. (Ed.), *Handbook of school violence* (pp. 273–84). New York: Haworth Reference Press.

Brock, S.E., Jimerson, S.R., & Hart, S.R. (2006). Preventing, preparing for, and responding to school violence with the National Incident Management System. In S.R. Jimerson & M.J. Furlong (Eds.), *Handbook of school violence and school safety: From research to practice* (pp. 443–58). Mahwah, NJ: Erlbaum.

Brock, S.E., Nickerson, A.B., Reeves, M.A., Jimerson, S.R., Lieberman, R.A., & Feinberg, T.A. (2009). *School crisis prevention and intervention: The PREPaRE model*. Bethesda, MD: National Association of School Psychologists.

Brock, S.E., Sandoval, J., & Lewis, S. (1996). *Preparing for crises in the schools: A manual for building school crisis response teams*. Brandon, VT: Wiley.

Brock, S.E., Sandoval, J., & Lewis, S. (2001). *Preparing for crises in the schools: A manual for building school crisis response teams* (2nd ed.). New York: Wiley.Brooks, B., & Siegel, P.M. (1996). *The scared child: Helping kids overcome traumatic events*. New York: Wiley.

Brooks, B., & Siegel, P.M. (1996). *The scared child: Helping kids overcome traumatic events*. New York: Wiley.

Brooks, R.B., & Goldstein, S. (2001). *Raising resilient children*. Chicago: Contemporary Books.

Brown, E.J., & Bobrow, A.L. (2004). School entry after a community-wide trauma:Challenges and lessons learned from September 11th, 2001. *Clinical Child and Family Psychology Review, 7*, 211-21.

Brymer, M., Jacobs, A., Layne, C., Pynoos, R., Ruzek, J., Steinberg, A., Watson, P.(2006). *Psychological first aid: Field operations guide* (2nd ed.). Rockville, MD: National Child Traumatic Stress Network and National Center for PTSD.

Brymer, M. J., Pynoos, R. S., Vivrette, R. L., & Taylor, M. A. (2012a). Providing school crisis interventions. In S. E. Brock & S. R. Jimerson (Eds.) *Best practices in school crisis prevention and intervention* (pp. 317–36; 2nd ed.). Bethesda, MD: National Association of School Psychologists.

Brymer, M., Taylor, M., Escudero, P., Jacobs, A., Kronenberg, M., Macy, R., Mock, L., Payne, L., Pynoos, R., & Vogel, J. (2012b). *Psychological first aid for schools: Field operations guide* (2nd ed.). Los Angeles, CA: National Child Traumatic Stress Network.

Caplan, G. (1964). *Principles of preventive psychiatry*. New York: Basic Books.

344

Caplan, G. (1970). *The theory and practice of mental health consultation.* New York: Basic Books.

Carlson, E.B. (1997). *Trauma assessments: A clinician's guide.* New York: Guilford Press.

Carrion, V.G., Weems, C.F., Ray, R.D., & Reiss, A.L., (2002). Towards an empirical definition of pediatric PTSD: The phenomenology of PTSD symptoms in youth. *Journal of the American Academy of Child & Adolescent Psychiatry, 41,* 166–173.

Charney, R.S. (1992). *Teaching children to care: Management in the Responsive Classroom.* Greenfield, MA: Northeast Foundation for Children.

Charney, R.S., & Wood, R. (1981). *The Responsive Classroom approach to instruction.* Greenfield, MA: Northeast Foundation for Children.

Christner, R.W., Forrest, E., Morely, J. & Weinstein, E. (2007). Taking cognitive-behavior therapy to school: A school-based mental health approach. *Journal of Contemporary Psychotherapy, 37,* 175–183.

Conolly-Wilson, C. (2008). *Conducting psychological triage.* Waukegan, IL: Waukegan Public Schools.

Creamer, T.L., & Liddle, B.J. (2005). Secondary traumatic stress among mental health workers responding to the September 11 attacks. *Journal of Traumatic Stress, 18,* 89–96.

Crepeau-Hobson, F. & Kanan, L. M. (2013/2014, December/January). After the tragedy: Caring for the caregivers. *Phi Delta Kappan, 95(4),* 33–7.

Demaria, T. & Schonfeld, D. J. (2013/2014, December/January). Do it now: Short-term responses to traumatic events. *Phi Delta Kappan, 95(4),* 13–17.

DiRaddo, J. D., & Brock, S. E., (2012, May). Is it a crisis? *Principal Leadership, 12(9),* 12–16.

Doll, B., Brehm, K., & Zucker, S. (2014). *Resilient classrooms: Creating healthy environments for learning* (2nd ed.). New York: Guilford Press.

Dorn, M., Thomas, G., Wong, M., Shepherd, S., Kelly, J., & Stephens, R. (2004). *Jane's school safety handbook* (2nd ed.). Surrey, UK: Jane's Information Group.

Dugger, S.M. (Hobson), & Carlson, L.A. (2007). *Critical incidents in counseling children.* American Counseling Association.

Durlak, J. A., Weissberg, R. P., Dymnicki, A. B., Taylor, R. D., & Schellinger, K. B. (2011). The impact of enhancing students' social and emotional learning: A meta-analysis of school-based interventions. *Child Development, 82,* 405–32.

Dwyer, K., & Jimerson, S.R. (2002). Enabling prevention through planning. In S.E. Brock, P.J. Lazarus, & S.R. Jimerson (Eds.), *Best practices in school crisis prevention and intervention* (pp. 23-46). Bethesda, MD: National Association of School Psychologists.

Dwyer, K., Osher, D., & Warger, C. (1998). *Early warning, timely response: A guide to safe schools.* U.S. Department of Education.

Dyregrov, A. & Yule, W. (2006). A review of PTSD in children. *Child and Adolescent Mental Health, 11,* 176–184.

Ehrenreich, J.H. (2001). Coping with disasters: A guidebook to psychosocial intervention. *Mental Health Workers without Borders.*

Eksi, A., Braum, K. L., Ertem-Vehid, H., Peykerli, G., Saydam, R., Toparlak, D., et al. (2007). Risk factors for the development of PTSD and depression among child and adolescent victims following a 7.4 magnitude earthquake. *International Journal of Psychiatry in Clinical Practice, 11,* 190–9.

Erbacher, T.A., Singer, J.B., & Poland, S. (2015). *Suicide in schools: A practitioner's guide to multi-level prevention, assessment, intervention, and postvention.* New York: Routledge.

Eth, S. (2002) Television viewing as risk factor. *Psychiatry, 65,* 301–3.

Everly, G.S. (1999). Toward a model of psychological triage: Who will most need assistance? *International Journal of Emergency Mental Health, 3,* 151–4.

346

Everly, Jr.,G.S. (2011). *Fostering human resilience in crisis: A primer on psychological body armor and psychological first aid and resilient leadership.* Ellicott City, MD: Chevron.

Everly, Jr., G.S., & Brown, S. (2009). *The resilient child.* New York, NY: Diamedica Publishing.

Everly, Jr., G.S., & Mitchell, J.T. (2003, 2nd ed.). *CISM: Individual crisis intervention and peer support.* International Critical Incident Stress Foundation. Baltimore, MD.

Everly, Jr., G.S., & Mitchell, J.T. (2010). *A primer on critical incident stress management (CISM).* Ellicott City, MD: International Critical Incident Stress Foundation.

Fein, A.H., Carlisle, C.S. & Isaacson, N.S. (2008). School shootings and counselor leadership: Four lessons from the field. *Professional School Counseling, 11,* 246–52.

Feinberg, T., Pfohl, W., & Cowan, K. (2004). Crisis: Tips for Caregivers. In A. Canter, L. Paige, M. Roth, I. Romaro, & S. Carroll (Eds.), *Helping children at home and school II: Handouts for families and educators.* Bethesda, MD: National Association of School Psychologists.

Fiedler, F. E. (1967). *A theory of leadership effectiveness.* New York: McGraw-Hill.

Fiedler, F. E. (1994). *Leadership experience and leadership performance.* Alexandria, VA: US Army Research Institute for the Behavioral and Social Sciences.

Fiedler, F.E., Chemers, M. M., & Mahar, L. (1976). *Improving leadership effectiveness: The leader match concept.* New York: John Wiley.

Figley, C.R. (Ed.) (1995). *Compassion fatigue: Coping with secondary traumatic stress disorder in those who treat the traumatized.* New York, NY: Brunner/Mazel.

Figley, C.R. (1999). Compassion fatigue: Towards a new understanding of the costs of caring. In B. H. Stamm (Ed.), *Secondary Traumatic Stress: Self-care issues for clinicians, researchers, & educators* (2nd ed., pp. 3–28). Lutherville, MD: Sidran Press.

Figley, C.R. (2002). *Treating compassion fatigue.* New York, NY: Brunner-Routledge.

Flynn, B.W., & Norwood, A.E. (2004). Defining normal psychological reactions to disaster. *Psychiatric Annals, 34,* 597–603.

Fraiberg, S. (1959). *The Magic Years.* New York, NY: Scribners.

Freeman, W., & Spears, B. (2009, November). *Preparedness.* U.S. Department of Education, Office of Safe and Drug-Free Schools Readiness and Emergency Management for Schools Initial Grantee Meeting. Irving, TX.

Garro, A., Brandwein, D., Calafiore, T. & Rittenhouse, N. (2011). Understanding and addressing early childhood trauma. NASP *Communiqué.* November, 2011, 40, (3).

Gilman, R., Huebner, E.S. and Furlong, M.J. (Eds) (2009). *Handbook of Positive Psychology in Schools.* New York, NY: Routledge.

Gordon, R. S. (1983). An operational classificationof disease prevention. *U.S. Department of Health and Human Services Public Health Report 1983, 98,* 107–9.

Grollman, E. (Ed.). (1967). *Explaining death to children.* Boston, MA: Beacon Press.

Hackman, J. R. & Wageman, R. (2005a). A theory of team coaching. *Academy of Management Review.* 30:2, 269 287.

Hackman, J. R. & Wageman, R. (2005b). When and how team leaders matter. *Research in Organizational Behavior, 26,* 37–74.

Hackman, J. R. & Walton, R. E. (1986). Leading groups in organizations. In P. S. Goodman (Ed.) *Designing effective work groups* (pp. 72–119). San Francisco: Jossey- Bass.

Harris, A. (2008). Distributed school leadership: Developing tomorrow's leaders. London: Routledge.

Hart, S. R. (2012). Student suicide: Suicide postvention. In S. E. Brock & S. R. Jimerson (Eds.) *Best practices in school crisis prevention and intervention* (pp. 525–47; 2nd ed.). Bethesda, MD: National Association of School Psychologists.

Heath, M.A., Bingham, R., Dean, B. (2008). The role of memorials in helping children heal. *School Psychology Forum: Research in Practice, 2,* 17–29.

Heath, M. A. & Cole, B. V. (2012). Identifying complicated grief

348

reactions in children. In S. E. Brock & S. R. Jimerson (Eds.) *Best practices in school crisis prevention and intervention* (pp. 649–70; 2nd ed.). Bethesda, MD: National Association of School Psychologists.

Heath, M.A., Sheen, D., Annandale, N.O., & Lyman, B. (2005). Responding to a crisis. In M.S. Heath and D. Sheen (Eds.), *School-based crisis intervention: Preparing all personnel to assist* (pp. 23–43). New York: Guilford Press.

Hersey, P. (1985). *The situational leader.* New York, NY: Warner Books.

Hersey, P. & Blanchard, K.H. (1977). *Management of organizational behavior: Utilizing human resources (3rd ed.).* New Jersey: Prentice Hall.

Holland, M. L. (2012). Identifying psychopathological crisis reactions. In S. E. Brock & S. R. Jimerson (Eds.) *Best practices in school crisis prevention and intervention* (pp. 613–29; 2nd ed.). Bethesda, MD: National Association of School Psychologists.

Horowitz, K., McKay, M., & Marshall, R. (2005). Community violence and urban families: Experiences, effects, and directions for intervention. *American Journal of Orthopsychiatry, 75,* 356–68.

International Critical Incident Stress Foundation, Inc. (2006). *A murder in the family.* Retrieved June 27, 2009 from http://www.thisisawar.com/GriefMurderFamily.htm

Ivey, A. E., Ivey, M. B., & Zalaquett, C. P. (2010). *Intentional interviewing & counseling: Facilitating client development in a multicultural society* (7th ed.). Belmont, CA: Brooks/Cole.

Jaycox, L. (2004). *Cognitive behavioral intervention for trauma in schools.* Longmont, CO: Sopris West.

Jellinek, M. S. & Okoli, U. D. (2012). When a student dies: Organizing the school's response. *Child and Adolescent Psychiatric Clinics of North America, 21,* 57–67.

Jimerson, S. R., Stein, R., & Rime, J. (2012a). Developmental considerations regarding psychological trauma and grief. In S. E. Brock & S. R. Jimerson (Eds.) *Best practices in school crisis prevention and intervention* (pp. 377–99; 2nd ed.). Bethesda, MD: National Association of School Psychologists.

Jimerson, S. R., Brown, J. A., & Stewart, K.T. (2012b). Sudden and unexpected student death: Preparing for and responding to the unpredictable. In S. E. Brock & S. R. Jimerson (Eds.) *Best practices in school crisis prevention and intervention* (pp. 469–83; 2nd ed.). Bethesda, MD: National Association of School Psychologists.

Johnson, K. (1998). *Trauma in the lives of children: Crisis and stress management techniques for counselors, teachers, and other professionals.* Alameda, CA: Hunter House.

Johnson, K. (2004). *Crisis in the classroom: The teacher's guide: Quick and proven techniques for stabilizing your students and yourself.* Alameda, CA: Hunter House.

Johnson, K. (2006). *After the storm: Healing after trauma, tragedy and terror.* Alameda, CA: Hunter House, Inc.

Jones, J.M. (2007). Exposure to chronic community violence: Resilience in African American children. *Journal of Black Psychology, 33,* 125–49.

Katzenbach, J.R., & Smith, D.K. (1993). *The wisdom of teams: Creating the high- performance organization.* New York, NY: Harper Collins.

Kemple, A.E., Heath, M.A., Hansen, K., Annandale, N.O., Fischer, L., Young, E.L., et al. (2006). Cultural sensitivity in a school-based crisis intervention. NASP *Communiqué, 34* (7), 34–7.

Kendall, P.C. (Ed.), (2011). *Child and adolescent therapy: Cognitive-behavioral procedures.* New York, NY: Guilford.

Kennedy-Paine, C., Reeves, M. A., & Brock, S. E. (2013/2014, December/January). How schools heal after a tragedy. *Phi Delta Kappan, 95(4),* 38–43.

Kim, H.K., & McKenry, P. (1998). Social networks and support: A comparison of African Americans, Asian Americans, Caucasians, and Hispanics. *Journal of Comparative Family Studies, 29,* 313–34.

Klingman, A. & Cohen, E. (2004). *School-based multisystem interventions for mass trauma.* New York, NY: Kluwer Academic/Plenum Publishers.

Kouzes, J. & Posner, B. (2012). *The leadership challenge: How to make extraordinary things happen in organizations* (5th ed.). CA: The Leadership Challenge.

Kubler-Ross, E. (1997). *On Death and Dying.* Washington, DC: Abbe Publishing.

LaGreca, A.M., Silverman, W.K., Vernberg, E.M., & Robers, M.C. (Eds.) (2002). *Helping children cope with disasters and terrorism.* Washington, DC: American Psychological Association.

Lavin, C. (1998). Helping individuals with developmental disabilities. In K. Doka & J. Davison (Eds.*), Living with grief: Who we are, how we grieve* (pp. 161–80). Philadelphia, PA: Brunner & Mazel.

Levine, P.A. & Kline, M. (2007). *Trauma through a child's eyes: Awakening the ordinary miracle of healing, infancy through adolescence.* Berkley, CA: North Atlantic Books.

Lewin, K. (1951). *Field theory in social science.* New York, NY: Harper.

Lewin, K. Lippitt, R., & White, R.K. (1939). Patterns of aggressive behavior in experimentally created "social climates." *Journal of Social Psychology, 10,* 271–99.

Lieberman, R., & Davis, J.M. (2002). Suicide intervention. In S.E. Brock, P.J. Lazarus, & S.R. Jimerson (Eds.), *Best practices in school crisis prevention and intervention* (pp. 531–51). Bethesda, MD: NASP.

Lubit, R., Rovine, D., Defrancisi, L. & Eth, S. (2003). Impact of trauma on children. *Journal of Psychiatric Practice, 9*(2), 128–38.

McNally, R.J., Bryant, R.A., & Ehlers, A. (2003). Does early psychological intervention promote recovery from posttraumatic stress? *Psychological Sciences in the Public Interest, 4,* 45–80.

Mears, C.L. (Ed.) (2012). *Reclaiming school in the aftermath of trauma: Advice based on experience.* New York: Palgrave MacMillan.

Mennuti, R.B., Freeman, A., & Christner, R.W. (Eds.), (2006).

Cognitive-behavioral/interventions in educational settings: A handbook for practice. New York, NY: Routledge.

Meyers, J., Parsons, R.D., & Martin, R. (1979). *Mental health consultation in the schools.* San Francisco, CA: Jossey-Bass.

Meyers, J. & Pitt, N. (1976). A consultation approach to help a school cope with the bereavement process. *Professional Psychology, 7,* 559–64.

Minuchin, S. (1974). *Families & family therapy.* Cambridge, MA: Harvard University Press.

Mitchell, J.T. (1983). When disaster strikes: The critical incident stress debriefing process. *Journal of Emergency Medical Services, 8,* 36–9.

Mitchell, J.T. (1993). Critical Incident Stress Management: The First Decade. *Life Net, A Publication of the International Critical Incident Stress Foundation, Inc.,* 4(4), 1, 2.

Mitchell, J.T., & Everly, Jr., G.S. (1996). *Critical incident stress debriefing.* Ellicott City, MD: Chevron.

Mitchell, J.T., Everly, G.S. (1998). *Critical incident stress management: The basic course workbook* (2nd ed.). Ellicott City, MD: International Critical Incident Stress Foundation.

Mitchell, J. & Everly, G. (2001). *Critical incident stress debriefing: An operations manual for CISD, defusing, and other group crisis intervention services.* Ellicott City, MD: Chevron.

Molaison, V. (2003). *School survival kit: Helping students cope with grief in the school setting.* Supporting Kidds: www.supportingkidds.org.

Molock, S.D., Puri, R., Mtlin, S., & Barksdale, C. (2006). Relationship between religious coping and suicidal behavior among African American adolescents. *Journal of Black Psychology, 32,* 366–89.

National Association of School Psychologists. (2003). *Helping children cope with loss, death, and grief: Tips for teachers and parents.* Bethesda, MD.

National Association of School Psychologists. (2004). *Culturally competent crisis response: Information for school psychologists and crisis teams.* Bethesda, MD.

National Association of School Psychologists. (2006). *Responsible media coverage of crisis events impacting children.* Bethesda, MD.

Nickerson, A.B., & Heath, M.A. (2008). *Developing and strengthening crisis response teams. School Psychology Forum,* 2(2), 1–16.

Nickerson, A.B., Reeves, M.A., Brock, S.E., & Jimerson, S.R. (2009). *Identifying, assessing, and treating posttraumatic stress disorder at school.* New York, NY: Springer.

Office of Safe and Drug-Free Schools (OSDFS), U.S. Department of Education. (2007). *Practical information on crisis planning: A guide for schools and communities.* Washington, DC.

Ortiz, S. O., & Voutsinas, M. (2012). Cultural considerations in crisis intervention. In S. E. Brock & S. R. Jimerson (Eds.) *Best practices in school crisis prevention and intervention* (pp. 337–57; 2nd ed.). Bethesda, MD: National Association of School Psychologists.

Osofsky, J.D. (Ed.). (2004). *Young children and trauma: Intervention and treatment.* New York, NY: Guilford Press.

Osofsky, J.D. (Ed.). (2011). *Clinical work with traumatized young children.* New York, NY: Guilford Press.

Parson, E.R. (1994). *Inner city children of trauma: Urban violence traumatic stress response syndrome (U-VTS) and therapists' responses.* Retrieved June 28, 2009, from http://www.giftfromwithin.org/pdf/parson.pdf

Pedersen, P.B. (2003). Culturally biased assumptions in counseling psychology. *The Counseling Psychologist, 31,* 396–403.

Petersen, S. & Straub, R.L. (1992). *School crisis survival guide: Management techniques and materials for counselors and administrators.* San Francisco, CA: Jossey-Bass.

Pfohl, W., Jimerson, S.R. & Lazarus, P.J. (2002). Developmental aspects of psychological trauma and grief. In S.E. Brock, P.J. Lazarus, & S.R. Jimerson, (Eds.), *Best practices in school crisis prevention and intervention* (pp. 309–31). Bethesda, MD: National Association of School Psychologists Press.

Poland, S. (1997). School crisis teams. In A.Goldstein & J. Conoley (Eds.), *School violence intervention handbook*. New York, NY: Guilford Press.

Poland, S., & McCormick, J. (1999). *Coping with crisis: Lessons learned*. Longmont, CO: Sopris West.

Poland, S. & Poland, D. (2004, April). Dealing with death at school. *Principal Leadership, 4*, 8–12.

Poland, S. & Rosenberg, S. (2011). Brazilian school shooting mirrors school violence lessons from around the world. NASP *Communiqué*. November, 2011, 40, (3).

Pynoos, R.S., & Nader, K. (1990). Children's exposure to violence and traumatic death. *Psychiatric Annals, 20*, 334–44.

Rabalais, A.E., Ruggiero, K.J. & Scotti, J.R. (2002). Multicultural issues in the response of children to disasters. In A.M. La Greca, W.K. Silverman, E.M. Vernberg, & M.C. Roberts (Eds.). *Helping children cope with disasters and terrorism* (pp.73–99). Washington, D.C.: American Psychological Association.

Raundalen, M. & Dyregrov, A. (2004). *Terror: How to talk to children*. Center for Crisis Psychology, Bergen, Norway. www.icisf.org/articles

Reeves, M. & Cowan, K. (2008). Securing PREPaRE training in your district. NASP *Communiqué, 37*(4).

Reeves, M., Kanan, L., & Plog, A. (2010). *Comprehensive planning for safe learning environments: A school professional's guide to integrating physical and psychological safety—Prevention through recovery*. New York, NY: Routledge.

Reeves, M.A., Nickerson, A.B., Conolly-Wilson, C., Lazzaro, B., Susan, M.K., Pesce, R.C., & Jimerson, S.R. (2011). PREPaRE Workshop # 1: *Crisis prevention and preparedness: Comprehensive school safety planning*. (2nd ed.). Bethesda, MD. National Association of School Psychologists.

Reeves, M. A., Conolly-Wilson, C. N., Pesce, R. C., Lazarro, B. R., & Brock, S. E. (2012). Preparing for the comprehensive school crisis response. In S. E. Brock & S. R. Jimerson (Eds.) *Best practices in school crisis prevention and intervention* (pp. 245–64; 2nd ed.). Bethesda, MD: National Association of School Psychologists.

Ristuccia, J. (2013). Creating safe and supportive schools for students impacted by traumatic experience. In E. Rossen & R. Hull (Eds.). *Supporting and educating traumatized students: A guide for school-based professionals* (pp. 253–63). New York, NY: Oxford University Press.

Ritchie, R., and Woods, P.S. (2007). Degrees of distribution: Towards an understanding of variations in the nature of distributed leadership in schools. *School Leadership and Management, 27*(4), 363–86.

Ritchie, W.C., & Hamilton, S. (2004). Assessing mental health needs following disaster. *Psychiatric Annals, 34*, 605–10.

Rossen, E. & Cowan, K. (2013, November). The role of schools in supporting traumatized students. *Principal's Research Review, 8(6),* 1–8.

Roth, J. & Curtis, J. (1993). Operation cooperation: Conflict resolution and beyond. NASP *Communiqué, 22* (2).

Ruof, S., & Harris, J. (1988, May). Suicide contagion: Guilt and modeling. A series on suicide prevention. NASP *Communiqué, 16* (7), 8.

Ruzek, J.L., Brymer, M.J., Jacobs, A.K., Layne, C.M., Vernberg, E.M., & Watson, P.J. (2007). Psychological first aid. *Journal of Mental Health Counseling, 29*, 17–49.

Saltzman, W.R., Pynoos, R.S., Layne, C.M., Steinberg, A.M., & Aisenberg, E. (2001). Trauma-and grief-focused intervention for adolescents exposed to community violence: Results of a school-based screening and group treatment protocol. *Group Dynamics: Theory, Research and Practice, 5*, 291–303.

Sandoval, J., & Brock, S.E. (2009). Managing crisis: Prevention, intervention, and treatment. In C.R. Reynolds & T.B. Gutkin (Eds.), *The handbook of school psychology* (pp. 886–904). New York, NY: Wiley.

Sandoval, J. & Lewis, S. (2002). Cultural consideration in crisis intervention. In Brock, S.E., Lazarus, P.J., and Jimerson, S.R., (Eds.), *Best practices in school crisis prevention and intervention* (pp. 293–308). Bethesda, MD: National Association of School Psychologists.

Saylor, C.F., Belter, R., & Stokes, S.J. (1997). Children and families coping with disaster. In S.A. Wolchik & I.N. Sandler (Eds.). *Handbook of children's coping: Linking theory and intervention* (pp. 361–83). New York, NY: Plenum.

Seligman, M.E.P. (2007). *The optimistic child: A proven program to safeguard children against depression and build lifelong resilience.* Boston, MA: Houghton Mifflin.

Seligman, M.E.P., Reivich, K., Jaycox, L., & Gillham, J. (1995). *The optimistic child.* Boston, MA: Houghton Mifflin.

Senge, P.M. (2006). *The fifth discipline: The art and practice of the learning organization* (2nd ed.). Crown Business.

Silva, A. (2004). *Culturally competent crisis response: Information for school psychologists and crisis teams.* NASP. Retrieved from http://www.nasponline.org/resources/culturalcompetence/cc_crisis.aspx

Silva, A., & Klotz, M.B. (2006). *Culturally competent crisis response.* NASP. www.naspcenter.org/principals/cultcompcrisis.pdf

Singer, M.I., Flannery, D.J., Guo, S., Miller, D., & Leibbrandt, S. (2004). Exposure to violence, parental monitoring, and television viewing as contributors to children's psychological trauma. *Journal of community Psychology, 32,* 489–504.

Smallwood, D.L., Williams, B.B. & McDonald, D.M. (2006). Cognitive-behavioral approaches to school crisis response. In R.B. Mennuti, A. Freeman, & R.W. Christner (Eds.), *Cognitive-behavioral interventions in educational settings* (pp. 407–27). New York, NY: Routledge.

Spillane, J.P. (2006). *Distributed leadership.* San Francisco: Jossey-Bass.

Spillane, J.P., Halverson, R. & Diamond, J.B. (2004). Towards a theory of leadership practice: A distributed perspective. *Journal of Curriculum Studies, 36* (1), 3-34

Stamm, B.H. (1999*). Secondary traumatic stress: Self-care issues for clinicians, researchers & educators.* Baltimore, MD: The Sidron Press.

Sue, D. W., & Sue, D. (2003). *Counseling the culturally different: Theory and practice* (4th ed.). New York: John Wiley & Sons.

Sugai, G., & Horner, R. (2002). The evolution of discipline

practices: School-wide positive behavior supports. *Child and Family Behavior Therapy, 24*, 23–50.

Sugai, G. & Horner, R. (2006). A promising approach for expanding and sustaining the implementation of school-wide positive behavior support. *School Psychology Review, 35*, 245–59.

Susan, M.K. (2010). Crisis prevention, response, and recovery: Helping children with special needs. In A. Canter, L.Z. Paige, & S. Shaw (Eds.), *Helping children at home and school III: Handouts for families and educators* (pp. S9H4-1–S9H4-3). Bethesda, MD: National Association of School Psychologists.

Taylor, M. (2006, September). *Conducting effective table tops, drills and exercises.* Presentation of the Office of Safe and Drug-Free Schools, Santa Monica, CA.

Thompson, R.A. (2006). *Nurturing future generations: Promoting resilience in children and adolescents through, emotional, and cognitive skills.* New York: Routledge.

Tugade, M.M., & Frederickson, B.L. (2004). Resilient individuals use positive emotions to bounce back from negative emotional experiences. *Journal of Personality and Social Psychology, 86*(2), 320–33.

Ungar, M. (2008). Resilience across cultures. *British Journal of Social Work, 38*, 218–35.

Vaillancourt, K.M., & Gibson, N.A. (2114). Professional practice: Model school district policy for suicide prevention. *Communique, 43 (2)*, 1, 24-27.

Vasquez, C., & Janvier, R.A. (1991). The problem with interpreters: Communicating with Spanish-speaking patients. *Hospital and Community Psychiatry, 42*, 163–5.

Vernberg, E.M., LaGreca, A.M., Silverman, W.K., & Prinstein, M.J. (1996). Predictors of children's post-disaster functioning following Hurricane Andrew. *Journal of Abnormal Psychology, 105*, 237–48.

Vernberg, E.M., Steinberg, A.M., Jacobs, A.K., Brymer, M.J., Watson, P.J., Osofsky, J.D., et al. (2008). Innovations in disaster mental health: Psychological first aid. *Professional*

Psychology: Research and Practice, 39, 381–8.

Viorst, J. (1972). *The tenth good thing about Barney.* New York, NY: Atheneum.

Wachtel, P.L. (2011). Therapeutic communication: Knowing what to say when (2ⁿᵈ ed.). New York, NY: Guilford.

Webber, J., & Mascari, J.B., (2010). *Terrorism, trauma, and tragedies: A counselor's guide to preparing and responding.* (3ʳᵈ ed.). ACA Foundation.

Wolfelt, A. (2004). *A child's view of grief: A guide for parents, teachers, and counselors.* Fort Collins, CO: Companion Press.

Wong, M., Rosemond, M.E., Stein, B.D., Langley, A.K., Katoaka, S.H., & Nadeem, E. (2007). School-based intervention for adolescents exposed to violence. *The Prevention Researcher, 14*(1), 17–20.

Worden, J.W. (2009). *Grief counseling and grief therapy: A handbook for the mental health practitioner.* (4ᵗʰ ed.). New York, NY: Springer Publishing Company.

Young, M.A. (1997). *The community crisis response team training manual* (2ⁿᵈ ed.). Washington, D.C.: Office for Victims of Crime and the National Organization for Victim Assistance.

Yukl, G. (2012). *Leadership in Organizations.* (8ᵗʰ ed.). New Jersey: Prentice Hall.

Zautra, A.J., Hall, J.S., & Murray, K.E. (2010). Resilience: A new definition of health for people and communities. In J.W. Reich, A.J. Zautra, & J.S. Hall (Eds.), *Handbook of Adult Resilience* (pp. 3–29). New York, NY: Guilford, Press.

Zenere, F. J. (2009a). Suicide clusters and contagion. *Principal Leadership, 12*, 1–5.

Zenere, F. J. (2009b). Violent loss and urban children: Understanding the impact on grieving and development. NASP *Communiqué*, October, 2009, 38 (2).

Zhe, E.J. & Nickerson, A.B. (2007). The effects of an intruder crisis drill on children's self-perceptions of anxiety, school safety, and knowledge. *School Psychology Review, 36*, 501–8.

REFERENCES

Zibulsky, J. (2012). Preparing for the anniversaries of crisis events. In S. E. Brock & S. R. Jimerson (Eds.) *Best practices in school crisis prevention and intervention* (pp. 423–4; 2nd ed.). Bethesda, MD: National Association of School Psychologists.

Acknowledgements

The partnership with my wife Carol inspires me, and yes, she did help develop this manuscript. Long ago, daughter, Leah, and son, Michael, taught me what unselfish love is and how to overcome the desire to make it better all at once. Ted Weiner, friend as brother, first suggested I study school psychology.

I am grateful to school psychologist Joan English, who spent months alternating between sleeplessness and nightmares describing, for our district manual, how to respond to a litany of crises.

I have been strengthened by inspiring teachers throughout my public school experience, by my opportunity to teach at Project Learn, an amazing alternative school in Philadelphia, and by my graduate programs, Psychoeducational Processes and School Psychology at Temple University where the special inspiration of my dissertation committee — Patricia Minuchin, chair, Joel Meyers, Mel Silberman, and Eugene Stivers — remains with me.

I thank those gracious individuals who reviewed the manuscript including Patricia Minuchin, Joel Meyers, Melissa Reeves, George Bear, Cathy Moore, Carol Roth and Bonnie Britt. Your thoughtful suggestions have been on target and extremely helpful. I also wish to thank friends and colleagues whom I have interviewed during the research including Laurie Barkin, Laura Becker, Donald Bersoff, Leah Roth Booze, Raleigh Booze, Leslie Carlson, Nancy Carney, Donna Carroll, Beth Couto, Elliot Davis, Marqueia Davis, Al DiEmedio, Doug DiRaddo, Joan English, Susan Gleich, Sara Castro- Olivo, Olivia Roane, Michael Roth, Pat Stone, Becky Stone, Marty Tracy, Iman Turner, Ted Weiner, and Eleanor Weinglass. I have learned so much from your work and your perspectives.

I am thankful to the Brandywine School District for the years I served, the support afforded crisis response teams, and the experiences recorded here that may help other districts respond to traumatic events. I am grateful to Mark Holodick, district superintendent, and Amanda Salvatore and Sue Breckenridge in administrative support.

I value the dedicated members of our district crisis response team and their profound commitment to helping people in pain begin to heal.

About the Author

A Nationally Certified School Psychologist, Jeffrey C. Roth joined the Brandywine School District in Delaware where he initiated Operation Cooperation—a school-wide approach to conflict resolution. He wrote a middle school crisis manual, helped initiate and lead the district Crisis Response Team, and was named School Psychologist of the Year by the Delaware Association of School Psychologists.

He coordinated school psychologists, developed Instructional Support and Positive Behavior Support Teams, and a social skills program for students with social challenges. He also developed a program of self-directed professional development for school psychologists and attended workshops in the PREPaRE Model, Critical Incident Stress Management, and Red Cross Disaster Mental Health. He is an American Red Cross Disaster Mental Health volunteer.

Dr. Roth received his undergraduate degree in psychology at Temple University. After serving in the Air Force, he practiced social work and returned to graduate school at Temple where he earned his doctorate. During graduate school, he worked as a recreational therapist at St. Christopher's Hospital for Children and taught graduate courses at Arcadia University. He is a Licensed Psychologist in Delaware.

Dr. Roth is an adjunct professor and advisor at Wilmington University, Delaware. He co-developed a mentoring program for new school psychologists for the state Department of Education.

Personal Insights on Formative Experiences

Several formative experiences contributed to my leadership in crisis response. My earliest model for response was my father, Martin Roth, a World War II navy veteran. I recall from childhood that he sometimes yelled out in his sleep, shattering the silence of the evening with recurring nightmares of traumatic battles at sea. Martin said little about his war experiences.

When I was 10, spending an idyllic summer with my extended family in Atlantic City, my father stayed working in Philadelphia. Nearing the end of vacation, we had no idea that my grandmother Leah had suddenly died in Philadelphia. My father jumped in his old Pontiac and raced to the Jersey shore where he found us on the boardwalk at dusk, awaiting the Miss America Pageant parade. Leah's daughters rushed toward him, knowing he brought bad news, and all three found comfort in his arms. His demeanor signaled sorrow, but quietly, he expressed calmness and caring. The festivities lost all meaning. We followed my father, walking quickly with our grief, but deriving from him a sense of strength and support.

Other life experiences influenced who I am as a crisis responder. My father died suddenly while I was stationed overseas in the Air Force. I felt profound sorrow, but also calmness on the journey home.

While working as a recreational therapist at a children's hospital, I was exposed to the death of young people. Hospital staff grieved with their families, but adhered to the hospital ethic — bounce back, continue to function, no matter what our feelings.

The sudden death of a colleague, Janet Newsome, constituted the loss of a professional partner and friend who had taught me many valued lessons.

Caring for my aging mother Yetta—as she declined in a nursing home, and keeping vigil as she died—was an unexpected spiritual experience that inspired me to greater service.

INDEX

A

administration,
      district, 60, 71, 144, 146, 193
      school, 4, 7, 9–10, 35, 59, 92, 129, 153, 157, 269, 287
      support, 3, 9–10, 15, 19, 27–30, 32–3, 35–7, 43, 47–8,
51–3, 56–60, 63, 73–7
adolescents, teenagers,
adult reactions, 191
African Americans, 12–13, 15, 191, 265, 267–8, 272–3, 277, 279
      kinship support, 14–15, 268
aggression. *See* violence and aggression
anger, 4, 5, 7, 21, 36, 45, 62, 89, 94, 113–4, 119, 125, 127–9,
155, 158–9, 162, 186, 190–4, 196–7, 204, 235, 237–9, 241, 245,
271, 279,
      off target, 129, 194, 239, 245
anniversaries of traumatic incidents,
Asian Americans, 11, 277–8
at-risk students, 76, 80–1, 102–3, 127–8, 155, 157–60, 165–8,
208, 227, 232, 242–3, 255, 265, 271

B

bibliotherapy, 78, 105, 108–9, 119, 135, 288
blame, 14, 124, 128, 187–8, 194, 196, 245, 287
      blaming the victim, 187
briefing, crisis team 4, 15, 27, 29, 53, 59, 72, 75, 80, 82, 100, 107,
134, 181, 183–5, 208, 241–2, 251, 254, 257, 262, 269, 270–1,
      initial, 72, 80, 184, 190, 269–70
bullying. *See* violence and aggression
burnout, 29, 199, 202, 252

C

caregivers, 10, 42, 51, 58–9, 70, 79, 81, 83, 99, 120, 120, 127,
144, 150, 154, 177, 181, 199–210, 234, 236, 242
      caring for, 51–9, 141, 199–211
      training, 58, 88, 100, 106, 122, 151, 122, 151, 153–5,

N

National Emergency Assistance Team (NEAT), 44
natural disasters, 70, 201
National Organization for Victim Assistance (NOVA), 44, 261
normal routines/normalcy, 8, 72, 74, 228–9, 157–60
    reestablish, 23, 74, 92, 102, 118, 121, 124–5, 135–6, 145, 154–5, 181, 188–9, 208, 217–8, 228, 232, 243–4, 268, 271, 273, 287

O

opportunities for students to take action, 77, 81, 91, 136, 155, 168, 242, 274–5, 287
outcome evaluation. *See* examining response effectiveness

P

partnerships, 24
    community, 132, 255–6
    district "buddy" system, 62, 208, 255
personal vulnerability risk factors, 43, 102–4, 98–9, 226, 286
phases of crisis team development, 27–30
physical proximity. *See* psychological triage/evaluating risk
positive behavior support (PBS), 213–4
Post-Traumatic Stress Disorder (PTSD), 31, 43, 102–4,120–2, 159–60, 204–5, 236
    mitigation, 52, 150,160
    symptoms, 120–2, 160, 204–5, 235–6, 266–7
pre-crisis capacity, 210, 225–6, 234, 284
PREPaRE, acronym, xv, 24
PREPaRE Model, 24, 33–8, 47, 52, 66, 82, 86, 99, 106, 117, 132–3, 150–1, 183, 214, 237, 267–8
preparedness. *See* crisis response, preparedness
prevention. *See* crises/ traumatic incidents, prevention/ mitigation
primary language, 131–7
principal, 32, 34
    leadership, 32–3, 35, 52, 59, 85, 87, 185, 190, 249–53
    reciprocal support for, 35, 254–5
    roles and functions during crisis, 27, 35, 72, 78, 87, 90
problem solving, 8, 23, 79, 117–8, 122, 124, 159, 200, 228, 231,